Effective study skills

We work with leading authors to develop the strongest educational materials in study skills, bringing cutting-edge thinking and best learning practice to a global market.

Under a range of well-known imprints, including Prentice Hall, we craft high quality print and electronic publications which help readers to understand and apply their content, whether studying or at work.

To find out more about the complete range of our publishing, please visit us on the World Wide Web at:
www.pearsoned.co.uk

Effective study skills

Geraldine Price and Pat Maier

Harlow, England • London • New York • Boston • San Francisco • Toronto • Sydney • Singapore • Hong Kong
Tokyo • Seoul • Taipei • New Delhi • Cape Town • Madrid • Mexico City • Amsterdam • Munich • Paris • Milan

Pearson Education Limited
Edinburgh Gate
Harlow
Essex CM20 2JE
England

and Associated Companies throughout the world

Visit us on the World Wide Web at:
www.pearsoned.co.uk

First published 2007

ISBN: 978-1-4058-4073-6

British Library Cataloguing-in-Publication Data
A catalogue record for this book is available from the British Library

Library of Congress Cataloging-in-Publication Data
Price, Geraldine.
Effective study skills / Geraldine Price and Pat Maier.
p. cm.
Includes bibliographical references and index.
ISBN-13: 978-1-4058-4073-6 (pbk.)
1. Study skills. I. Maier, Pat. II. Title.
LB1049.P746 2007
378.1'70281--dc22
2007024140

10 9 8 7 6 5 4 3 2
11 10 09 08

Typeset in 10/12 Helvetica by 30
Printed and bound in Great Britain by Ashford Colour Press Ltd, Gosport

The publisher's policy is to use paper manufactured from sustainable forests.

Contents

Foreword

The authors of this study skills book would like to congratulate you for deciding to go on to further study; you will find it a true 'rite of passage' for later life, so it is important that you make the most of your time both socially and academically.

Your time in higher education should be seen as an opportunity to develop yourself through study. The authors have designed the chapters to encourage self-reflection and personal development rather than a 'tips for' approach, as this will encourage a professional attitude to your work. A self-reflective and 'can do' approach will mark you out as an independent lifelong learner, a vital attribute for anyone today.

Don't forget to update your personal development planners (PDPs) as you go through the book and your studies, as this will help you make your learning explicit.

Finally, we would like to wish you all the best with your studies and beyond.

Geraldine Price
Pat Maier

How to use this book

Why this book?

Academic study skills are a set of skills that set you up as a life-long learner within and beyond your official study period. The tone of the book is one of personal development, encouraging you to reflect on your skills, develop a 'can do' attitude and know what you need to do to improve. These are qualities that will set you up for life and increase your employability.

The book can be used by individual students or tutors wishing to embed these skills in the curriculum and link into personal development planners. We are living through a period of rapid change where our knowledge needs updating regularly throughout our lives in order to remain current. Lifelong learning skills therefore become important and enable us to improve and keep up to date throughout our working life and beyond.

For you - the student

This book explores the challenges of university life and how you can move from a novice to an experienced learner in your field. The challenges for you are at many levels: your engagement with the subject, your ability to manage your time and your motivation to take responsibility for your own learning. Those of you who take up the challenges and develop a deeper understanding of your subject are more likely to succeed and do well. The book helps you to take control of your own learning, with self-management being an overarching skill underlying in each of the chapters. Self-knowledge and reflection will improve your grades and give you the qualities employers seek. It is an interactive book which prompts and guides you to more effective and efficient working habits.

To help you do this, each chapter provides *activities* which enable you to increase your skills. The activities in the book are not a once-and-for-all activity and should be revisited throughout your stay at university as your skills develop. It is important, therefore, that you reflect on your stages of learning by completing the *personal development planner* (PDP) section at the end of each chapter. These PDPs can be used with your tutor, or linked into your department's own PDP to encourage you to move ever forward and onward.

It is advisable to start with the first chapter as this will give you that broad brush view on getting started in Higher Education. If you are already in later years, you will also gain from the focus in this chapter.

For you – the tutor

Tutors wanting to use this book may be working centrally as learning advisers or with a department as a subject tutor. As a learning adviser you may be working individually with students, outside their curriculum or collaboratively with subject tutors. Whichever role you have, this activity-focused book could be adapted to your own circumstances and slot in easily with other material.

The authors, as subject and skills tutors themselves, have developed this material from their own practice and tested the material with their students. Some suggestions for using the book are as follows:

- *Induction for first years*. It is useful to include information from 'Learning in Higher Education' which gives a broad brush view on moving into Higher Education. The chapters on stress and time management are also useful for adaptation in induction sessions, at undergraduate and postgraduate level.
- *Personal development planners*. Every chapter encourages students to reflect on the skills they are developing. You may expect students to carry out some of the activities in this book for initial proof of their reflective ability.
- *Reading critically*. As tutors we are all aware of the difficulty students have in rising above writing simple descriptive texts. Criticality is a skill that is valued and encouraging criticality in later study years becomes an issue. The section on reading could be used in a project unit, along with the writing section that encourages students to think of the writing process. Activity 3 in Chapter 3.3, 'Reading Critically' could be used as a warm-up exercise to encourage a more critical approach to reading.

- *Presentation skills*. The chapters on teamwork and presenting your work have proved very useful for giving students guidance on poster preparation, oral presentations and working in real teams.
- *Learning outcomes.* Each of the chapters conforms to academic practice and includes learning outcomes. There is no assessment, but informal reflective exercises at the beginning and the end could serve to 'assess' increased awareness.

Getting the most out of the book

Each chapter opens with a *navigation page* giving a brief overview of the sections within the chapter along with the learning outcomes. This means that you can easily dip into the section and activities you want. Each chapter begins and ends with your own reflection on how you feel your skills are developing. It is valuable to reflect on your skills prior to reading the chapter and then see how you have increased your awareness as a result of working through the activities. These mini PDPs are intended to be used as part of your institution's own system.

Some of the *activities* require you to take stock of your own skills while others give you valuable practice, i.e. putting into operation what you have read. Towards the end of each chapter you will find a *summary map* combining all the parts of the chapter into a visible whole. Finally, each chapter also gives you advice on where you might go for further help, if you still feel unsure of your performance.

Unlock your potential

You have the potential to do well, obtain good grades and be employed in an area that interests you. So, use this book as part of your strategy for personal development and realise your potential.

> *In times of change, learners inherit the Earth, while the learned find themselves beautifully equipped to deal with a world that no longer exists.*
>
> Eric Hoffer, an important social thinker/writer of the twentieth century.

Additional student support is available at: www.pearsoned.co.uk.effectivestudy

Learning in Higher Education

Learning in Higher Education is, and should be, challenging. The challenges for you are at many levels: your engagement with the subject, your ability to manage your time and your motivation to take responsibility for your own learning. Those who take up the challenges and develop a deep understanding of their subject are more likely to succeed and do well. Those of you who do the minimum work and take a 'surface' approach to learning are more likely to fail or drop out. Although your tutors and advisers are there to give you the support you need, the decision to take this responsibility, to reflect and act on your development, is yours and yours alone. Take it and succeed.

We don't receive wisdom; we must discover it for ourselves after a journey that no one can take for us or spare us.
Marcel Proust (French novelist, 1871–1922)

In this chapter you will learn how to:

1. recognise what makes you a proficient learner
2. understand what plagiarism is and how to avoid it
3. identify the key documents that describe your programme and units
4. know how to start thinking about your own employability.

USING THIS CHAPTER

Your learning	A	B	Generally me (A or B)
Time	Tutors tend to set coursework deadlines too close together, so when I try to get the work done I am having to cram everything in at the same time to meet these deadlines. I prefer working to tight deadlines and this means I leave all my work to the last minute. It would be better if tutors spread out the deadlines as that would suit me better.	Although we get coursework deadlines set close together, we are told in advance and I try where possible to set my own staggered deadlines so that I am not working on all coursework at the same time.	
Reflection on learning	I find little opportunity in my studies to do this and we are generally not encouraged to do it either, so why bother. I had to do this in school and feel that it should be left there.	I am keen to reflect on what and how I learn. Tutorials and seminars are good for this as discussion helps me see what I understand and don't understand. I always want to know how I can improve.	

Are you predominantly A or B? You may have guessed that A represents a dependent learner while B an independent learner.

How independent and responsible do you feel you are with regard to your learning? What might you do to improve this – write three things in the box below. Read the remainder of this chapter and identify the later chapters you think could be relevant to you.

1.

2.

3.

NOTE Your tutors can only do so much. It is up to you to be prepared to take full advantage of what is on offer.

Know yourself as a learner

At this stage of your studies you are really preparing yourself for work and part of that, as indicated earlier, is about being a lifelong, independent learner. Increasingly companies will expect you to learn on the job, take further study or follow a continuing professional development programme. Being able therefore to reflect on how best you learn, on the skills you are acquiring and on improvements you need to make will be vital as you progress your career. Take a look at some of the relevant later chapters in areas you feel you could do with checking.

What kind of learner are you?

In Chapter 2.3, 'Working in a real team', you are asked to identify the kind of learner you feel you are based on the learning styles proposed by two psychologists, Peter Honey and Alan Mumford (1992):

An activist: you like to learn by doing things. You are happier with project work, and all kinds of active learning. You are less happy reading long papers, analysing data and sitting in lectures.	***A reflector:*** you are more cautious and like to weigh up all the issues before acting. When you make a decision, it is thought through. You are probably happy to work on a project, if you are given time to observe all the facts before making a decision. You dislike having work dumped on you and get worried by tight deadlines.
A pragmatist: you like taking theories and putting them into practice and you need to see the benefit and relevance of what you are doing. If you are learning something you feel has no practical value, you lose interest. You may want to ask your tutor 'why are we learning this?' If you are a student who says 'I don't like this course as it is all theory' then your learning preference is probably 'pragmatist' or 'activist'.	***A theorist:*** you like to understand what is behind certain actions and enjoy working through issues theoretically and in a well-structured way and whether you apply it or not doesn't interest you so much. You may be the one to ask questions as to why and how something occurs. You dislike unstructured sessions and dislike it when you are asked to reflect on some activity or say what you felt about it.

Each of these learning styles represents a point on the learning cycle proposed by David Kolb in 1975 (Figure 1) showing that when we learn something we need concrete experience, time to observe and reflect on abstract concepts and theories before we apply these ideas in new situations. We can start this learning cycle at any point, and as a learner we are happier in some of the stages than others and it is this that gives us our learning preferences.

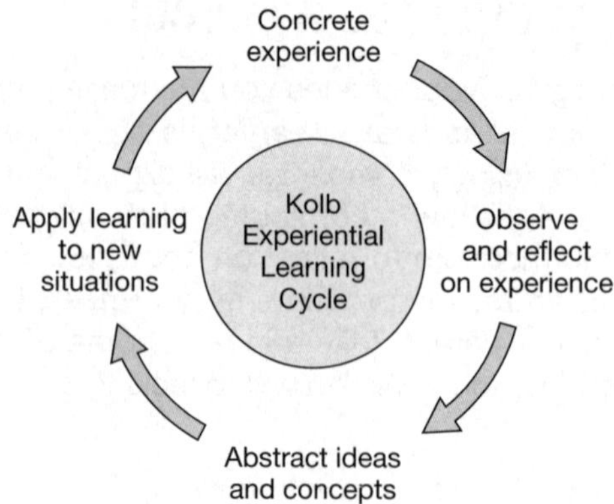

Figure 1 Kolb experiential learning cycle
Adapted from Smith (2001)

Which part of the learning cycle do you feel more comfortable with and how might this affect your learning? Can you find ways of working around other aspects of the learning cycle that you don't feel so comfortable with? To be a successful learner you will need to be able to at least function on all points of the learning cycle, even though you may be happier in one area.

Move from novice to expert

Knowing how novices see things and how experts see things is a helpful shorthand in understanding how we learn. No one is expecting you to become an expert overnight, but you will see your tutors as experts and wonder why you can't understand things that appear so simple to them, and vice versa they may be puzzled why you can't understand something. But just remember you are probably much better on mobile phone technology than any of your lecturers!

How often have you felt that you just don't know what your brain can do with yet another piece of information? These pieces seem to be all unconnected. You feel frustrated as you panic about trying to remember it all. This is because you haven't yet been able to process this information into chunks and store it away ready for retrieval when you want it. The more you learn, reflect and revise a subject, the more you will start to see patterns in the information and you can start to group things. At that point, these chunks of information become knowledge and you can then start applying it.

One of the major things that experts do that you won't do as a novice is find order and patterns in information and they do this by chunking pieces of information together; they know how to make these chunks and identify the patterns. This means that, unlike novices, they are not working with discrete pieces of information, they already know how it fits into a larger jigsaw. Experts therefore have that bigger picture.

One way to help you integrate these pieces of information, and start to build the bigger picture, is to draw a concept map (see Activity 2). This technique was developed by Joseph Novak in the 1960s and is a visual method of showing linkages between ideas, concepts or topics. Each topic is linked by a line that indicates the nature of that relationship. See the example below.

Concept maps can be drawn as hierarchies, flow charts or networks (as below). If you prefer a more linear approach, use an indented list that indicates at least a hierarchical relationship. However, a list on its own is less useful as you need to see the relationships between things.

Concept maps enable you to see the relationship between concepts and how chunks of things belong together. You may find this difficult at the beginning of a topic but if you persist it will pay off and you will develop an integrated view of your topic and start to mimic the experts. Also, for each topic you are revising for an exam, finalise your revision with a concept map. Then use your concept maps for quick revision prior to the exam.

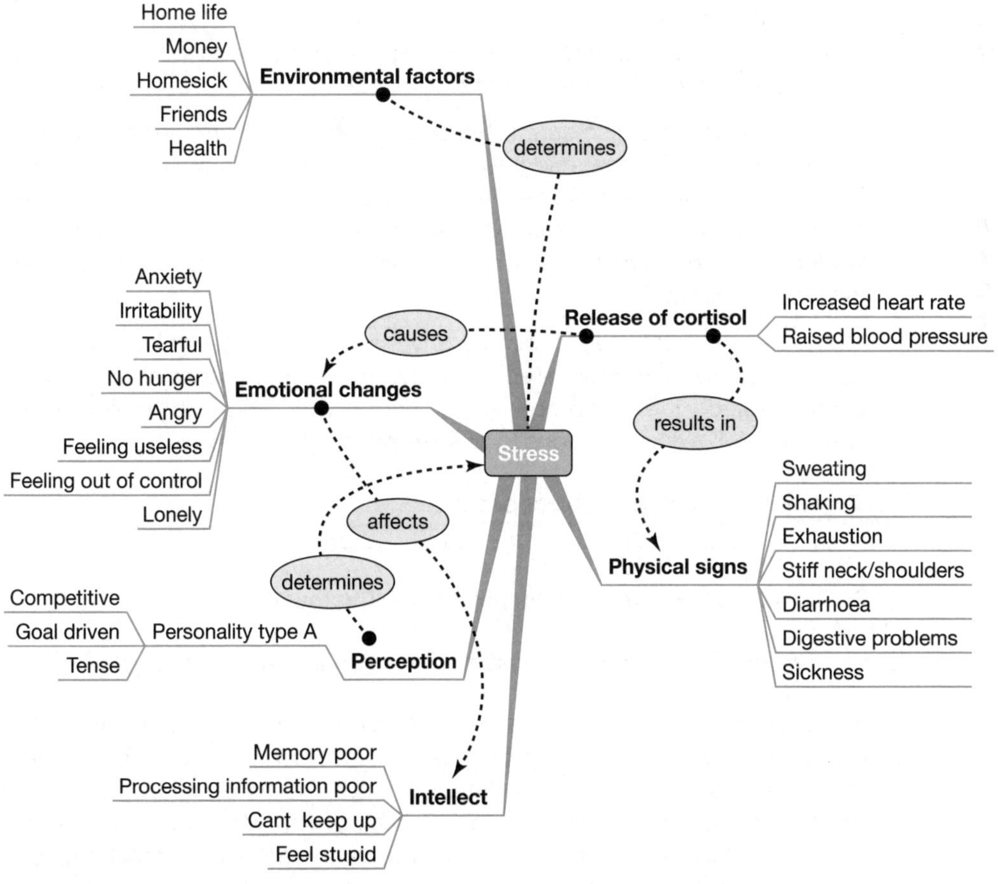

Produced using MindManager

ACTIVITY 2 Create a concept map

Look at Chapter 1.2, 'Managing your time', and develop a concept map for your current approach to time management using the concepts in that chapter. How well can you piece information together into a set of related topics? Try using this technique when you are note-taking. You may first have to take a set of linear notes as you read through a text, but then afterwards you can link it together through a concept map. If you really don't like creating concept maps write out a hierarchical list or flow chart.

Get organised

In order to be an effective learner you need to understand how you learn and how you manage yourself in order to learn. Sue Drew from Sheffield Hallam University carried out a piece of research in 2001 asking students what helped or hindered their academic achievement (Drew, 2001). She reported that students came up with four main areas:

- self-management, including taking responsibility for their own learning
- motivation to study
- understanding and reflection of their learning experience
- support from their tutors and the institution.

These findings were also supported by a report on the first-year experience of UK Higher Education students (Yorke *et al.*, 2007). Some of the features that first-year students do not like are: workload and time management, confusion about assessments and lack of feedback. If you are a first-year student then you need to work on your time management and be prepared to ask for feedback.

Motivation to study is your primary driver in being successful in your studies. If you don't feel motivated to study, or you feel you have chosen the wrong subject, then stop now and consider what you want to do. Select one of the following questions to answer privately:

1. I want to study this subject because ...
2. I know I want to study, but I'd prefer to study ...
3. I don't really know why I am here, I would rather do ...

From now on, it will be assumed that you are motivated to study.

Self-management is an overarching skill you need to develop. As an 18-year-old first-year student this may be the first time you have left home and you have to sort out accommodation, finance, new friendship groups and understand all the documentation associated with your study programme as well as start to learn something. If you are a mature or international student you will have additional issues to contend with. So, being able to manage all these aspects of your 'new life' can be daunting.

You need to quickly identify where you can get support for your needs. The Students Union is an excellent place to start. They will have an overview of all the services available to you at your institution. Your teaching department will probably have a student office where you can sort out specific things relating to your study. Get familiar with what is available and build a rapport with key people.

If you feel that self-management is an issue for you take a look at the chapters on stress and time management and develop your own strategies.

Develop an attitude

> *The greatest discovery of my generation is that a human being can alter his life by altering his attitudes of mind.*
>
> William James (1842–1910), US Pragmatist philosopher and psychologist

Developing a 'can do' attitude is going to help you enormously. This will enable you to manage yourself and feel in control of events around you. Your confidence will develop and you will easily be able to manage your time and stress. Chapter 1.1, 'Managing your stress', will help you work through the concept of self-belief or 'self efficacy', a term that was first coined by the psychologist Albert Bandura. For self-belief to gain a hold you need to:

1. be motivated in what you do
2. believe in yourself
3. recognise and deal with things that stress you so you can control your anxiety
4. look for solutions not obstacles
5. organise your time so you feel on top of things and in control
6. reflect and recognise your strengths and weaknesses in order to make informed choices.

If you feel this is an issue for you, you may want to look Chapter 1.1 on managing stress now.

Reflect on your learning

If someone said to you 'Just reflect on what you have just said for a moment ...' you know that you would be expected to think about what you have just said, and then reconsider the implications of it and what you've learned from it. What you are actually doing is: (a) recapping on what you said (replay), (b) taking a more objective look at the implications of what you said (reframing your actions) and (c) learning from it (re-assessing your actions and future actions). Activity 3 helps you reflect on your learning.

ACTIVITY 3 How do you feel about reflecting on your progress?

What I feel ...	Usually me	Think again ...
I find reflection difficult because I can't see what I am learning.		Work with a friend. Sometimes it is difficult when you first start to be objective about your own skills, especially when we are encouraged to be modest most of the time.
I find it a waste of time.		OK, don't call it reflecting, but make a list of the things you can do well, OK, or poorly and work out how you can improve. If someone asked you in an interview if you were a good team player how would you answer and if they asked what makes a good team player, what would you say?
I can't see where I'm developing skills in my courses.		Each course/unit should have a description of what you'll be expected to learn along with the assessment. Check the assessments and the learning outcomes (these should also include of list of skills you're learning) and from this you can see what skills and knowledge you are developing.
I don't know what to do with my personal development profile (PDP) when I complete it.		Your PDP should be part of every year in your degree. In some degrees it is built into the first year and then vaguely mentioned in years after that. Try and keep it up to date, this is for you and you can use it to adjust your CV and keep you prepared for those interviews and even for part-time work.
Sum up your own feelings about reflecting on your own skills and knowledge		

Reflection is important if you are to develop your understanding of your skills, yourself and your knowledge. You will be expected to work in teams, write essays and give presentations, etc., and through reflection you will be able to recap, reframe and re-assess your learning. Many students dislike the reflection aspect, but once they get used to doing it they see the value.

For most of the time we go about our business, interacting with people, developing skills and gaining knowledge without really being aware that we are doing this. A lot of what we learn is 'implicit', which means we are not aware that we are learning. Sometimes it takes another person to say what you have been learning in order to realise how you are developing. Implicit learning therefore comprises skills and knowledge you have, but you don't know you have. However, if you reflect on what you have been doing and you are able to objectively 'stand back' and think about it, you start to see the skills and knowledge you have and these then become 'explicit', i.e. we are conscious of them. Once these are explicit we are able to refer to them in our CV, talk about them at an interview and plan to use them again. On the other hand, while our skills and knowledge remain implicit, we can only react to our environment and when someone asks us what we can do, we tend to look a bit vague and trot out the usual 'I don't know.' Good reflection therefore enables us to be more strategic and create opportunities to improve ourselves, while having a better understanding of how we will perform in a similar event. This is the hallmark of a good graduate.

Reflection is not just thinking about what happened at the end of some event; it occurs at various stages. For an assignment it is:

- at the beginning when you reflect on what you have to do
- during the assignment where you adjust your plans in light of your experience
- afterwards, and it is this reflection that you resent. However, post-reflection provides you with the strategic information you need to take forward to the next assignment and it also makes you articulate what you have learnt.

Students in clinical practice for example will be familiar (if not now, then later) with 'reflection **in** action' and 'reflection **on** action'. This is a term coined by Donald Schön (1930–1997), an American philosopher whose work has been adopted by many in the health professions in order to develop the 'reflective practitioner'.

When studying, reflection can take many forms, such as:

Personal development planner	This is a record of your own assessment of your developing skills, which should include any part-time or volunteering work you do.
Reflective aspects of coursework, e.g. working in groups	Sometimes a formal part of your coursework assessment.
Tutor feedback	Feedback from your tutors is important for your learning. Most students complain they don't have enough feedback. Try asking for specific feedback when you hand in your coursework if you feel you are not getting the feedback you want. Remember good feedback enables you to make an action plan for improvement.
Peer feedback	Sometimes you may be asked to assess your peers, e.g. on an oral presentation, part of a report or their ability to work in a group. Once again, be objective and act fairly. Don't give marks on your likes or dislikes for that person. Be professional.

End-of-unit evaluation	This allows you to reflect on the whole unit, how coherent it was, how much you've learned, the organisation and how well you've been taught. Think about this objectively and professionally and reflect fairly. Don't give your tutor a low score because you simply don't like him or her or because you got some low marks.
Tutorials and seminars	An opportunity to go over difficult topics and discuss.
A student representative on a department committee	A chance to represent fellow students and reflect on your educational provision constructively.
Study groups with friends	Informal opportunity.

The personal development profile (PDP) is the key document for recording your reflections. Ensure you keep this up to date, whether your tutors ask you or not. This is primarily **for you** and the more explicit you can be with what you know and can do, the easier it is to talk about it to a potential employer. All the chapters in this book have been designed to incorporate reflective aspects; try using these activities to get you in the habit of reflecting. Activity 4 asks you to consider what you know about reflection.

2 Academic integrity – plagiarism

A Times Higher Education UK survey (March 2006) found that one in six students admitted to copying from friends, one in ten to looking for essays online and four in ten said they knew someone who had passed off work of someone else for their own. This is now recognised as an international problem and universities across the world are starting to tackle it. The main problem with academic cheating, particularly if it escalates, is that it is unfair to those students who don't cheat and eventually will undermine the value of degree awards, as its standard cannot then be guaranteed. Would you like to be treated by a doctor or a nurse who you knew cheated throughout their degree? Would you like to walk over a bridge where the structural calculations were checked by the structural engineer who cheated through his/her degree? I am sure the answer is a resounding 'no'.

Violating academic integrity can take several forms:

1. No referencing

- You must have read some authors' work, even if it is in a textbook, to give you ideas for your paper. Make sure you have the correct reference at the back of your paper. Ensure you use the correct referencing style for your subject. If you are not sure, ask your tutor or a librarian in your institution.

ACTIVITY 4 How's your writing?

Look at the concept map below on reflection and write a paragraph to describe it. This map below could reflect your notes from reading a chapter on reflective practice. Try and capture the main ideas in a coherent paragraph or two.

You may want to give your description to a friend for them to check your writing. If you found this very difficult, you may want to go to Part 4, 'Develop your writing.

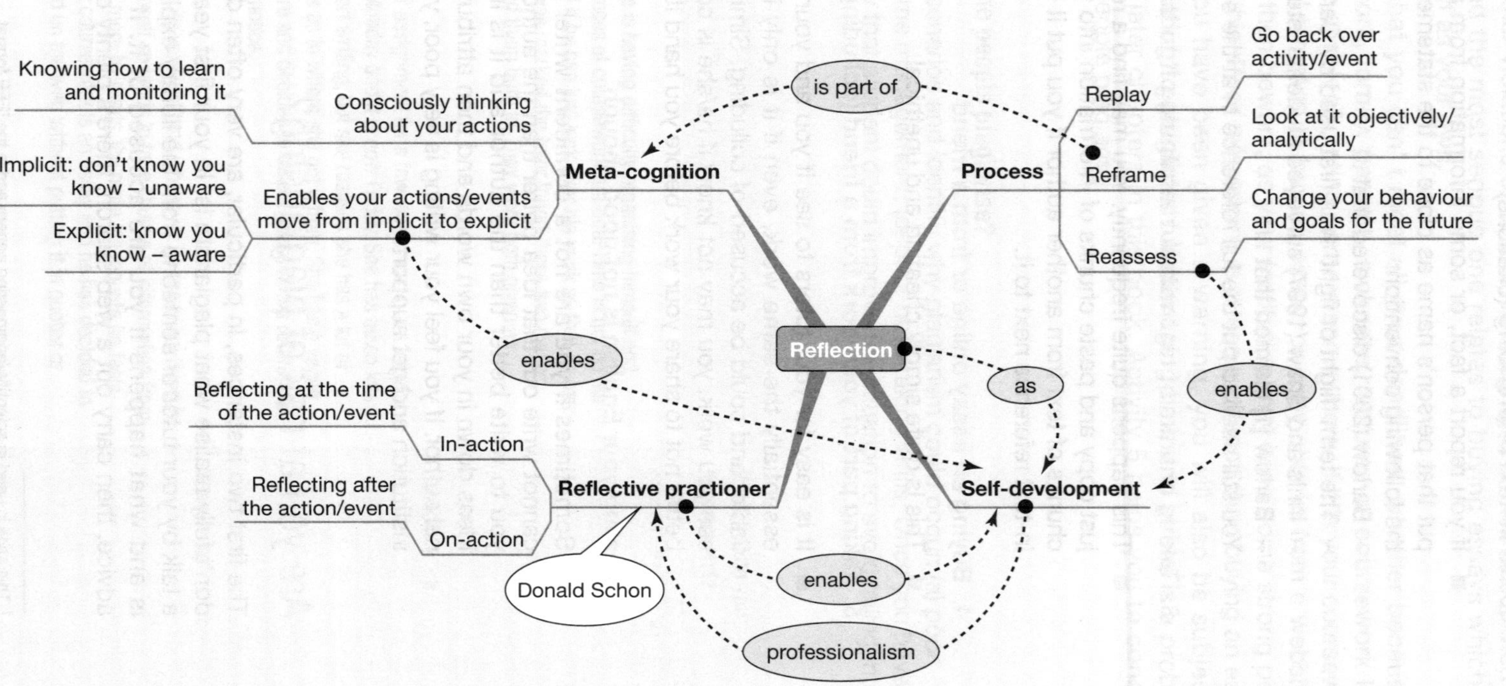

NOTE When you take chunks of text and place them in your own work, it is obvious as the style changes dramatically. You don't have to be a forensic linguist to notice it.

In all of the scenarios above, there was no malicious attempt to cheat, but it has resulted from the various pressures and lack of skill that you can easily find yourself in. Be careful, plagiarism is on the rise and institutions are under pressure to crack down. Some tutors are using anti-plagiarism software, and the most well known one for UK universities is 'Turnitin' which highlights potentially copied work (see **www.plagiarism.org/**).

For more information on plagiarism, or academic integrity as it is now called, see Part 4, 'Develop your writing'.

3 Understand your programme or course

Your institution and lecturers would have spent a surprisingly large amount of time preparing programme and course information for you. You might just see it as a heap of information that you may get round to reading one day, and then when you do get around to reading some of it, you don't understand all that educational mumbo-jumbo. So let's try and dissect some of the things that go into these documents.

The programme specification

The programme refers to the degree you are studying for, whether it is a BSc in Textiles, a BA in History or an MEng in Engineering. The programme specification tells you the aim of the programme as a whole across the three or four years of your study. It also gives you some idea of what you will learn through a list of learning outcomes. The learning outcomes indicate what you should know and be able to do at the end of your studies. If you read nothing else, read the learning outcomes. There will also be information on how you get support while at the institution.

This document should be available to you either on request or on your department's website. Ideally you should look at this before you sign up for your degree, but not many students realise that this document exists.

Module/unit/course description

Every programme will be supported by units, modules or courses (each departments seems to have different names for these). The unit is where the learning and teaching takes place. You may find you have core units and elective units. Each of these units also has a description outlining the aims of the unit, the learning outcomes and the assessments.

It is important to read the unit description, as your assessment will be based on the learning outcomes stated there.

About credits

In the UK institutions of High Education use a Credit Accumulation and Transfer Scheme (CATS), sometime written as Credits. This system allows us to value and measure the size of a unit. A three-year honours degree will accumulate 360 credits (120 each year). Each institution will package the number of credits you have to do in different ways.

NOTE It is a good idea to ask your tutors how many hours of learning (this includes face-to-face teaching and private study time) a credit is worth. This will give you some idea of the credit value of the unit. For example, if one credit equates to 10 hours of learning, then you are looking at 100 hours of learning for a 10-credit unit. Check how many face-to-face hours you have and then you can see the amount of work expected of you as private study for this unit.

As the European Higher Education systems become more aligned, we shall be moving to a European Credit Transfer and Accumulation System (ECTS), and currently 10 UK credits are worth approximately 5 ECTS. If you go on an exchange visit with the Erasmus/Socrates scheme and have to collect credits for your course, make sure you check out how many you have to do.

4 Your employability

If you are in your first few years of study, you may wonder why you should be thinking of employability now. Well, you should be. Employability is about you consciously developing your knowledge and a wide range of skills even if you still don't know what you want to do later. You record your developing skills in your personal development planner (PDP), which will enable you to see your progress across the years. You should take advantage of what is on offer now, be that sponsorship schemes, volunteering, work placements, career talks, talks from past students, career sessions or full career management courses (with or without credits), as this will help you develop yourself and focus on what you really want. It will also help you with part-time work.

If you are in your final year of studies, you may still not know what you want to do, you may want to take a gap year or you may have found the job you want. Make sure you complete your PDP as this will enable you to articulate what you know and can do as well as remind you where the evidence is to support this. You should visit your Careers Service for advice – most institutions allow you to use this service for several years after graduation.

What is the difference between employability and employment?

Employability refers to your personal qualities, your attitude to work, the knowledge you have and the skills, both practical and intellectual, that you have developed. This refers therefore to your ability to find a job, stay in that job and progress to the next step. Employment on the other hand refers to simply 'getting a job'. One of the aims of Higher Education is to make you more employable and by doing that also develop your interests in a particular topic.

What do employers want?

Your degree is only the first tick in the box. For the graduate jobs that you will be expecting to do once you have finished, your degree will just enable you to apply, not necessarily get the job. A recent Government report (Leitch Review, 2007) stated that 40% of the adult population should have a first degree by 2020. So if you want to get noticed, you will have to develop some aspect of yourself that marks you out individually.

Some employers want graduates with discipline-specific knowledge while others are interested in the graduate quality regardless of discipline. The graduateness qualities that employers refer to are: knowledge of a subject area, analytical skills, interpersonal skills, communication skills, time management skills, personal belief in yourself, taking responsibility for your own learning, and the ability to reflect and improve yourself. You will have the opportunity to work on all of these areas while at university, if you take the opportunities available.

What's the knowledge economy – and why should it concern me?

We are living through a knowledge explosion. New communications technologies enable research and new knowledge to be exchanged much faster than ever before. Knowledge becomes a valuable resource and since it is moving so fast the life span of knowledge, especially technologies, is ever shortened. We are all in a vicious circle of trying to 'keep up' with the latest knowledge.

During your studies, therefore, you will learn knowledge that could be out of date in 5 years, and sometimes less. It is important, therefore, that you learn a set of skills that enable you to update your knowledge and make you a proficient lifelong learner. The whole purpose of this book hinges on this point. This book aims to help with personal development where you can enhance your skills rather than immediate quick-fix tips. It is valuable, therefore, to understand the current thrust of Higher Education worldwide.

Look at the map below and see if you can add any more aspects of employability that apply to you.

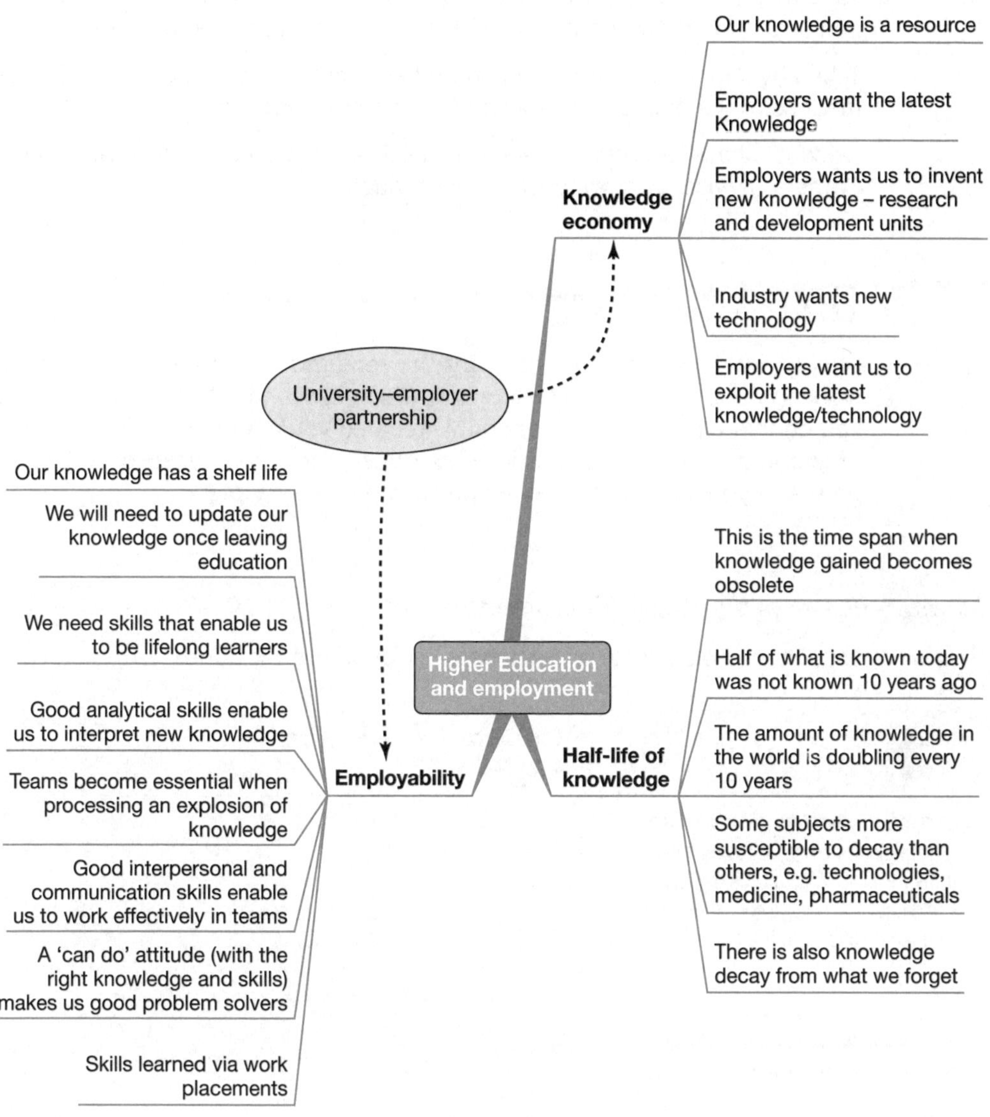

Source of information on half-life of knowledge from Peter Knight-Moore (1997)

What should I be doing now?

You will probably have been given a PDP by your department. Some departments will fully develop this with you, while others will have it very much on the side. The PDP is for YOU and regardless of how your tutors feel about this, it is in your interest to keep it as up to date as you can. This really is your evidence of how you are developing, within and outside your studies.

Use your part-time job to your advantage and include what you are learning in your PDP. If you are alert to what you are learning, you will be able to articulate it. Even sitting in a checkout in a supermarket will mean that you have to learn to deal with difficult customers. Take note on how you do this and how effective (or not!) you are. How have you improved this skill?

Take advantage of volunteering and other similar schemes, career management sessions or courses, talks and visits from employers.

Once you have left your university, you will find that most offer access to the Careers Service for a few years after graduation.

5 Going forward

This chapter has set the scene for the remainder of the book, and from working through it you may know now which section to dip into next. Before you do that take time to assess how prepared you are to take full advantage of learning in Higher Education. How does your current assessment compare with your assessment at the beginning of the chapter?

Activity 6 Update your personal development planner

Grade your confidence on a scale of 1–5 where 1 = poor and 5 = good

Moving into Higher Education – my plan	Confidence level 1–5	Plans to improve
I understand what I can do to become a proficient learner, e.g. be responsible for my own learning, understand myself as a learner, get organised, see the value of reflection (via PDPs). *Section 1*		
I understand the principles of plagiarism and realise why it has to be controlled. *Section 2*		
I understand the key documents relating to my programme and courses. *Section 3*		
I understand why employability is something I should consider throughout my studies and what to do about it. *Section 4*		

Getting extra help

- Your local Students Union as well as the National Students Union at: www.nusonline.co.uk.
- If you have any kind of condition that you feel could interfere with your studies, check out your own institution. There are usually units within student services that are available for all kinds of help.
- If you feel you aren't coping, first check with your personal tutor (or someone in your department), and then go and get help from one of the specialist units in your institution.
- There is always someone in student services, or the Students Union, to show you where to get help with finances.
- If you feel you are on the wrong course, talk to your personal tutor and see if you can change. Do this early in your first year if possible.
- If you want to do some volunteering first go to your Students Union; they will know of schemes within your institution.
- Don't forget the library. Staff are usually very friendly and more than happy to help you. Libraries can appear daunting, but don't be afraid to ask.

References

- Argyris, M. and Schön, D. (1974) *Theory in Practice. Increasing Professional Effectiveness*. San Francisco, Jossey-Bass. Landmark statement of 'double-loop' learning' and distinction between espoused theory and theory-in-action.
- Drew, S. (2001) 'Student perceptions of what helps them learn and develop in High Education', *Teaching in Higher Education*, 6(3), 309–31.
- Honey, P. and Mumford, A. (1992) *The Manual of Learning Styles*. Maidenhead, Peter Honey.
- Kolb, D. A. and Fry, R. (1975) 'Toward an applied theory of experiential learning', in C. Cooper (ed.) *Theories of Group Process*. London, John Wiley.
- Knight-Moore, P. T. (1997) 'The half-life of knowledge and structural reform of the education sector for the global knowledge-based economy', Paper prepared for the Forum on Education in the Information Age organized by the Inter-American Development Bank and the Global Information Infrastructure Commission and hosted by the Universidad de los Andes Cartagena, Colombia, 9–11 July 1997. Available at: **www.knight-moore.com/pubs/halflife.html** [last accessed March 2007].
- Leitch Review (2007) *Prosperity for all in the Global Economy: World Class Skills*, H.M. Treasury, UK Government, available at: **www.hm-treasury.gov.uk/leitch** [last accessed March 2007].
- Schön, D. A. at Informal Education (Infed), available at: **www.infed.org/thinkers/et-schon.htm** [last accessed March 2007].

[illegible]
accessed March 2007).

- Smith, M. K. (2001) 'David A. Kolb on experiential learning', The encyclopaedia of informal education. [illegible] (last accessed March 2007).

[illegible]

1.1 Managing your stress

Most of your time at university will be a happy and enjoyable one. There may be times, however, when you feel things are getting out of control and you feel uncomfortably stressed. This can be related to your studies, your personal life, or both. Knowing what stress does to our bodies, our own tendencies towards being stressed, and the approaches we use to handle stressful events is an important life skill.

In this chapter you will learn how to:

1. identify signs of stress in yourself and others
2. develop proactive strategies to dealing with stress
3. recognise a personal tendency to be more stressed
4. recognise what your stressors are and how to manage them.

USING THIS CHAPTER

Estimate your current levels of confidence. At the end of the chapter you will have the chance to re-assess these levels where you can incorporate this into your personal development planner (PDP). Mark between 1 (poor) and 5 (good) for the following:

I can recognise my own signs of stress.	I can recognise what stresses me.	I can apply proactive strategies to combat stress.

Date: ________________

1 Introduction

Of students surveyed for the Student Experience Report in 2006, 98% said that university life is a happy one. You may well be one of those and may look at the title of this chapter and feel that you are not particularly stressed and that, if you were, you could cope with it. However, 56% of those students also said that since being at university they were under a lot more stress than before.

If you are thinking of not reading this chapter because you currently don't feel stressed, **stop now** and consider the following: I know what happens to my body when I am stressed, I can recognise the symptoms and I fully understand what stresses me. I have also reflected on my attitude to things in my life and realise this plays a role in how stressed I feel and I have enough belief in myself to solve any issues that cause anxiety. If you are happy with all these statements, move on. If not, and you wish to develop or hone this life skill, read on.

2 What happens to our bodies under stress?

Richard Lazarus, an eminent psychologist who won the prestigious award of 'American Psychologist' in 2002, claimed that stress and anxiety mainly occur when we believe we can't cope with the problem we perceive as stressful (Lazarus and Folkman, 1984). When we see this problem as overwhelming and feel we have no way of escaping or solving it, we experience anxiety or stress. However, we don't all see the same events as stressful.

We have different perceptions of what is stressful, we have different levels of confidence in dealing with it and different ways of coping with it. There is therefore no one solution, but in general, it is the feeling of being out of control that makes us anxious and stressed.

How do our bodies respond to stress?

When we perceive an event as stressful, our bodies react physiologically to it. The Harvard physiologist Walter Cannon coined the term 'fight or flight' in the 1920s and it refers to our body's physiological response to a threatening situation, be this physical or emotional. When we feel threatened our heart rate speeds up, our blood pressure rises and our muscles tighten. At the same time our body releases the hormone cortisol that increases the flow of energy to our muscles. This makes us ready for action; we either stay and fight or run. Once we have dealt with the threat our body returns to normal. However, if our perceived threat doesn't result in action, then cortisol takes longer to disappear. If we 'run away' from a piece of coursework, for example, it isn't going to help very much. We may find ourselves even more stressed. 'Running away' from many of our stressors often means making excuses, and this can make things worse in the long run, making us feel even more stressed. If this continues over a long period of time, it attacks our immune system, our cardiovascular system, digestive system and musculoskeletal system until we are exhausted and eventually become ill.

Excess cortisol also affects the part of the brain that is central to learning and memory by interfering with how our brain cells communicate with one another. In a crisis, we often don't remember what went on exactly; it is as if our 'lines are down' and we only react to that which is vital. So, not handling stress well, or being under constant stress will affect our ability to learn.

Being alert to what creates stress in our lives, and developing techniques that can enable us to cope with these, and reduce excess flow of cortisol, is therefore an essential life skill.

NOTE Although stressors increase the amount of cortisol in our bloodstream, we also have 'daily shots' of cortisol throughout our daily cycle (circadian rhythm). This helps to keep us alert, by maintaining our blood pressure and enabling us to react to our environment.

3 What are the symptoms of stress?

When we feel stressed we notice changes in our emotions and our behaviour. Activities 1 and 2 help you to identify stress in yourself and others.

ACTIVITY 1 Identifying signs of stress

Look at the scenarios below and complete the table.

Carlos is a very outgoing and confident person and has decided to study abroad. He is now reaching the end of his first semester. He is very gregarious and has a good friendship group. However, his friends are noticing that he is becoming increasingly withdrawn, is not eating properly and appears 'on edge' a lot of the time. When they try to talk to him he becomes irritable and no one feels they should pry any further.

Lucy is a third-year student and has always had a very full social life. Her tutors have spoken to her many times for handing work in late and missing classes. However, she always seemed to pull things together at the last minute. Just recently, however, you have noticed that she has started drinking more and when you pointed this out to her she said she wasn't sleeping well and needed some alcohol to help. You have also noticed that your fun-loving friend has little interest in the things you used to do together. She is also getting into difficulties with her third-year project group who are complaining of her forgetfulness and lack of interest in the project.

	Signs of stress	**What he/she might be feeling**	**What he/she should do**
Carlos			
Lucy			

Check the feedback section for more information.

ACTIVITY 2 Recognising your own symptoms of stress

When **you** feel stressed what symptoms do you have? List them under how you **feel** – including physical characteristics (e.g. heart pounding, feeling sick, tired) and how you **act** (e.g. irritable, lack of interest, get emotional).

How do you feel? (include physical and emotional characteristics	How do you act and behave?

Check the feedback section for more information.

Let's keep things in proportion. We all get stressed at times. Most of the time symptoms are uncomfortable but short lived and manageable. Sometimes we aren't even aware of feeling stressed until someone points out how irritable we are. However, we can get chronic stress symptoms and this needs to be dealt with.

Is all stress bad?

Stress can be both positive and negative. Positive stress is having just about enough stress to motivate and challenge us. It can give us a buzz. However, generally when we hear the word 'stress' we associate it as a negative state, as our symptoms above show. So, for some a group project, an essay or a presentation may be seen as positive and challenging while for others it could be seen as negative and worrying.

Also, we need some stress in our lives to keep us alert and ready for that challenge. We have probably all experienced a rise in our heart rate just as we are about to do something we feel challenging or stressful, but often that is what we need to get us up and running – a healthy dose of cortisol that dissipates quite soon afterwards. How many of us have put off a task because the deadline is just too far away? As the deadline approaches, we get the 'rush' and this stimulates us into activity. The trick is knowing when this can flip over from being the kick-start you need to being stressful.

Reflect on how you deal with deadlines; are you generally operating too close for comfort or just about right? You will probably find you have a particular tendency (see Chapter 1.2 'Managing your time'). You need to identify this so you can tackle it, if you need to.

Some symptoms of positive stress are:

- I feel excited
- I get motivated
- it gives me a buzz
- it stretches me intellectually or physically
- it enables me to learn.

4 Personal development in handling stress

Broadly speaking our attitudes will affect how we relate to others, how we cast blame when things don't work out, how we go about our tasks and the degree of control we feel over our lives. We need to develop our self-awareness in identifying stress and stressful events as well as confidence (self-belief) in being able to regain control over our lives.

Making personal changes – developing emotional intelligence

Daniel Goleman, author of the popular book *Emotional Intelligence* (1995), claims that intellectual IQ alone does not give us all the skills needed to be successful in everyday life. We need to develop self-awareness and recognise what others are feeling (empathy), know how to handle our emotions and to have self-discipline. This, Goleman claims, is emotional intelligence or emotional quotient (EQ). Group work projects, for example, if taken seriously, develop our interpersonal skills (emotional literacy). Similarly, effective use of the personal development planner (PDP) enables us to reflect on our progress and personal development. These aspects of the curriculum therefore have good reasons for being there.

Activities 1 and 2 have been included so that you can see the importance of being aware of your own and your friends' behaviour as an initial step in dealing with stress.

Emotional intelligence comprises, in essence, three areas: know yourself, choose yourself, give yourself. These are summarised in the table below.

By developing your emotional intelligence, you have the grounding to develop your self-belief and self-confidence, which gives you confidence to become more in control of your life. You also become aware of your own behaviour and how this can limit you as well as increasing your empathy towards your friends' troubles.

Emotional intelligence categories	Questions	Application to your studies
Know yourself	• What makes you think and feel the way you do? • What parts of your reactions are habitual or consciously thought through? • What are you afraid/ anxious of?	Being honest with yourself enables you to reflect on your qualities and faults. You learn from your experiences. Reflect on this through your studies, part-time work, etc., and make notes in your personal development planner. This reflection should alert you to habitual actions – possibly fear of exams, particular coursework, etc. When you become aware of this you can then try to prevent yourself being a hostage to previously learned negative reactions.
Choose yourself	• How do you know what's right for you? • If you were not afraid or anxious what would you do? • Can you increase your awareness of your actions?	Manage your feelings. If something starts to stress you, identify exactly what it is and objectively assess why this is a stressor for you. Can you manage it yourself or do you need help?
Give yourself	• Am I helping or hurting people? • Am I working interdependently with others? • Have I developed empathy? • Do I work by a set of personal standards?	Be aware of your fellow students. When working together be alert to their needs as well as yours (be empathic).

Adapted from the Emotional Intelligence Network, **http://6seconds.org/index.php**.

Making personal changes – developing self-belief

As we have mentioned, an important aspect of dealing with stress is this ability to feel you can control your life. The modern day reaction to the 'flight or fight' is our ability to change things that stress us and to do that we need to have confidence in ourselves (see Activity 3).

Albert Bandura, a famous Canadian professor in Psychology, began to see personality as an interaction between psychological processes, the environment and our behaviour. He noticed that those who felt more in control of their lives (had high self-efficacy) behaved differently and personally achieved more (Bandura, 1997).

ACTIVITY 3 Is it all down to fate?

Look at the following statements – do you agree with them or not?

	Agree	Disagree
When things go wrong for me, it is just bad luck.		
It doesn't matter how well I plan, what's going to be, will be.		
Friendships are a result of chemistry – they work or they don't.		
Some people have all the luck.		
When things go wrong, I can usually find out who is to blame		

As you probably realised, these are statements that reflect someone who has little self-belief in their own ability to make changes. Take a note of where your tendency lies. Check the feedback section for comments on these statements.

Write a new list of statements below that reflects someone who has self-belief.

	Generally me	Generally not me

Check the feedback section for some more examples once you have written your own.

Strategies for improving self-belief

1. Select a specific task/activity you want to improve and feel confident about. Thinking specifically is vital.
2. This activity needs to be important to you as this will give you the motivation to work on it.
3. Has your previous experience of doing this activity been negative? If so, identify the specific negative aspects so you can work on them (don't generalise because you can't work with generalisations).

4. Develop a picture of yourself, or someone, doing this activity well. What makes it good? Make sure you 'see' your negative aspects performed well. Keep that picture in mind.
5. Set yourself specific and short-term goals to deal with aspects of the activity you have identified. See the section below on approaches to dealing with stressful events.
6. Seek feedback and work with it positively. If you feel you 'can't do something' always say 'I can't do that YET.' It has a powerfully confident feel about it.
7. Verbalise (write it out) your strategy for achieving your short-term goals. This way you have articulated your success and you can 'hear' it, and it primes you for action.
8. Small successes breeds overall success.

NOTE Being 'in control' of events in your life is not about being a 'control freak'. It is about feeling that you can DO something to help. The higher your emotional intelligence, the better you will be at trusting others in order to give and receive help. Recognise when you need support and be proactive in seeking it out.

Checklist for signs of stress

Take the list of symptoms here as a warning signal. If these symptoms become chronic you must seek help.

Physical

Headaches, backache, exhaustion, insomnia, pounding heart, diarrhoea or constipation, stiff neck and shoulders, rashes, nausea.

Emotional

Feeling useless, worthless, not confident of abilities, not recognising your strengths, talking yourself down, feeling lonely, feeling 'out of control', feeling irritable and angry.

Intellectual

Feeling you can't learn another thing, you can't remember things, you don't process information very well in class, you have to keep going over something to make it 'stick'.

As a result of some of these symptoms you may find that you have negative reactions, such as: withdrawal from friends, mood swings, angry outbursts, inability to make decisions, weepy, not hungry or eating too much, feeling sick when you open 'that' book or go past the library, possibly excessive drinking, drug abuse or self-harming.

NOTE If things have gone on too long or have become worse you may start to show more serious symptoms such as obsessive behaviour, suicidal feelings or depression. If you feel your symptoms are getting worse and you are worried, you must get professional help either from your doctor or the counselling service at your institution. If you do this, make sure you tell your personal tutor so that he/she can make allowances for late work or postpone certain assignments.

5 Do I have a personality that stresses me out?

We are all aware that some of our friends get more stressed out than others and we may envy them if we are the one that gets stressed out while they remain calm. We should be aware by now that there are (a) individual differences in how stressful or challenging we see particular events, and (b) individual differences in our perceptions of our own ability to deal with these events, once we see them as stressful. One of the factors for these individual differences is our different personality styles.

How does your personality affect your stress levels?

In the 1950s, two cardiologists, Dr Meyer Friedman and Dr Ray Rosenman, observed that there was more heart disease in their male patients with high-pressured jobs. This may seem obvious to us now but it wasn't at the time. They also noted that particular personality types were also more prone to heart disease. The personality type they felt was more 'at risk' was their so-called 'Personality A' person. Incidentally, Friedman regarded himself as a 'recovering type A'. The type A personality has now become synonymous with 'driven' people, obsessed with time and perfection. The counter to that is the type B personality that is laid-back and easy going.

Are you a type A or a type B?

Type A and type B is essentially a continuum of personality traits from being uptight to laid-back. It is not an intricate measure of your personality but serves to give you a guideline of where your tendencies are.

Type A personalities tend to:

- be very goal driven (in the extreme often at all costs)
- be competitive
- need recognition and advancement

- multi-task when under time pressure
- be keen to get things finished
- be mentally and physically alert (above average).

NOTE There is continuing debate as to whether type A personality people are more at risk from heart disease. But the potential anger and hostility aspect of this personality type does seem to be a factor.

Type B personalities tend to:

- be more relaxed
- be more easy-going
- socialise a lot
- be less competitive
- set realistic goals that don't overstretch them.

If you are not sure which personality type you are, the Science Museum has a short online fun quiz that allows you to find out. This can be found at: **www.sciencemuseum.org.uk**. Search on 'stress' from their search engine.

Help! I'm a type A personality and I'm already stressed out about it

Not all characteristics of type A people are bad. You will know yourself if you feel too driven or uptight. If you feel you are a type A person you may feel stressed out, for example, if you can't achieve what you set out to do, or if you see coursework deadlines looming and you think you are going to be late. You may need to re-adjust your personal standards and become a little more relaxed, if you feel you are overdoing things. Some of your friends may hint at your behaviour and you may want to consider if you are being too 'driven'.

Think about yourself and develop your emotional intelligence. Are there ways you can tone down your type A characteristics? Identify some of your characteristics you think you can work on. Also, check out the stress busting techniques to help you when you need them.

Why bother – I'm a type B personality?

Not all the characteristics of extreme type B personalities are good. You may find yourself too laid-back where nothing stresses you until things get out of hand. You need to submit work tomorrow and suddenly you have got to get into action and you may not have the time to give your best. But, if you are an extreme type B this may not worry you either! However, try and balance your relaxed style and ensure you are keeping to the goals you have set.

We need to get a balance

As with everything, we need a balance of drive and relaxation. Ideally you should be halfway between a type A and type B person. This way you can deal with unexpected deadlines and other stressors by calm planning. You feel in control and not stressed out.

So once you have become self-aware, emotionally literate and believe in yourself, how do you approach stressful events?

6 Proactive strategies for dealing with stress

Stress-busting techniques are one way of coping with stress (see Section 8), but they are just that, 'techniques', and they are good to have. However, a more fundamental way of dealing with stress is to be **proactive** in your management of it. Psychologists have identified two broad types of coping strategy:

- problem-focused strategy
- emotion-focused strategy.

Problem-focused strategy	• Know your stressors. • Analyse what stresses you about an event. • Break down the various components of the situation into manageable chunks. • Identify which part is the problem. • Look at the options. • Develop an action plan. • Check your resources – do you need help?
Emotion-focused strategy	• Know your stressors. • Reflect on how you *feel* when confronted with this stressor. • Resist your feeling to avoid thinking about this. • Reflect on how you can start to change this emotion. • Trust in others and discuss with a friend or counsellor.

Source: Coping strategies from Lazarus and Folkman (1984)

If you are already a proactive stress-buster, you may find you have a preference for one or other of the strategies above. Ideally, you should be using both strategies and they tap into your self-belief and your emotional intelligence. Activity 4 asks you to think about how you solve problems.

ACTIVITY 4 Problem solving as a way of dealing with stress

Now think of an example that is pertinent to you. How would you use this problem solving strategy?

1. Identify a stressful problem.
2. What makes it stressful?
3. How do I feel about it?
4. What can I do now to manage it?

Are you ready to test your stress?

The Science Museum website has an excellent **stressometer**, which gives you a fun score from 'totally chilled' to 'melt down'. Follow the link to this on their website at: **www.sciencemuseum.org.uk**. Search on 'stress' to find it.

Checklist for proactive coping strategies	
	Need to work on this ✓
Personal development: • Self-belief (I am a 'can do' person) • Emotional intelligence (I know myself and trust others)	
Personality type: • Type A (perfectionist, driven, high standards) • Type B (relaxed)	
Strategies: • Problem-focused (analyse, action plan) • Emotion-focused (realign emotions)	

7 What makes studying stressful?

Learning does cause stress and your ability to handle some degree of stress will help you. You may well find you are in your comfort zone at the beginning of a course where you feel in control of your learning and you can predict what is going on. However, very soon you may find that as the difficulty increases you feel less in control of what you know and don't know and very soon fall outside your comfort zone. At this stage you are learning! It is important to recognise that you must go through this stage in order for your new knowledge to find its place and become your new comfort zone. It is important to get back into your new comfort zone, although for some students this takes until the exams before everything starts to fall into place. Look at the graph in Figure 1.[1] Where do you feel you are now? Are you happy to be outside your comfort zone while you learn?

Becoming a student can be seen as a 'rite of passage'. It is something you probably feel you want to do; it does mature you. You leave home, make a new home for yourself, make new friends and learn about something you are interested in. These are all exciting challenges and can give you such a buzz – **or** – completely stress you out. Which is it for you? Activity 5 asks you to identify stressors in academic life.

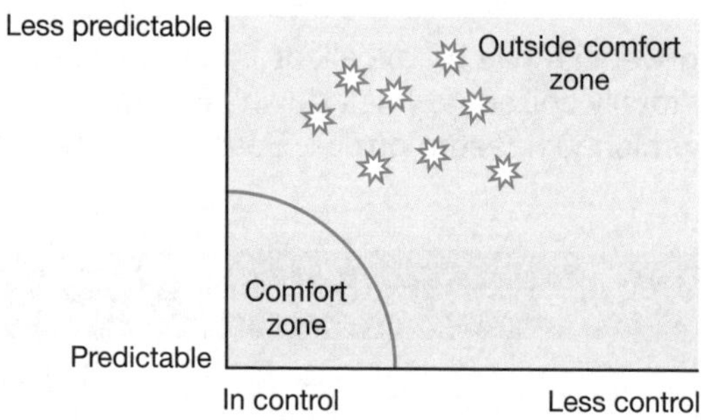

Figure 1 Are you in your comfort zone?

ACTIVITY 5 Stressors in academic life

Identify some of the stressors in academic life from this typical scenario. What do you think Joanne should do? Then identify academic stressors that particularly affect you.

> Joanne was the first of her family to go on to further study and she was very excited at studying engineering. She made friends quickly through her studies and the clubs she joined. However, now in her third year, money, or lack of it, is an increasing worry. She has taken out several loans but has now decided to take a part-time job to make ends meet and has found herself a job in a local restaurant. She works two evenings a week on four-hour shifts finishing at midnight. She has also taken on another small job in the local supermarket working a busy afternoon shift. While her bank balance is now looking healthier, she feels that the late nights and the extra supermarket job are beginning to affect her work. Her studies are increasingly complex and she has several projects to complete. As this is her third year she needs good grades to get the degree she wants. She is beginning to feel there are too many demands on her life and doesn't know how to cope, especially since her boss is pressurising her to work more shifts.

[1] Thanks to Professor Mark Lutman from the University of Southampton who discussed these ideas. He feels that a good learner is one who can cope with being outside their comfort zone – as long as it is not for too long.

	Academic stressors	Coping strategies
Joanne		
You		

Will I/do I fit in?

When you leave home to study you leave behind something you have grown familiar with: your friends, your town, your boyfriend/girlfriend and your family. This familiar environment has helped make you and support you. Although you are excited by leaving all this behind, you may find that once you are away things do not feel as comfortable or safe as they did at home. You are basically homesick. Many of your fellow students will also be feeling the same and you know you have to make an effort to fit in, find new friends and belong. The best time to do this is right at the beginning of your studies when everyone is looking out for new friends. You may find that you don't mix with the right group in the first instance, but by the second semester you will be feeling confident enough to know who you'd like to be with and how to go about it. Being shy may make this process slower, but try and join clubs you are interested in and that should automatically link you with like-minded people.

I never seem to have enough money

The Student Experience Report 2006, carried out by MORI (Unite, 2006), with over a 1000 face-to-face interviews with undergraduate and postgraduate students, found that of those sampled, over half reported difficulties managing their finances and one-third had already asked their families to help them out in a crisis. Postgraduate and mature students, however, were least likely to turn to their families for financial support.

Finances are an increasing source of stress for students and finding part-time work is an obvious solution. The trend towards part-time work when in full-time education is growing. The Student Experience Report 2006 reported that four in ten of those interviewed had done part-time work during their studies, and this is set to increase. In a *Guardian Unlimited* article in 2002 it was reported that the National Union of Students in the UK estimated that approximately 42% of students worked part time, whereas the Trade Union Council's survey in 2000 claimed that 60% of students needed to work to meet basic living costs (Henessey, 2002). Although working gives you that added work experience and responsibility, too much can damage your studies. The Government recommends that you spend no more than 10 hours/week in part-time employment.

Lack of money is the route cause of other stressors, e.g. poor accommodation, cheap food and lack of course materials. So getting your finances right is crucial (see Activity 6).

ACTIVITY 6 Budgeting

Budgeting is something we have to do all our lives. However, if finance is a particular stressor for you then you must get to grips with budgeting. This is rarely anyone's favourite activity, but to prevent debts building up you need to know what comes in and what goes out and work within that budget as much as you can.

How do your finances look? Work on a weekly or monthly basis, whichever suits you best.

	Amount incoming weekly/monthly	**Amount outgoing weekly/monthly**
INCOME:		
Loan		
Part-time work		
Family		
Savings		
Other		
ACCOMMODATION:		
Rent		
Electricity		
Gas		
Water		
Telephone		
Council tax		
Other		

	Amount incoming weekly/monthly	Amount outgoing weekly/monthly
STUDIES:		
Tuition fees		
Field trips		
Stationery		
Project costs		
Other		
LIVING COSTS:		
Food		
Eating out (evening and day)		
Toiletries		
Mobile phone		
Travel: car		
Travel: bus fares – daily		
Travel: long-distance trips (home?)		
Clothes		
Other (dentist, doctor, prescription, etc.)		
SOCIAL LIFE:		
The pub		
Cinema, clubs		
Sporting activities		
Other		
TOTAL		

Do the incoming and outgoing columns balance?

What should you do if you find yourself in need of financial support ? Your institution will have a student support centre where you can find out information on the student hardship fund that they operate. They may have other schemes to help you budget more effectively. These are people in your institution whose job it is to help you; you should be proactive and seek them out.

I don't know what my tutors expect of me

A problem for first-year students is that move into Higher Education. You may have come from an 'A' level course in the UK, be an international student or a mature student returning to full-time education.

Always check your programme and course documentation (see 'Learning in Higher Education') as this describes the aims of your courses and the learning outcomes. Always make sure you know exactly what is needed in an assignment, never assume. Remember you will be expected to develop an independent style of learning (see 'Learning in Higher Education'). If you are in doubt regarding what is expected either ask your tutor or a student in the second or third year.

If you have a study buddy or peer mentoring scheme in your institution, take full advantage of it. If not, you may want to ask if one can be set up. See the Peer Assisted Learning website at Bournemouth University, **www.peer-learning.ac.uk**.

I just can't learn everything I am expected to

The academic load and demands of coursework are another area that has been identified as a cause of stress. You may find that your assignments are bunched towards the end of the semester and you struggle to hand in on the deadlines.

Assignment deadline bunching is a problem. But, if you are given the task way ahead of time, you will be expected to time manage all your assignments (see Chapter 1.2, 'Managing your time'). Plan when you can fit each assignment in given the amount of knowledge you know at the time. Sometimes you may have to get started before you have had the lecture, seminar or laboratory class. You can make an outline plan and fit in as much as you can as you go along.

Academic load in terms of sheer quantity of what you are expected to learn will mean that you need to develop some effective academic skills. The chapters in this book are designed to do just that. Actively take what you need from each chapter and **act on it** and this will start to reduce your stress as you begin to feel in control. Activity 7 asks you to identify your stressful events.

The complexity of the material you have to learn will also increase with the years and this has been shown to be another stressor. Don't suffer in silence over something you are struggling with. Ask your tutor and possibly a postgraduate teaching assistant who may be helping on the course. Don't forget you can ask your friends or student mentors, if you have this set up in your programme.

In 'Learning in Higher Education', we discussed the characteristics of a novice and an expert; you may want to check this out again later.

ACTIVITY 7 Identifying your stressful events

Which of the following, if any, do you find stressful:

- bunched assignment deadlines
- the sheer quantity of work to get through
- complexity of the work
- anything else?

How can you be proactive in managing these potential stressors for you?

Complete the concept map below with the different types of study stressors and list ways of dealing with them. Place each study stressor on the first branch and the ways of dealing with it on the lower branches.

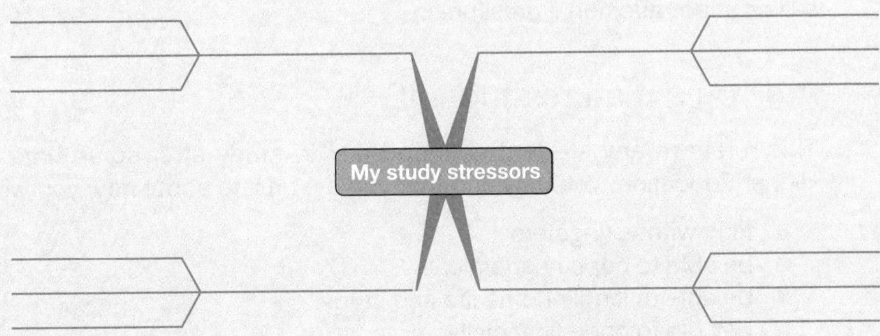

See feedback section for a map of the result of stress on study.

Dropping out: a response to stress?

Dropping out from your studies can be a response to stress, but not necessarily. If you feel that you really have chosen the wrong subject, the wrong place to study and you now know exactly what you want to do and it is not studying, then leave. You will become even more stressed if you stay and will only be staying because you want to 'save face' or not offend someone. According to a BBC article (BBC News, 2004) one in seven students in the UK drop out. However, this varies greatly across institutions. Learning how to keep stress under control and not letting it ruin your life is vital.

If you want to leave because you feel you can't cope or you are generally unhappy, **think again**. With the help of your personal tutor, a student adviser, a friend, or a religious leader, discuss why you are unhappy and what your options really are. You will find there are various options and one could be just right for you, enabling you to go on and graduate. **Don't let wanting to leave be a flight reaction to stress.**

Who gets more stressed out?

As we should know by now, being stressed out varies between individuals. However, some groups of students are more likely to feel the pressures than others. Stressors can be external or internal. External stressors refer to things outside of us that we have to deal with, e.g. exams, coursework, finances, etc. Internal stress refers to our own personality characteristics, or if we are dealing with some incapacity or illness. So, all stress is an interplay between what we bring to the event and the event itself. The imbalance between internal and external stressors can affect our psychological and physiological well-being and cause stress (Lazarus and Cohen, 1977).

Since external factors play a role in stress, certain students may find themselves under additional pressures.

Are you a mature student?

This refers to any student coming back to study after some time out of Higher Education. You may find that you are unsure about how you will:

- fit in with youngsters
- be able to cope academically
- be able to juggle home life and study
- be able to cope financially.

Are you an international student?

As an international student you also have additional things that add pressure. You will have to deal with:

- setting up home in another country
- being homesick
- understanding the cultural differences (socially and academically)
- working in a language that is not your native language
- facing, possibly, racist comments. Do report this if within the university.

External pressures are discussed in Activity 8.

NOTE You are probably a happy and well-adjusted student even though you may have these added pressures. Please don't feel you have to be stressed out. If you are coping well, you may want to be alert to students in a similar situation to you who are not coping well and you may be able to give them some support (develop your emotional intelligence).

ACTIVITY 8 My external pressures

	Applies to me	Do I need to do anything?
Just returning to full-time education after many years and wonder how I will cope.		
I'm homesick (or may become).		
My English is not good enough.		
I'm not giving enough time to my family.		
I miss my friends back home.		
Can I cope?		

List more pressures that apply to you and check if you think you need to do something about it to keep it in check. What personality type are you – could this influence your reaction to stress? Are you proactive and use problem- and emotion-focused coping strategies (see Sections 4, 5 and 6 above)?

8 Stress-busting techniques: a maintenance strategy

In addition to the personal development and proactive strategies above, we can develop a maintenance programme that enables us to cope with on-going stress that hits us once in a while. Some basic techniques are:

- **Exercise**. This will help the physiological aspect of stress and the release of endorphins will give you a feeling of euphoria as well as help your heart. It is also ideal for getting rid of anger and frustrations. If you want to choose only one stress-busting technique, then choose this one.
- **Relax**. When you are feeling stressed out it is difficult to unwind. You may find you have to make a big effort to do this. It may be better to go to classes such as yoga or tai-chi. Exercising also helps you to relax. If you want to develop your own relaxation techniques then try deep breathing or meditation. Go out with friends and have a good laugh.

- **Eat well**. Avoid junk food and too much alcohol – both of these can sap your energy and make you feel low.
- **Talk**. Open up to friends and family. They will feel honoured that you trust them enough to discuss your problems. Talking allows you to see things in perspective and get another view.
- **Stress diary**. By keeping a diary you start to articulate what your feelings are and what stresses you out. Once you do this you become conscious and self-aware, which is where you must start in order to cope. You can couple this with talking to your friends.
- **Focus**. When we are stressed we start to feel overwhelmed. Go back and look at the strategies for developing self-belief above and focus on each part of your plan.
- **Get support from others**. There are some problems you can't and shouldn't face on your own. Don't try and be superman or superwoman. Most Higher Education institutions are caring and will have support in place for you. You should make yourself familiar with what is available, for example: student services, Students Union, religious chaplains, counselling services, medical services, your personal tutor and, of course, your friends and family.

Exams – the special case

During revision:

- plan a realistic revision timetable – this will help you stay on top of things
- summarise your notes, make key points, highlight important information and use concept maps for quick overviews
- take breaks so you can stay alert.

During the exam:

- 'feel' calm – breathe slowly and deeply
- feel in control
- read the instructions carefully (very often students don't do this)
- read the questions calmly – underlining key aspects
- mark the questions you want to do first
- allocate time for each question
- allow time to check your work.

9 On reflection

Stress management, as you have seen, is much more than learning a few techniques; it is life changing. It cannot guarantee you a stress-free life, and would you want one? But, it will enable you to manage it and keep the health-threatening aspects of stress under control.

Summary of this chapter

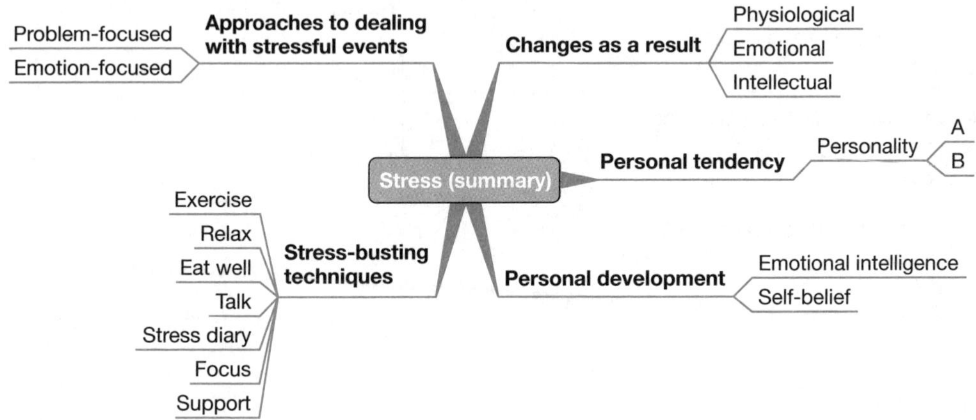

Now reflect on your current abilities to work through a stress-management plan and consider what you need to do to improve. You may want to transfer this information to your own institution's personal development planner scheme.

ACTIVITY 9 Update your personal development planner

Having read this chapter, gauge your confidence again – how does this compare to your confidence levels at the start of the chapter? What can you do to improve? You can incorporate this in to your own personal development planner and of course add anything else that you feel is appropriate.

Grade your confidence on a scale of 1–5 where 1 = poor and 5 = good.

My stress management plan	Confidence level 1–5	Plans to improve
Recognise my personal tendency to being stressed (personality type A, B). *Section 5*		
Identify what stresses me. *Section 7*		
Recognise how I react to stress. *Section 3*		
Check my self-belief. *Section 4*		

My stress management plan	Confidence level 1–5	Plans to improve
Improve my emotional intelligence *Section 4*		
Identify proactive strategies in dealing with stress that suit me best. *Section 6*		
Identify and use the best stress-busting techniques for me. *Section 8*		

Date:______________________

Getting extra help

- Talk to your university counsellor. He or she will be able to give advice on how best to deal with the common problems associated with the stresses of studying.
- Ask friends how they cope with stress – not only will you discover that it's more common than you think, but also they may have some useful stress-busting tips for you.

Consult a few interesting websites:

- Student Mental Stress: Dstress. This site is produced by Loughborough University and is full of useful information. It is a good interactive site. See: **www.d-stress.org.uk** [last accessed December 2006].
- **Mind: How to Cope with the Stress of Student Life**. They have a guide and a series of tips for getting help if you need it. Search on 'student stress' using their search engine: **www.mind.org.uk** [last accessed December 2006].
- **Channel 4, 4Health**, Student Stress, Wendy Moore. Search on 'stress' using their search engine. 'Most students will feel the effects of stress at some point in their studies and a small number of students may feel stressed or depressed for a lot of the time.' See: **www.channel4.com/health** [last accessed December 2006].

Feedback on activities

ACTIVITY 1 Identifying signs of stress

	Signs of stress	What he/she might be feeling	What he/she should do
Carlos	Becoming withdrawn Not eating properly On edge/irritable	Emotional. This can be weepy, or aggressive. Emotional exhaustion	Notice that things aren't right and something needs to be done before you get too behind with your studies. Talk to someone you trust – friend, tutor or counsellor. Make sure this doesn't go on for too long.
Lucy	Heavy drinking Not sleeping well Disinterested, forgetful	Feeling unwell and possibly depressed from too much alcohol and not enough sleep. Mental exhaustion.	Be alert to a change in behaviour that is unhelpful. Identify the first thing that needs to be done, i.e. stop drinking. Seek help from a friend or counsellor to prevent serious alcohol damage.

NOTE In these case studies the key to moving on is being alert to your own stress patterns and recognising when they are becoming overwhelming. Seek help and allow your friends to help you. As a friend, you may have to help someone who is trying to push you away. Be patient and try not to abandon him or her during this difficult phase of your friendship.

ACTIVITY 2 Recognising your own symptoms of stress

Here are some symptoms of stress. Check the ones that you have identified. You may recognise more symptoms that you didn't realise indicated stress. ▶

How do you feel? (including physical and emotional characteristics)	How do you act and behave?
Feeling overwhelmed	You are disorganised and forgetful. You are over-cautious and have difficulty making decisions. You panic. You have lost your confidence. You can't concentrate on your work. Mental exhaustion.
Feeling tired and exhausted	You have no or little interest in things. You don't sleep well. You cry about things easily.
Feeling anxious and nervous	You are moody, irritable, aggressive and get angry easily. You may resort to recreational drugs to alleviate symptoms.
Feeling very emotional and tearful	You react emotionally and are often near to tears … emotional exhaustion.
Feeling sick/tight feeling in stomach/not hungry	You have diarrhoea and/or lose interest in food.
Heart is pounding	You perspire more than usual.
Feeling homesick	You withdraw from your friends.
Being anti-social	You want to be on your own. People irritate you and you get short tempered.
Feeling depressed	Everything becomes too much and you have little interest in doing anything.

NOTE If your list was rather short, you might now recognise some of the symptoms you have. Add them to your list in this activity. Being aware of our stress symptoms is very important, as we saw in Activity 1.

ACTIVITY 3 Is it all down to fate?

	Comments
When things go wrong for me, it is just bad luck.	This means that you feel your behaviour doesn't contribute, or contribute much to things that go wrong for you. You are placing the blame on something external – 'bad luck'.
It doesn't matter how well I plan, what's going to be, will be.	You feel you have no control as your whole life is already mapped out for you.
Friendships are a result of chemistry – they work or they don't.	Chemistry is definitely part of friendship, but not everything. If you don't work at finding and keeping friends, you will be on your own. Social well-being is very important in controlling stress.
Some people have all the luck.	See the first statement above. In this case you assume other people's successes are a result of 'good luck' rather than their efforts.
When things go wrong, I can usually find out who is to blame.	See the first statement above.

Statements of self-belief

I can influence what happens to me.
If I make specific short-term plans I know I will be able to keep to them.
I know friends are attracted to each other, but I can still influence how well I integrate with my friends. I have the interpersonal and emotional intelligence to do that.
When things go wrong, I work out why and sort it out so that it doesn't happen again.

ACTIVITY 7 Identifying your stressful events

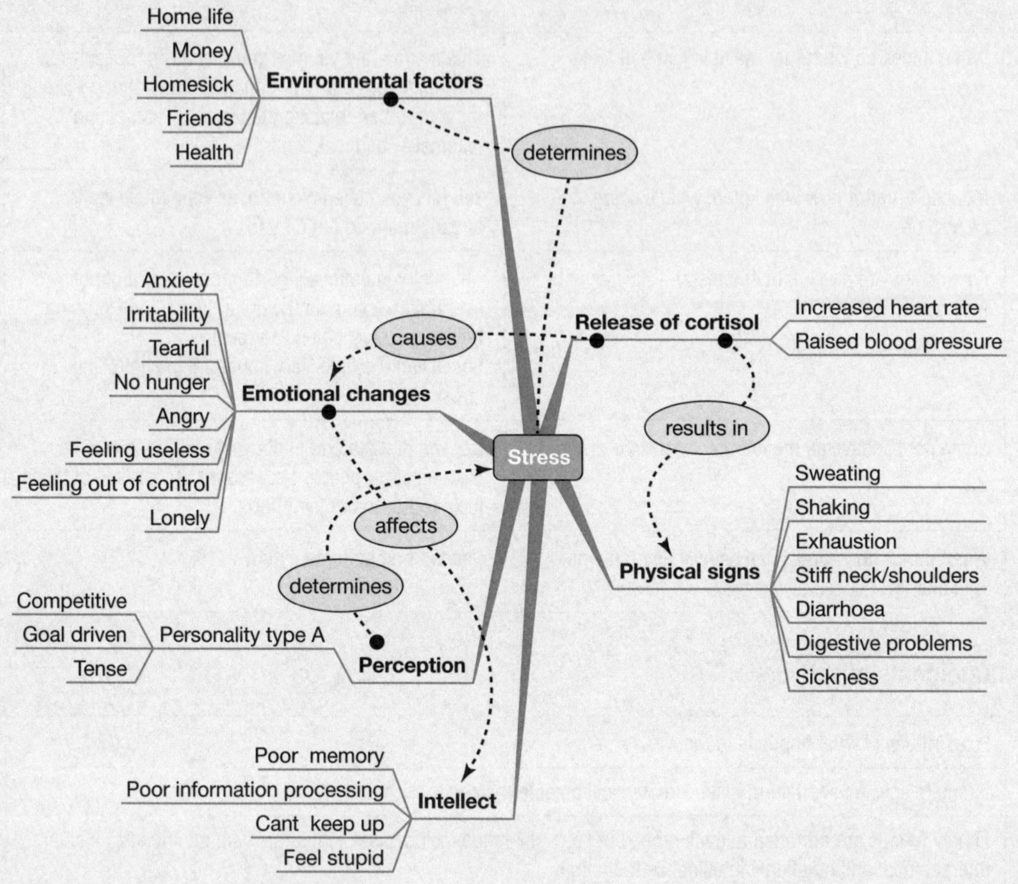

Map of study stressors – summary chart

References

- 6Seconds: Emotional Intelligence Network, at **http://6seconds.org/index.php** [last accessed December 2006].
- Bandura, A. (1997) *Self Efficacy in Changing Societies.* Cambridge, Cambridge University Press.
- BBC News (2004) 'One in seven students to drop out', 30 September available at: **http://news.bbc.co.uk/1/hi/education/3703468.stm** [last accessed December 2006].
- Bournemouth University, Peer Assisted Learning, at **www.peerlearning.ac.uk** [last accessed December 2006].
- Goleman, D. P. (1995) *Emotional Intelligence: Why It Can Matter More Than IQ for Character, Health and Lifelong Achievement*, New York, Bantam Books.
- Hennessy, K. (2002) 'All work and no play makes ... a student', *Guardian Unlimited*, 30 September, available at: **http://education.guardian.co.uk/students/story/0,,802009,00.html** [last accessed March 2007].
- Lazarus, R. S. and Cohen, J. B. (1977) 'Environmental Stress', in I. Altman and J. F. Wohlwill (eds.), *Human Behavior and Environment*, Vol. 2. New York, Plenum.
- Lazarus, R. S., and Folkman, S. (1984) *Stress, Appraisal, and Coping.* New York, Springer.
- Science Museum, **www.sciencemuseum.org.uk** [last accessed December 2006].
- Unite, Student Experience Report 2006, MORI, available at: **www.mori.com/polls/2005/unite.shtml** [last accessed December 2006].

1.2 Managing your time

Managing our time is something like dieting. We know what we should eat, we know why we should eat that way and we know the benefits it will bring. However, how often do we start with good intentions and then let things slip? Time management can be similar. We know why we should manage our time, we often know what to do, but we just can't keep to it.

In this chapter you will learn how to:

1. identify your relationship with time and understand how this affects your time management
2. consider your life goals as part of your time management
3. manage your time efficiently and effectively.

USING THIS CHAPTER

Estimate your current levels of confidence. At the end of the chapter you will have the chance to re-assess these levels where you can incorporate this into your personal development planner (PDP). Mark between 1 (poor) and 5 (good) for the following:

I can identify my relationship with time and understand how this affects my time management.	I can identify my life goals as part of my time management.	I can get the best out of my time.	I can manage my time effectively.

Date: ____________________

1 Introduction

How many of us have started each day by stumbling from lecture to seminar to the café, to the pub, and then to bed, only to do the same the next day with little thought of what we are doing? How many of us start the day by looking at the electronic messages and using that as a driver for the morning's activities? At the end of the day you get to bed exhausted because you have been so busy 'reacting'. But what have you actually done that is important in moving you forward? Are you a proactive time manager or a reactive one?

Our relationship to food, stress and time is very personal and in order to move on in all these areas we need to identify our relationship with them. This chapter enables you to identify your own relationship with time and recognise how you time manage now. You will look at the importance of the whole picture in order for you to fulfil all aspects of your life, not just your studies. Finally, we shall look at the mechanics of time management in order to make things happen.

Seeing time as a resource

We have only to look at the number of idioms in English that relate to time to see that we regard time as a resource. Most of these idioms refer to either spending, wasting or saving time, as shown overleaf.

We are living in an increasingly global world with technological communications that give us instant access to information and we find ourselves in an environment that demands even quicker responses from us than ever

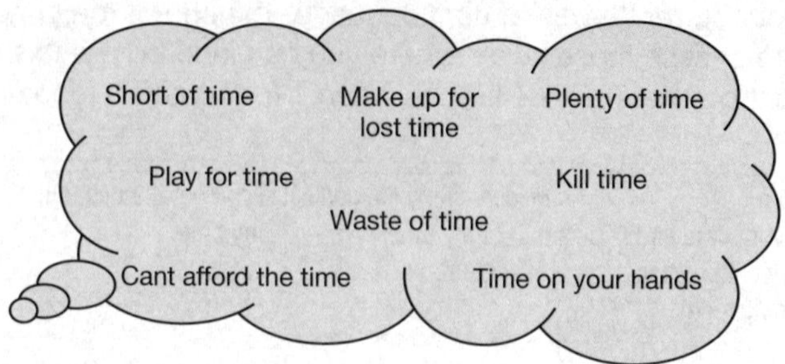

before. We are living in social cultures, be this industry, college, or social spheres, where the volume of activity each week has rocketed. This can result in us feeling controlled by time. In a study of how North Americans use their time, the researchers found that 61% of the population reported never having excess time with 40% feeling that time is a bigger problem for them than money (work by Robinson and Godbey, 1997, cited in Boniwell, 2005).

The life of a student is tightly constrained by deadlines, time slots and timetables. How many times have fellow students you know complained about the amount of coursework they have to do and the bunching of deadlines? We increasingly work and play in environments that demand multi-tasking and that suits some and not others. Time affects us all, but how we **perceive time** and handle it varies between individuals.

2 Recognising your relationship with time

We can get an insight into how we deal with time by recognising if we generally 'look forward', 'look to the past', 'work to the wire' or finish one thing before starting the next. When we look at time like this, we realise there can be no 'one size fits all' as we have individual preferences.

First let us look at our preferences for particular time perspectives, as this is one aspect that affects our motivation to study.

Time perspectives

Professor Philip Zimbardo, an award-winning social psychologist from the University of Stanford, looked at how our dominant orientation to the past, present and the future influences our behaviour and especially our ability to manage our time (Zimbardo and Boyd, 1999). Activity 1 helps you to identify different time perspectives in other people.

ACTIVITY 1 Recognising different time perspectives in others

In this activity there are no absolute answers, and it is used to prepare you for recognising your own relationship with time later. Use the scenarios to give you a flavour of the characters and then estimate the following:

1. What time perspective dominates these students' lives at present: past, present or future? There could also be a mixture of these time perspectives.
2. Who do you think are multi-taskers and single-taskers?
3. Estimate their motivation to study.

Adrian is a second-year student living in a house with other students. He is very sociable and really enjoys his time with friends. The highlight of his week is Thursday night when he goes out with friends until the early hours of the morning. These Thursday nights have been so enjoyable he has started extending them to a few more nights as well, as Adrian's philosophy in life is 'to live for today'. Now, in the second semester, coursework and work difficulty is increasing and he is finding it hard to cope with everything, apart from his social life. He has had several warnings from tutors for late hand-ins, but just can't get around to doing more work, but he knows he has to. He finds it quite difficult to juggle social life and coursework.

Ismet is someone you can rely on to have a good time. He often arranges great evenings that are cheap but great fun. He is now in his third year and knows exactly what he wants to do when he finishes studying. His great planning abilities have helped him manage a busy social life and a challenging course. However, he knows he could probably have got a better degree grade if he had put more work in, but he gets such a buzz from juggling all these parts of his life that he is prepared to accept that. Although, having said that, he is heading for an upper-second degree classification.

Rachael always wanted to be an engineer and as a child was fascinated by those Victorian civil engineers who laid the foundations of our cities today. She knows it is tough, and is determined to get a good degree. She works very hard and is setting up volunteering and vacation work to get as much hands-on experience as possible. She also manages to have several pieces of coursework on the go at the same time and seems to be able to cope with it, although she gets a little irritated if she is interrupted while working. Her friends think she needs to relax a bit and at least take some time to enjoy herself now.

Student	Time perspective (past, present, future)	Preference to multi-tasking or single-tasking	Motivation to study (high, medium, low)	Estimated time management skills (poor, OK, good)
Adrian				
Ismet				
Rachael				

Check the feedback section at the end of the chapter.

Now, think about some of your friends. What time perspective dominates their lives? Do you think they are multi-taskers?

What's your time perspective?

Sometimes it is easier to recognise characteristics in others than ourselves, so now you've looked at others, it is time to take a look at yourself and see if you can identify which time perspective dominates you during semester time: in Activity 2 you can select several time perspectives. It would be interesting to see which one feels like you **now**.

ACTIVITY 2 Identifying your own time perspective

Look at the different time perspectives – which one(s) do you feel dominate(s) you during the semester?

Time persective 1	Time perspective 2
I tend to be impulsive and love excitement. I am happy to take risks as this makes life exciting. My motto is 'Live for today because I don't know what tomorrow will bring.'	My past life was not very pleasant and I too frequently recall events or things I regret doing and it can sometimes affect me now.
Time persective 3	**Time perspective 4**
I know where I want to go and I put plans in place to help me get there. I am prepared to work through boring pieces of coursework as I know it is laying a foundation for later work.	My motto is 'Whatever will be, will be.' I generally feel that I shouldn't worry too much about the future as it will take care of itself and luck plays a large part in how successful one is anyway.
Time persective 5	
I get a warm feeling when I think about the past, my family or cultural traditions. It makes me know who I am. It is very important for me to keep track of my old friends.	

Check the feedback section at the end of the chapter.

Consider how these time perspectives could effect your time management behaviour. Do you think you need to make adjustments to enable your studies?

Ideally we should be balanced between the different positive time perspectives, but not perspectives 2 and 4 as they have a negative effect on our life. Most successful people have a tendency to be 'future oriented' (perspective 3). When you are engaged in your academic studies this should motivate you sufficiently to encourage you to be future oriented. If you are not motivated, then it is going to be hard to engage with your learning or manage your time effectively. However, too much of this orientation can make you a workaholic; so you do need a balance.

We have seen that our time perspective affects our behaviour and our motivation to study and subsequently how we manage time. Our preference to being a multi- or linear tasker reflects our perception of time and how we manage time to complete tasks.

Are you comfortable multi-tasking or not?

An important anthropologist, Edward T. Hall, observed that different cultures had particular preferences when structuring their time. Cultures that see time as linear tend to emphasise the usage of time in discrete slots and complete tasks in a linear manner. Those cultures that see time as more fluid and less exact tend to carry out their tasks in a more non-linear manner and do lots of things at the same time. Work has continued in this field and these characteristics are also observed in individuals and particular jobs.

Different jobs have different time cultures where different time personalities can thrive. Those working with disaster teams, transport crews and surgical teams need people who can estimate time accurately and know what has to be done, when it has to be done, and do it. Those working in more creative fields may find such colleagues stifling. The academic time culture is deadline driven and many institutions will penalise you if your work is not handed in on time. If working to deadlines is not your preferred style then it is important to acknowledge that first and devise ways of coping.

With regard to individuals, those preferring to do one task at a time are seen as 'linear taskers' while those happy to juggle lots of tasks at the same time are seen as 'multi-taskers'. If you see time as being discrete then you are able to identify slots in which to work and control your time. If, on the other hand, you see time as fluid and continuous you may not see much of a separation between work and your social life and you carry out tasks when the mood takes you rather than working to rigid time plans. How you think of time therefore can influence your tendency to multi-task or not. Activity 3 helps you to identify if you are a multi-tasker.

NOTE If you want to learn some jargon; a multi-tasker is a **polychron** (a term first coined by Hall, 1959) and someone who focuses on one task at a time is a **monochron**! Can you recognise monochrons and polychrons in your friendship group?

ACTIVITY 3 Are you a multi-tasker?

Some of the key time management behaviours that can distinguish multi-taskers from others are: planning, focus and attention, reaction to change, and performing under pressure. You may already know if you are a multi-tasker, but have a look at a few of these statements and check the feedback. Remember, we can all be multi- or linear taskers but we prefer to operate in one or the other. Your preference will determine how you manage your time and how you meet your deadlines.

▶

	Ideally me	But in practice ... I do/don't do this ...
Planning		
1. I like to plan what I am going to do. Although I find it hard, I need to plan my time quite carefully. Without a plan, I feel a little bit lost. [linear tasker] 2. I don't like working to a detailed time plan. It makes me feel constrained and irritable. [multi-tasker]		
Focus and attention		
3. Once I start on a task I give it my full attention and I dislike it when I am interrupted. [linear tasker] 4. My focus and attention tends to be spread across lots of different tasks I am doing. It doesn't bother me if I am interrupted, I just deal with that and then carry on. [multi-tasker]		
Reaction to change		
5. I can make rough plans, but happily change them too. [multi-tasker] 6. Once I have worked out my plan of action, I get annoyed if I have to change it. [linear tasker]		
Performance under pressure		
7. I like to keep track of the tasks I have to do and can prioritise very well. This gives me breathing space and so I can do the work before the pressure gets too strong. [linear tasker] 8. I work best when I feel under time pressure. I am usually juggling several pieces of work to meet my deadlines. Prioritising is a last minute approach for me, but I tend to get everything done. [multi-tasker]		
Is your preference multi-tasking or linear tasking?		

Check the feedback section at the end of this chapter for more information

NOTE These characteristics are just some indicators of multi- and linear tasking.

Advantages for the multi-tasker

You will probably feel less intimated by the time pressure as you are able to juggle your coursework. You will probably find this stimulating. You may be a procrastinator as you are happy to leave things to the last minute and get started on many things simultaneously, but make sure you finish them! You have a very flexible working style and can deal with interruptions and changes to your schedule.

Dangers for the multi-tasker

Your preference for working under pressure and leaving things to the last minute does not allow for any mishaps. What if you suddenly realise you don't understand something the night before you hand in your coursework or that you should have completed a set of data before now? Since you can juggle lots of tasks, you may react to all your tasks in the same way. You must remember to plan and schedule and prioritise your activities, at least to some degree. If you try to do too much at one time you can be inefficient as you may just get overloaded and find you don't do anything very well. It may be better to allocate quality time for particularly difficult or important tasks. You may find you are a multi-tasker because you are an urgency addict (see Section 3 below). Now is your time to reveal your true colours!

Advantages for the linear tasker

You consciously want to have control over your time and if you are able to plan and identify time periods when things should be done, you can probably deal with the pressure. As a result of your prioritising and planning, you will be able to focus on key pieces of work.

Dangers for the linear tasker

Studying and the bunching of coursework deadlines can lead to a sense of time stress and the feeling that you can't do anything properly. You need to break down your tasks into smaller chunks and schedule at that level so you feel you are working in a linear mode. You may also need to be flexible enough to find those quality slots at short notice.

Checklist for dealing with your relationship with time

1. Identify your time preference.
2. Recognise if you are a multi- or a linear tasker.
3. Note if you can improve your relationship with time.
4. Recognise how this impacts on your time management.

3 Addressing your life goals: getting a balance

Time management is more than just organising ourselves and writing 'to-do lists'. We also need to make room for our wider goals in life, relationships, friends and family – we need a balance. Just planning and prioritising the tasks we have been given can be rather reactive and in order to account for all aspects of our life that are important to us, we also need to be proactive and ensure we work at them too. In our busy world there is a tendency to be 'urgency driven', reacting to all those demands that cross our path, rather than by those things that are important. We need to make sure we can plan, create and fit in all the things that are important to us in our life.

Traditionally time management training has been concerned with giving us tips to enable us to organise our time and deal with those ever increasing urgent activities, generally in a very linear manner. Stephen Covey, father of nine children, professor of business management and author of one of the most influential business books, *First things First*, believes that we need to change our paradigm of time management from being addicted to dealing with what we perceive as urgent to proactively determining what is important. 'Importance' then becomes the new framework for managing our time.

The framework below was devised by Covey *et al*. (1994) to enable us to clarify what is urgent, not urgent, important and not important. Activity 4 asks what is important in your life.

	Urgent	**Not urgent**
Important	**I** Lectures, seminars etc. Coursework preparation Assignment deadlines Crises	**II** Preparation – long-term goals Planning – long-term goals Relationship building Creating Personal development
Not important	**III** Interruptions (some) Meetings (some) Some e-mails	**IV** Trivia Junk mail Time-wasting activities

Adapted from Covey, *et al.* (1994)

Quadrant I

Activities here are important and urgent; they have to be dealt with. To deal with activities here, we have to have organise and prioritise what needs to be done. If we procrastinate with activities here, there will be serious consequences. In this quadrant we can feel driven and constrained by time, resulting in feeling stressed.

Quadrant II

This quadrant is where we deal with important issues such as planning (to keep quadrant I in check), creating new ideas and working towards our goals for both university and life in general. Keeping fit, doing exercise, broadening our mind, making intellectual leaps in our studies, volunteering, reading, helping friends and family, and developing meaningful relationships are all part of quadrant II. In this quadrant, we feel empowered and we need to proactively deal with items in this quadrant. Don't neglect it.

Quadrant III

Many of us who are urgency addicted will deal with items that seem urgent but are not important. You may find you are reacting to other people's priorities at the expense of your own – try and keep a balance, and say 'no' to a few more non-urgent things.

Quadrant IV

This is where we generally waste our time. We might slump in front of the television, read trashy novels, etc. We are all in this quadrant from time to time, but try to limit how much time you spend here. You will find yourself in this quadrant often if you are driven by urgency as you will be stressed and exhausted and this is where you 'drop'. Also, when you procrastinate, you will find yourself in this quadrant.

ACTIVITY 4 What's important in your life?

You may feel very tempted to skip this activity. Please take time to think about it. The questions are quite challenging, but answers will come.

1. What things are important to me across my life?
2. What gives me a buzz?
3. What kind of work would I like to do after my studies? Do I need to be getting experience in place for that?

Now think of some of the steps you need to take in order to operationalise these goals. What could your plan look like if you include some of these things. Remember these are your quadrant II activities and you need to be proactive in order to make them happen. Quadrant II activities are easier for those with a future time perspective.

This activity is something you need to do on an annual basis as your views do change, and it may need to be revitalised.

NOTE You should be motivated to study and successfully completing your degree should be one of your life goals. If this does not appear in your list, you need to ask yourself why you are studying or if you are studying the wrong subject.

4 Organising yourself

Organising yourself involves planning your time and organising your study space. Your plan tells you what you should do and when you should do it and for how long. Your study space enables that to happen. If you are a multi-tasker you may want to skip this section, but stop and read this as you may be able to maintain your spontaneity and couple this with some degree of planning that can help you. In addition, you should be able to determine the kind of environment that gets the best out of you. Linear taskers will probably be competent planners by now but check where you best learn and ensure you can make that happen.

Of course your degree of motivation for this will depend, to some extent, on your time perspective. Planning encourages the development of a future orientation. If you are dominantly oriented towards the present, you will find it hard to fufil your plans even if you make them. Be careful of this.

How do you organise your time through planning?

Even the worst students of time management don't lurch unconsciously from one thing to another during the day, every day. There is always some degree of planning. However, what is your general pattern on time planning during a week? A plan will give you some idea of where all that time is going and how effective you are at getting those important things done (see Activities 5 and 6). Interestingly, a study in 1997 found that students at a particular university had more study work activity on Monday, Tuesday and Thursday, and fewer studied at weekends. They found that typically students spend 38.8 hours on study-related tasks (the range was 34–48 hours depending on age, gender and year). Of that study time, 35.5% was spent on assessed work, 12.8% in lectures, 8% on non-assessed work, 7.6% of time in tutorials and 3.2% searching books in the library (Innis and Shaw, 1997).

ACTIVITY 5 Developing a weekly schedule

Look back on a typical week during semester time and try to remember how you spent your time. Include sleep, going out, paid work, private study, group/course work etc. as well as attendance at lectures/seminars. Note it down on the schedule below and estimate the time for your activities, using time slots. Are you happy with this or would you have liked it to be different? Is it similar or wildly different to the research above?

A typical week

Approx times	Mon	Tues	Wed	Thurs	Fri	Sat	Sun
8.00–10.00am				9.00–10.00 Lecture			Catching up with sleep
10.00–12.00		11.00–12.00 Lecture	Seminar				Catching up with sleep
12.00–2.00pm						Paid work	Seeing friends
2.00–4.00pm			**Sport**				
4.00–6.00pm			**Sport**				
6.00–8.00pm			Paid work				
8.00–10.00pm			Paid work				
10.00–12.00pm							

Now think of next week and plan how you should spend your time, given the deadlines you have.

Approx times	Mon	Tues	Wed	Thurs	Fri	Sat	Sun
6.00–8.00am	Sleep	Sleep	Sleep	Sleep	Sleep	Sleep	Sleep
8.00–10.00am				9.00–10.00 Lecture			Catching up with sleep
10.00–12.00		11.00–12.00 Lecture	Seminar				Catching up with sleep
12.00–2.00pm						Paid work	Seeing friends
2.00–4.00pm			**Sport**				
4.00–6.00pm			**Sport**				
6.00–8.00pm			Paid work				
8.00–10.00pm			Paid work				
10.00–12.00pm							

Next week my main goals are: ______________________________

ACTIVITY 6 Balancing your time

Look at the activities on your weekly plan:

1. Can you identify the quadrants? Label them: QI, QII, QIII and QIV.
   - Are any of your activities labelled QI really QIII? You can gain time by weeding out QIII type activities.
2. Make a new empty weekly planner and start by putting in events/activities that are time sensitive, e.g. a lecture, as these are immovable.
3. Add QII type activities in the free slots (these may not be on a weekly basis, but possibly a monthly basis). These will be taken from Activity 4, above, 'What's important in your life?' Remember to use the time slots to free up time to do things you want to do.

Organising your study space

You may have read in time management books that you need to have a clear desk (represents a clear head!), be somewhere quiet and not be disturbed. However, when you actually talk to students and ask them their organisational preferences, it varies. What do you prefer? See Activity 7.

ACTIVITY 7 Your current and ideal study space

Imagine you have to complete a piece of coursework, which could, for example, be an essay or a laboratory report. You know you have to begin this piece of work today and so you sit down to start. Answer the questions in the table below. The examples are just prompts, you can also add your own. You may be happy with what you do, then say so; if not, say what would be ideal for you.

	What you do currently	**Is this ideal? If not, what is ideal?**
1. Where do you prefer to work?	*At home, in the library*	
2. Generally how is your work space organised?	*Cleared desk, work on top of other things, work on floor, have papers in a folder, have loose papers*	
3. When you sit down to work do you find yourself getting up soon afterwards?	*You are hungry, thirsty, just need to sort something out quickly. Check the ritual you have before you finally get started*	

	What you do currently	Is this ideal? If not, what is ideal?
4. How long do you think it takes you to feel settled and start work?		
5. Do you like to have music on at the same time as studying or have other people around you?	*Some people need to be alone and quiet and others need a certain background noise. What is your ambient preference?*	

There are no correct answers for this except to say that it is advisable to have all the papers you need to start an assignment at hand, as well as knowing **exactly** (not roughly) what you have to do and how long you have to do it. Having a messy desk and working with music and people around you may be what works for you. If so, then keep to it but do check you get the best out of this and it is not just a habit. The essence of this activity is for you to identify how you currently organise yourself, recognise your rituals (this is like doing stretches in the gym prior to your workout; you prime yourself for activity) and recognise that you are getting ready for work. However, if your 'rituals' go on for too long, you may be procrastinating. So be aware. If you are currently working in a space that is not conducive to your learning, now is the time to identify what the problems are and make changes.

Making a piece of work manageable

Some pieces of coursework can be rather daunting, so you need to create smaller chunks that are easier to manage:

- clarify what is needed in your coursework
  - identify any data you need from experimental or practical work
  - identify the pieces of information you need
- make a list of all the parts/chunks you need to complete
  - order the list
- check your hand-in date for your coursework
  - add a time frame to each chunk.

If you are a multi-tasker you may be happy with the main points. If you are a linear tasker, you may want to further develop the sub-points in your list.

5 Time management strategies

In the earlier sections we have looked at individual preferences with respect to our perceptions of time and how this influences the way we organise our time. In some cases time may be handled well and for others, the majority of us, there will be room for improvement.

Time is a resource that cannot be reused or recycled as with some other resources. We have a fixed number of hours in a semester and the only way of doing all those things we want to do and need to do is to manage this resource more efficiently. If you consider how much effort you put in each day you need to ask yourself what the net effect or outcome of all this effort is.

Mechanics of time management – planning, scheduling and using to-do lists

To do this effectively you need to take different time frames and the most appropriate is the semester, the week and the day. Your semester plan enables you to see the overall picture for your studies and plan those important things that can get lost once the semester starts, e.g. develop a new sport, start up a new hobby, do some volunteering work or attending the careers advisory talks/workshops.

The weekly schedule fills in those time constrained activities like lectures, etc., leaving you slots for other important activities.

The 'to-do' list relates to each day and is where all your planning stops and the 'doing' takes place. This time frame is critical. If you consistently don't deliver within this time frame and you are predominantly a linear tasker, you start to feel overwhelmed and out of control. Multi-taskers may condense their 'to-do' lists in a flurry of activity, possibly at the last minute.

The table opposite gives some idea of how these time management aids work for your studies, but remember this should also include important things you want to do outside of your studies.

NOTE To-do lists is where the action happens and they should have a time frame and be able to support your goals. Make them SMART: specific, manageable, relevant and timely.

Recommending a time management strategy

Good time management is about working smart and not about working long hours. Your time is precious and you don't want to squander it on things that are not important, so be:

1. *S*pecific – quieten your mind and focus on what needs to be done now, later this week and this month. Concentrate on the first two. Make sure your work space is organised for best effect.
2. *M*anageable – manage your time so that it **suits you**. Break large pieces of work into manageable chunks that enable successful/staged completion.
3. *A*ppropriate – work on things that are right for now.
4. *R*elevant – don't just rush into any job, this will make you 'urgency driven'. Remember to be driven by what is important and reduce those activities that just waste your time.

4. *T*imely – your time management should be organised in a way that enables you to work through important tasks within a given time frame. Your plan can be rough or detailed, depending on your preference, but whatever your style, the hand-in date is just that.

Long-term planning	Mid-term planning	Short-term planning
Planning ⟶		Doing (outcome from your time planning)
Semester plan	Weekly schedule	Daily to-do list
Identify your academic goals for this semester.	This is similar to the weekly planner in Activity 5, above. Ensure items identified in your semester plan get transferred to appropriate weekly planner.	This is your present time perspective. Apart from your time-sensitive slots, you should prioritise your other activities according to their importance.
Read unit descriptions to see what is expected of you.		
Select options.		
Note assignments and hand-in dates for your courses.	Enter your time-sensitive items like lectures, tasks/event that satisfy your key goals and those urgent things that just must get done.	Start your day by setting your 'to-do' list and then **prioritising** tasks according to their **importance** and 'due date'.
Find out who you need to see regarding possible work placements, Erasmus exchange, etc.	Make sure your weekly planner includes your whole life and not just your studies. Many people are increasingly turning to electronic means for this through mobile phones or PDAs.*	PDAs usually have a 'to-do list' function, you may want to use that.
Note any software you need to learn or be expected to know and find out how you can train yourself.		Highlight the high priority tasks.
Promise yourself to complete your personal development planner as this will enable you to articulate what you are learning and identify where your strengths and weaknesses are.	Carefully estimate the time it will take you to complete tasks. This takes experience, but it is a characteristic of good time management.	

*PDA is a personal digital assistant. It can be integrated in your mobile phone or a standalone tool. There are also several desktop tools that can be used like a PDA, e.g. Google has a selection of tools and Microsoft Outlook has a PDA-like function built into it.

Checklist for developing good time management strategies

1. Balance short-term with long-term (life) goals.
2. Be importance rather than urgency driven.
3. Plan – in detail for linear tasker and roughly for multi-tasker.
4. Know how and where you learn best.

ACTIVITY 8 Recommending time management strategies

How should these students improve their time management skills? Can you identify their issues with regard to time management? A summary of time management is included below to help you work through this activity.

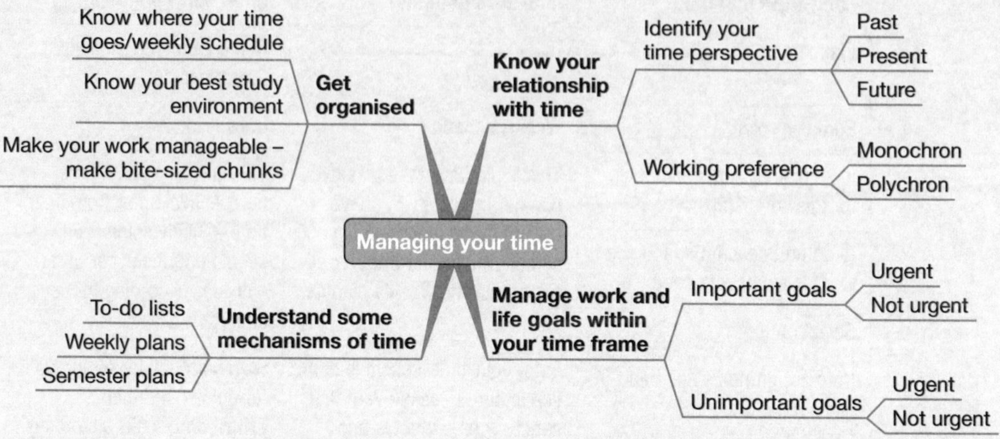

Jane is the first of her family to study at university and she is very excited by it. She lives with a long-term boyfriend who is just finishing a modern apprenticeship scheme. She is in her first year and, although she has worked before, she was not prepared for the amount of independent work she would have to do in addition to keeping her 'old life' together. Jane knows what her goals are, but finds the juggling of tasks difficult as there seems to be so many demands on her time.

Winston has been in the UK for about a year and is enjoying his studies. He knows what he wants to do when he finishes but has difficulty around exam times. He is fine during the year and manages to get his coursework in on time. Revision for exams is somehow different. He doesn't have a set place to revise and some days goes to the library, other times he sits on the floor of his bedroom or in the kitchen. He knows that when he starts to revise he will suddenly feel hungry and then goes to make something to eat. He will come back, ready to start, and then realises he hasn't made a promised phone call, so he does that. He is now ready to start, and a friend calls and they have a chat. By late afternoon he gets some work done but then his friends ring up and invite him out. Since he feels that his day is already wasted, he decides to go. He feels bad about this, but promises himself he will start revising properly tomorrow.

Can you write your own scenario?

NOTE If you are dyslexic you may have difficulty putting things (mentally and physically) in order. It is important for you to try and identify what you need to do and create a slot for it. If you have persistent problems with this, then it would be advisable to consult a learning differences unit at your institution as it is essential you find a strategy that suits you.

6 On reflection

Time management is about understanding your relationship with time and how that affects you ability to manage time. Looking forward motivates you and enables you to identify your life's goals. Keeping up with old friends, and enjoying yourself now, also balances your life.

Planning, scheduling and 'to-do' lists are mechanisms you can use to keep yourself on track but ensure that your track is for important issues and not trivia. This will give you a sense of achievement and a feeling of control over your time.

Now, reflect on your own relationship with time and how you intend adapting your behaviour so that you can spend your time more effectively. You may want to transfer this information to your own institution's personal development planner scheme.

ACTIVITY 9 Update your personal development planner

Having read this chapter, gauge your confidence again. How does this compare with your confidence levels at the start of the chapter? What can you do to improve? You can incorporate this into your own personal development planner. Add anything else you feel appropriate.

Grade your confidence on a scale of 1–5 where 1 = poor and 5 = good.

My time management plan	Confidence level 1–5	Plans to improve
I recognise that my relationship with time affects how I manage my time. *Section 2*		
I recognise that my life goals are as much a part of my time management as course deadlines. *Section 3*		
I know how to get the best out of my time as I know how I study best. *Section 4*		
I now know how I can manage my time effectively and can develop strategies that suit me. *Section 5*		

Date:____________________

Getting extra help

At your institution:

- Consult the Careers Advisory Service or Student Services as they often hold key skill workshops on topics such as time management.
- Attend your institution's learning support unit (or similar) if you feel this is an issue for you.
- Check out your local Students Union as they often provide help in this area.

Books:

- Covey, S.R., Merrill, A. and Merrill, R. (1994) *First Things First: Coping with the Ever-increasing Demands of the Workplace*. London, Simon & Schuster.

A useful website:

- Mindtools, at: **www.mindtools.com** [last accessed December 2006].

Feedback on activities

ACTIVITY 1 Recognising different time perspectives in others

There are no absolute answers to this feedback. Here are some interpretations. If yours are different, it may be worth articulating your reasons.

Adrian

His time perspective is very much in the present, especially with respect to his social life and having a good time. From his short description, we might conclude that he is happier doing one type of activity at a time (his social life doesn't seem to vary much) rather than juggling a lot of different activities. His motivation to study appears to be low. His time management skills may be doubtful (poor).

Ismet

His time perspective is dominated by present and future. He is prepared to live now, but keeps his eye on coursework so that he doesn't fall behind. He seems to be a good organiser, and that takes some juggling. He has to do this as well as keep up with coursework, although I suspect he pulls back on his social life to get some of his coursework completed. He seems to be a multi-tasker and quite motivated in his studies as well as good at time management.

Rachael

Her time perspective is very much in the future and very much at the expense of living now. She should be careful that she doesn't experience burn-out and needs to re-balance her life. She appears to be a multi-tasker when it comes to her studies, but the fact that she gets irritated when interrupted could mean that she prefers to focus on single aspects of her coursework – doing one piece at a time and liking to stay focused. She is highly motivated and probably a good time manager (motivated people usually manage their time better than non-motivated people).

ACTIVITY 2 Identifying your own time perspective

If you are dominated by time perspective 1, you are 'present oriented'. You really focus on having a good time. For you, it is the now that counts. This is really a hedonistic perspective and we should all spend time in this perspective at some time during a week. If, however, it dominates you, you may find that you will be prone to giving up your work in favour of the addiction to seek excitement and having a good time. Being permanently in this time perspective is very unhealthy for your studies or career in the future as you succumb to temptations that appear more exciting at the time.

If you are dominated by time perspective 4, you are also 'present oriented' but in a negative, fatalistic way. You feel that life is outside your control and nothing you do will change that. You have a general feeling of helplessness. Being predominantly in this time perspective zaps your motivation. You see no point in putting in the effort so your studies and future work will really suffer.

If you are dominated by perspective 5, you are 'past oriented' in a positive way. Your happy memories have helped you develop a positive view of life and given you the stability to move on; we all need this. Research has shown that those in this perspective have a high sense of self-esteem (Boniwell, 2005).

If you are dominated by perspective 2, you are 'past oriented' in a negative way and you may not be able to get over something that was unpleasant in your past. If that is the case, and you feel it is an issue, you may be advised to seek professional help. It is important to deal with negative experiences so they don't run your life. In terms of your studies, you may find you are not meeting your full potential. Negative past events don't have to be traumatic; getting consistently bad marks for essay writing or maths tests, for example, could be enough to determine how you deal with these now.

If you are dominated by time perspective 3 you are future oriented. You have set out your goals and you make plans so that you can fulfil them. You seek out new challenges and opportunities where you can. Research has shown that this time perspective is associated with well-being, persistence and self confidence (Boniwell, 2005). You can, however, be so concerned with achieving that you forget to enjoy yourself, become a workaholic, experience burn-out and forget to live in the present. You need a balance.

ACTIVITY 3 Are you a multi-tasker?

You will probably find academic life is very much a polychronic culture. More than likely your coursework assignments will be bunched towards the end of your course just when you are thinking of revising for your exams. In some cases you are finishing coursework and writing exams in the same week. It is important to identify what your working preference is so that you can make adaptations to fit in with the actuality of study life.

If you have identified yourself as a multi-tasker then you will probably fit in well with academic structure. Be careful, however, that you give important pieces of coursework enough attention and don't leave things to the last minute.

If you have identified yourself as a linear tasker, then you need to prioritise your tasks, break them down into small tasks, create a time plan and carry out these smaller tasks in a linear way. You need to work in small chunks so you can get that piece of work finished within your schedule. This will keep you on track in a polychronic environment while you work in a linear fashion!

Multi-taskers (polychrons) prefer ...	Linear taskers (monochrons) prefer ...
time to be unstructured	structured time
not to make detailed plans	to work to detailed time plans
to work on tasks when they are in the mood	to work to their prioritised list of activities
to spread their focus and attention across lots of things	a very focussed approach
to go with the flow and if they are interrupted it doesn't matter.	to work without interruption.

ACTIVITY 7 Recommending time management strategies

Jane may have sorted out her major goals and planned well, but she does not seem to be handling her 'to-do' list well. She needs to prioritise, and that includes her home life, and stick to her daily tasks. If she carries on like this, she may feel that she can't cope with her studies and leave. She must work smart and really do what is important and work on the 20/80 rule.

Winston has problems revising for exams whereas structured assignments seem to be OK for him. He seems to be a classic procrastinator. He needs to first accept that this is what he is doing and then set himself small tasks. He should concentrate on the task at hand and not take or make phone calls during this period. He can then reward himself with a couple of hours out with his friends. He will feel good about himself and enjoy his time out a lot more.

References

- Boniwell, L. (2005) 'Beyond time management: how the latest research on time perspectives and perceived time use can assist clients with time related concerns', *International Journal of Evidence Based Coaching and Mentoring*, 3(2), 61.
- Covey, S. R., Merrill, A., and Merrill, R. (1994) *First Things First: Coping with the Ever-increasing Demands of the Workplace*. London, Simon & Schuster.
- Hall, Edward, T. (1959) *The Silent Language*. New York, Garden City.
- Innis, K. and Shaw, M. (1997) 'How do students spend their time?', *Quality Assurance in Education* 5(2), 85–89.
- Northgate, S. (2006) *Beyond 9–5: Your Life in Time*. London, Orion Publishing Group.
- Robinson, J. P. and Godbey, G. (1997) *Time for Life: The Surprising Ways Americans use their Time*. State College, The Pennsylvania State University Press.
- Zimbardo, P. and Boyd, J. (1999) 'Putting time in perspective: a valid, reliable individual differences metric', *Journal of Personality and Social Psychology*, 77, 1271–88.

2 Improve your work

This part emphasises what you can do to get the most out of some of the basic components of your education: note-making, lectures, presenting your work and exams. You may want to find out what your note-making style is and try out different approaches. Remember you will need your notes to structure your revision later. Lectures are often seen as a passive activity but you can get more out of them if you know how to be an active listener.

At some time during your studies, team work, oral presentations and poster presentations will be part of your assessment. Your tutors may refer to these as key or transferable skills. This means that once you are aware of how to improve these skills, you can transfer it to other contexts.

Exams are inevitable, so within your busy schedule it is important to know how to organise the revision process, identify the best way to present the information you need to learn and recognise how you best remember things.

Take time to reflect on the skills you are developing in this part through the questions in each chapter.

2.1 Making notes

The ability to make notes is an essential skill which will substantially enhance your university experience but which will also ensure that you maximise your performance in your career. Many students arrive at university with varying levels of expertise.

In this chapter you will:

1. learn the skills needed for efficient note-making
2. learn how to increase your expertise by trying out different strategies
3. explore a range of note presentation styles
4. learn how to select the most relevant presentation style related to your working context.

USING THIS CHAPTER

Estimate your current levels of confidence. At the end of the chapter you will have the chance to re-assess these levels where you can incorporate this into your personal development planner (PDP). Mark between 1 (poor) and 5 (good) for the following:

I am aware of a wide range of note-making styles.	I know the skills needed to make notes.	I know how to match notes format with context/task.

Date: _______________

Introduction

Making notes is an integral part of your university life. Yet it is surprising that your academic tutors assume that you have gained the necessary skills before you get to university. Many undergraduate and postgraduate courses do not put aside time to teach students these skills. Academic tutors will tell you that they expect students to have learned how to make effective notes. They maintain that they do not have the time to devout to this aspect of study. However, there may be online resources and general study skills support available. If you have acquired and developed these skills prior to entry, then you will need to reappraise your strategies to make sure that you are responding appropriately to your new academic demands. Note-making is an activity which supports all aspects of academic work. It is needed for:

- getting the most out of lectures
- your essay/assignment
- examination preparation.

1 Note-making profiles

Many students arrive at university having had experiences of note-making. However, it is vital that you consider if your strategies and methods are effective. For example, have they done the job you expected? The proof of the pudding is whether you have used your notes or left them gathering dust in files. Activity 1 asks you to consider what type of note-maker you are.

ACTIVITY 1 What sort of note-maker are you?

Which of these statements applies to you?	True	False
1. I rarely take notes.		
2. I jot down the odd word or two.		
3. I try to make sure that I take down every word.		
4. I find that I miss out junks of what has been said.		
5. My notes don't seem to make sense when I return to them at a later date.		
6. I can't listen and summarise what a person is saying at the same time.		
7. My handwriting is so untidy that my notes are illegible when I return to them at a later date.		
8. I write in sentences.		
9. I like to have my notes in paragraphs.		
10. I use different colours when taking notes.		
11. I panic when I can't spell a word I've heard.		
12. I use bullet points to take down information.		
13. I prefer to draw a map of the information.		
14. I can't keep up with notes if someone is speaking quickly.		
15. I am not sure what to leave out when someone is speaking.		
16. I keep all my notes in one file.		
17. I use abbreviations for ordinary words in my notes.		
18. I have my own system of abbreviations.		
19. I rarely go back to my notes at a later date.		
20. I make electronic notes.		
21. I use a recording device to take down notes in meetings and lectures.		

Of course, there are no right and wrong ways of making notes, but some techniques and skills will help you to produce better notes. You will have opportunities throughout this chapter to consider your strategies and methods and to consider ways of adapting to meet new demands.

What skills are needed?

The skills needed for note-making are those which will stand you in good stead for many academic activities. They are the skills which employers are looking for in their workforce. The generic skills are:

Selection of information.
Elimination of less important information.
Summary.
Critical thinking.
Reflection.
Analysis.

As you will see in the chapters on Reading and Essays, the above skills provide a toolkit for many operations.

Note-making: why bother?

Looking back over my three years at university, what advice would I give to others? This is a tricky one because there is so much. However, if I only have one piece of advice to pass on it would be to get a firm grip on your notes from the start. I thought I was an exemplary student because I took lots of notes – in lectures, seminars, as part of written coursework and for exam revision. Did I make use of all these notes? Certainly not! I found that the bulk of them were of no real use to me or gathered dust in files. I wish someone had told me something about how to write cool notes which would actually be used and how to organise them so I didn't have to spend so much time searching through files for the information I needed.

Gavin, third year Electrical Engineering student

Some students seem to be drowning under the weight of paper generated by notes – either of their own making or from course handouts and electronic downloads. Yet, as Gavin points out, how much use are they put to? If you consider why you need notes, this will help you to reflect upon your systems and presentation formats. One of the biggest issues for students is the time factor. Consequently, developing note-making skills and selecting a format which is appropriate for your information can make a difference.

2 Purposes of note-making

Having a clear idea about the purposes of note-making will have an impact upon the quality of the product. Ask yourself the following questions:

- Who are they for?
- Why take notes?
- How/when will they be used?

Who?

It is essential that you clarify this before you begin. The answer will have a knock-on effect upon the presentation of your notes and the type of abbreviations you choose. Most people take notes for themselves. If this is the case, you have only one master to please. **As long as the notes make sense to you**, and you can read them later then it shouldn't matter what sort of state they are in or what format you have chosen.

However, if you are carrying out this activity to share notes with others, you have to ensure that they are meaningful, legible, easy to understand and that the ideas flow with an obvious logic, pattern and framework. At times, in the course of group work, you may have the responsibility for providing a set of notes. It is important to come to some agreement with the group about layout and basic rules:

- use of abbreviations
- would the group prefer the notes to be linear?
- would they find a concept map format more helpful?

It is useful in these instances to decide in advance what the group expects so that you can choose the most appropriate way of presenting the notes. This will also give you guidance about what type of information the group would like to be selected, and what they are not so interested in.

Some students supplement their finances by becoming paid note-takers for students in receipt of the Disabled Students' Allowance (DSA). In many cases the reason students pay for the service is because they are dyslexic and need to have a set of notes which is complete after a lecture. In some cases, the reason may be that the students have some physical conditions, such as severe arthritis, which would affect the ability to 'write' notes quickly in lectures. Again, it is important to discuss with these students in advance their format preferences and to explain your systems for notes.

Why?

Most people make notes as **memory joggers**. Thus, important points, key terminology and definitions feature highly in the selection process of what to put in and what to leave out. Writing your own notes is much better than borrowing a friend's notes because you couldn't get to a lecture. Going through the process of listening to information, making decisions about what you need to remember and the physical act of writing all provide supportive memory joggers. The reason is that you have had to listen to and consider the information (analysis and summary) before deciding what to note. Writing out the notes also reinforces memory. Think about making a shopping list and then forgetting to take it with you. It is surprising how much we can remember because of the physical act of writing!

Notes are also **snap shots** of a lecture or a chapter in a book. This means that important terminology and facts need to be clearly recorded and presented so that they are accessible to you when you return to them. However, the snap shot must contain sufficient detail to strengthen your understanding and knowledge of a topic (selection and summary).

Notes are important **thinking tools**. Provided you have not simply copied information word for word, you will have engaged with the information, be it oral or written. Your notes, therefore, may contain critical comments which will help you to shape your ideas.

At times in a large lecture theatre, the warmth generated from hundreds of students, your own energy levels and the tone of the lecturer's voice have a soporific effect and could result in lapses in concentration. Some students use note-making as a way of keeping up their levels of **concentration**.

How?

There are a variety of methods of presenting notes which will be explored later in the chapter. You need to be aware of the different types of layout so that you can make appropriate choices according to the type of information with which you are dealing. If you are a History student, for example, a time-line format with annotations is clearer than bullet points. Would it be better to record what the lecturer is saying on a mini-disk? Is it more effective to use a laptop to take notes because they can then be incorporated with other electronic information?

When?

Another crucial question is when will you use the notes? Will they be used for:

- essay writing
- examination revision
- PowerPoint presentation to your group?

Again these decisions will determine the level of detail you wish to make and the way in which you organise and store your notes. For example, you may find that you take lots of notes in preparation for writing an essay. For revision purposes, these notes (and others) may be distilled and cut down to bare essentials.

3 Presentation of notes

Making notes is a skill which is essential not only for university or college but also for the workplace. You need to take stock of what your own notes are like now so that you are aware of what needs to be improved. This section will provide you with examples of many different formats for the presentation of notes. You may need to try out some that you have never used before to find out if they are effective. The old adage rings true: if you always do what you've always done, you'll always get what you've always got. In other words, if your notes are not effective now, and you carry on using the same methods of presentation, then they are not going to suddenly improve. The only way you can do this is by making changes.

Does presentation depend upon personal preferences?

Students are often told that personal preferences and individual learning style are the main factors which dictate note-making formats. It is true that some students prefer to use a visual style of note-making as opposed to the more traditional linear/bullet point format – and vice versa. Did you realise that there are other considerations of which you need to be aware? Some note-making styles require more advanced skills than others. For example, developing a concept map requires not only summary skills but also the ability to synthesise and make links between many aspects of the topic. The way you choose to present your notes may vary according to the type of information you are dealing with rather than your own preferred way of making notes. For example, if you are making notes about a process, it may be better to put the information into a flow chart format, which you can see in detail later in the chapter. If notes are a method of organising how information is stored, ready for access at a later date, the style of presentation, therefore, hinges upon the type of information and the best way to provide instant retrieval to jog the memory. Nevertheless, the added complication is that we do not have control over some of the factors, viz. the pace of the delivery of the information, and the way the information has been structured into a given framework. However, good notes do not rely solely upon their looks and presentation. The section below on 'Different types of notes' will help to inform your personal choices.

4 Different types of notes

Linear/Bullet points/Listing

This type of note-making style is the most traditional format. It shows a hierarchy of information. It can incorporate bullet points and numbered lists. If you are not an experienced note-taker this is the format which will be most appropriate for you to develop first.

It is worth remembering that many lecturers have developed the shape and structure of the lecture using a linear development of ideas. This means that the oral delivery of the information reflects this, and that they are probably 'talking' in bullet points and linear structures. Therefore, if you are an inexperienced note-maker it is easier for you to mirror this structure in your own notes. It takes more experience to listen to information delivered in one structure type and be able to convert this into a different structure on your pages of notes – especially as this has to be while thinking on your feet and trying to convert new and challenging concepts and information.

Sample notes:

Polar Bears

- **General information:**
  - Arctic dwellers
    - North Pole
    - Frozen environment
    - Well camouflaged
- Keeping warm
  - Fat = blubber
    - 8–10 cm layer
      - Retains heat
      - Got from eating seals
  - Outer fur
    - Thick
  - Inner fur
    - fluffy
- Diet
  - Carnivores
  - Eat prey animals

- **Adaptations:**
  - Feet
    - Width of paws
      - Large – give better grip
    - Soft pads
      - Rough texture to grip ice
    - Fur between toes
      - Good for slippery surfaces
    - Thick claws
      - Used to catch seals
      - Used for extra grip

Uses

This type of note format makes use of headings and sub-headings to show relationships between information. These notes can be readily converted into prose writing, and this may explain their popularity. They suit people who are logical and who think in layers of information (hierarchies). This format suits many subject disciplines. It is also conducive to the quick-fire response which is needed in the lecture environment. It requires the reduction of information. In other words, only the vital pieces of information are taken down. Of course, to make effective notes of this type you have to have:

- good listening skills
- excellent summary skills.

If you find that you are writing too much or trying to take down everything and not succeeding because you have no control over the pace of the delivery, then you need to work on these two skills **now**. You can find further guidance on improving your listening skills in Chapter 2.2, 'Getting the most out of lectures'.

Grids/tables

These are a useful way of categorising information. Look at the grid example:

Theorist	**Theory of intelligence**
Spearman	'g' factor – pervades performance on all mental ability tests. 's' factor – performance on a single type of performance test e.g. arithmetic.
Thurstone	7 Primary mental abilities: verbal comprehension verbal fluency inductive reasoning spatial visualisation number memory perceptual speed.
Guilford	Structure-of-intellect model 150 factors divided between: operations – mental processes like memory content – opinion based on reasoned thought products – responses required.
Cattell	Fluid ability – speed, accuracy Crystallised ability – accumulated knowledge.
Jensen	Neural conduction velocity – speed at which neural circuits conduct information.
Sternberg	Componential theory of analysis of intelligence. Information processing of complex tasks, e.g. analogies.

Take a look at a sample of tabular format:

Type of intelligence	Leading theorists	Brief overview	Comments
Single	Spearman	One type of mental ability governs actions and thought	Traditional view Easily measured Dependent upon speed of processing information Many opponents
Multiple	Gardner	Nine different types of intelligence, e.g. musical, linguistic, numerical, etc.	No agreement on the multiples involved Difficult to measure
Triarchic	Sternberg	Divided into three components	Analytical and practical are separated Grew out of Gardner's approach

As can be seen by this sample from a grid note-making system, it enables the information to be systematically correlated which eases analysis and comparison.

Uses

It is possible to take down notes in a lecture using this format if you are well prepared in advance. You would need to know the type of lecture you are attending. Thus, if it was an introductory lecture which is setting the scene for a series, the lecturer may be giving you a framework for detail in subsequent lectures. It is a broad-brush type of information-giver. How do you know in advance whether to choose this format? Go to Chapter 2.2, 'Getting the most out of lectures'.

In terms of skill and expertise, this type of format relies upon the ability to understand the big picture (the global thinker) and to be able to categorise information effectively because you have to be able to take information and slightly restructure it.

As you can see from the example above, the information is consolidated and would be a useful summary for revision notes. This format also lends itself to colour highlighting in the review stages.

Diagrams and hierarchies

These types of format provide a quick visual overview of how information is related and, depending upon the format, can make links between ideas, concepts and information very clear. There are a variety of ways of presenting hierarchies. It is important to remember that the information is closely linked. You can present them as pyramids of information as shown in Section 7: 'Labelling information: quick-start retrieval'. Look at the examples shown in Figures 1 and 2.

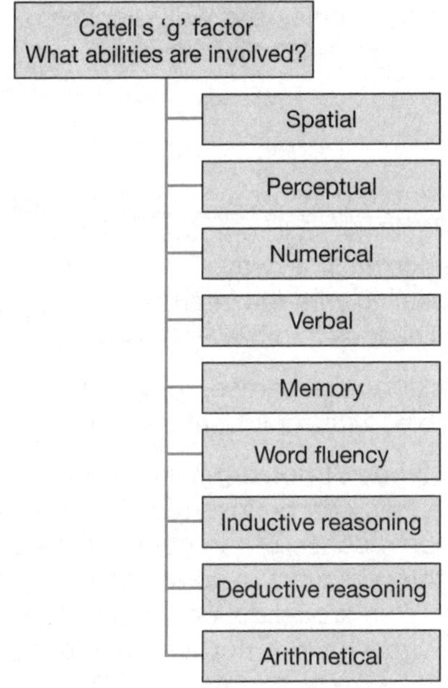

Figure 1 Example of branching diagram

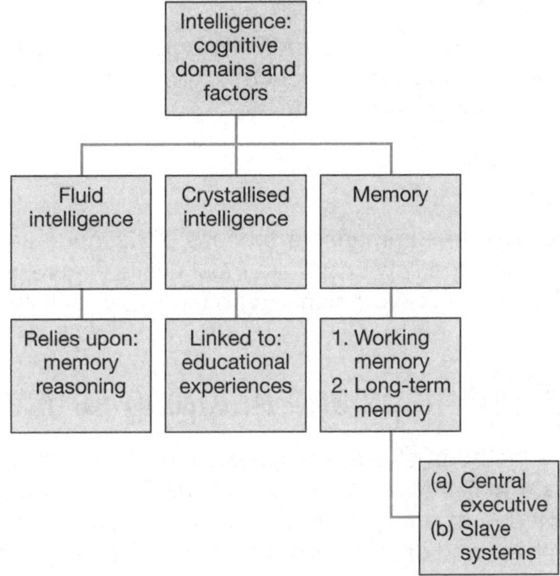

Figure 2 Example of hierarchies branching notes

The type of branching diagram shown in Figure 1 is suitable for lists. It can show the relationships between two layers of information. It is easily 'drawn' using the 'diagram/chart' facility in Microsoft Word. There are variations of this type of format.

Figure 2 shows another way of presenting this type of note format. As you can see, the hierarchies are well displayed. Some lecturers might refer to these as layers or levels of information.

Uses

You might want to consolidate and refine your lecture notes for revision purposes. Taking linear lecture notes and prose information, you can rearrange the information in this way. This means that you will be more actively involved in dealing with the information because you will have to make decisions about linkages and hierarchies/layers.

In terms of skill and expertise, they rank as a second-order type in that you have to be able to take information and slightly reconstruct it.

Often these types of notes rely heavily upon a pre-defined framework into which information can be inserted. This obviously requires prior knowledge or at least some sense of the connections and connectors of information. This is why they are often used after a lecture to help you to revisit the ideas and to develop your own concept mapping systems. They suit highly organised people who have a certain level of knowledge of the topic so that decisions can be made about how to link the information.

Cycles and flow charts

These are heavily reliant upon the type of information you are dealing with. They are often found in science textbooks such as anatomy, physics, chemistry, psychology, education, etc.

Uses

If you want to summarise a process or describe an operation of something then cycles and flow charts are most useful (Figure 3). The arrows help understanding and take your thinking from one part of the process to another.

Concept maps and mapping structures

These methods of presenting notes are often complex. They appeal to students who like to have visual notes as memory joggers and to help build up knowledge of a topic. They can incorporate colour and shape as ways of classifying and categorising information. The important feature to remember is that this type of format starts at the centre of a page and that it is better to turn your A4 paper around to the landscape view to ensure that you have as much space as possible at your command. They use branches, arrows and lines to show relationships (Figure 4).

1. What are the strengths and weaknesses of the individual?
2. Conduct a series of assessments to ascertain the individual profile of strengths and weaknesses. Analyse the results.
3. Formulate a teaching programme to meet the individual needs. Carry out the teaching.
4. Reflect upon the effectiveness (or otherwise) of the programme. Re-evaluate needs.

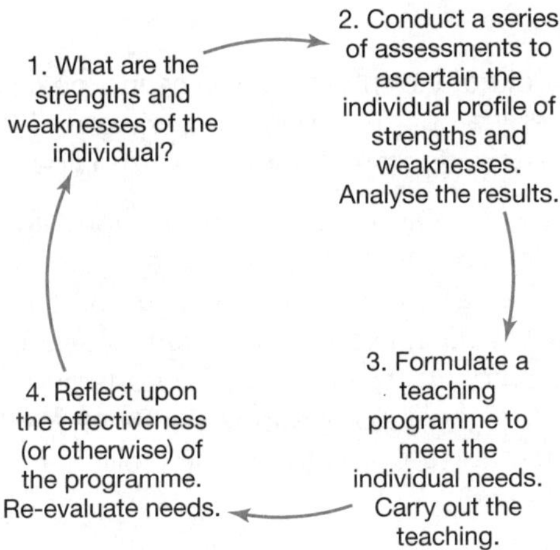

Figure 3 The assessment–teaching cycle

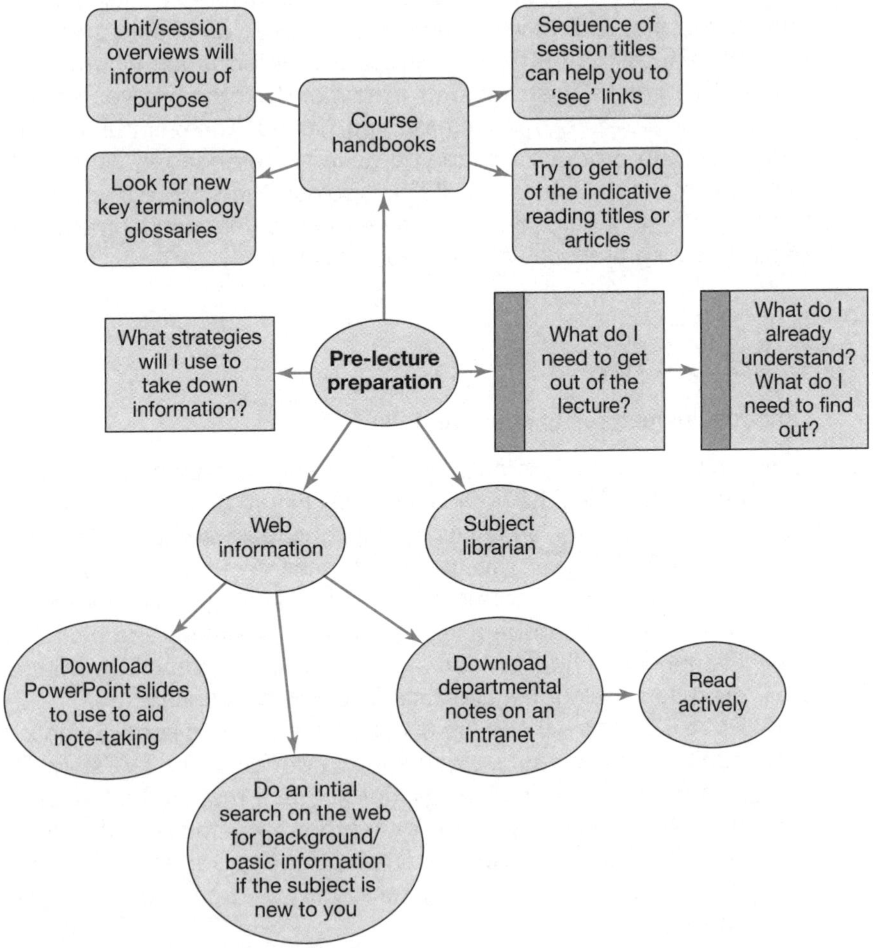

Unit/session overviews will inform you of purpose
Sequence of session titles can help you to 'see' links
Course handbooks
Look for new key terminology glossaries
Try to get hold of the indicative reading titles or articles
What strategies will I use to take down information?
Pre-lecture preparation
What do I need to get out of the lecture?
What do I already understand? What do I need to find out?
Web information
Subject librarian
Download PowerPoint slides to use to aid note-taking
Download departmental notes on an intranet
Read actively
Do an intial search on the web for background/ basic information if the subject is new to you

Figure 4 A sample concept map

Uses

This type of note format is not for the inexperienced note-taker. It requires not only expertise but an in-depth knowledge of the subject to be able to produce this type of format **at speed**, keeping pace with a lecturer's speech.

This type of format makes use of different signals for the brain. As you can see, sections of information are not only grouped together but are also identifiable by shape and colour. If you are consolidating and refining your lecture notes during your post-lecture activities, this format is useful for revision purposes. It might be worth considering these notes for your note section summary because they will force you to link up and connect ideas and concepts (see Chapter 2.5, 'Excelling in examinations', Section 'Good revision notes').

In addition, they have the advantage over linear notes in that they may be more flexible and more easily allow for the spontaneous additions in a talk. Similarly, if a speaker gives summaries at the end of each section, it is possible to add further boxes to the current framework. If your brain takes in information more effectively in this format then you should start practising this technique. It is better to practise with information where it does not matter if you make mistakes. For example, do this while you are watching television or a DVD film to increase your speed. There is the added advantage in that to produce a map you have to be engaged with the subject matter to make decisions about links, colour and shape. If you opt for this format during lectures, you will be sure to keep your concentration levels up because concentration is a key factor to success.

Other useful techniques

Other useful features of effective notes are:

- **Arrows** – to link information and to show connections and flow of information (see the cyclical example Figure 3).
- **Marking texts** – underlining; highlighting information in the post-lecture review stages. This makes information stand out and helps you to locate key and important facts and terminology more quickly.
- **Colour** – this can be used to group information and also to ensure that key and important facts and terminology stand out. But beware – overuse of colour negates its effect. So use it sparingly.
- **Post-it Notes** – these are excellent for bringing specific facts to your attention when you are gathering information for an essay. They are also useful for adding postscript notes. It may be that when you are reviewing your notes, you remember something or an idea comes into your mind but you have run out of space on your notes page. But beware – they are only temporary and can easily be dislodged and lost!

Abbreviations

R U OK? Go 2 bnk 4 xtra £. See U.

In a world where we are bombarded by text messages on mobile telephones and in e-mails to friends, most students have experience of the advantages of abbreviating language. There is a universal text language which is developing and can be utilised to good effect in note-making where the need to get down information at speed is crucial. It is quick to write and communicates the message effectively. You will have noticed that single letters can work for a whole word, 'U' for 'you', and that often the vowels (a, e, i, o, u) are missed out of words for speed, e.g. 'bnk' for bank. It is important to use your knowledge of text language abbreviations and apply it during lectures. Here is a list of common rules:

Rule	Example
Omit vowels	Hnd n wrk on frdy = Hand in work on Friday.
Omit some syllables or parts of a word	Devl't = development. Wd = would
Omit beginnings and endings of words (but beware of ambiguities)	Diffct = difficult Diffnt = different
Use a number to represent a word or part of a word	B4 = before

Of course there are many abbreviations which are in common use. Very few people nowadays have learnt the traditional Pitman's shorthand (which is a series of squiggles on the page, representing words). Nevertheless, you may already be familiar with these having seen them in books, magazines and articles. Symbols in Mathematics are also a useful source of abbreviation. Here is a list of the most commonly used:

Abbreviation	Meaning
e.g.	For example
Etc.	And the rest
Et al.	All the others
i.e.	That means, that is
N.B.	Note – important
Cf.	Compare
Viz.	Namely
& (or your own drawing of this)	And

Abbreviation	Meaning
p	Page
sp.	Spelling
Para	Paragraph
C20	20th century
>	More than, greater than[1]
<	Less than[1]
=	Equals, equal to, the same as
≠	Not the same as
∴	Therefore
∵	Because
+	In addition to
→	Consequently, leads to
↑	Rises, a rise in
↓	Decreases, decrease

[1]If you have memory difficulties and can never remember which one is which, it is best to concentrate on remembering only one of these.

Remember, abbreviations are supposed to speed up your ability to take down information. If you have your own system of abbreviating, then use this in preference because you are more likely to remember it when you review your notes. However, look at the above common abbreviations and analyse which ones could be of use to you and start to use them. The more you use them the quicker you will become.

5 Using technology for note-making

I forgot to name each file and when I came to find the information only a week later, I couldn't remember where it was on my system. It had miraculously saved itself with a name which turned out to be the first few words of the document. Of course, this meant nothing to me when I came to look for it. It was so frustrating to know that the information was in there somewhere. I now give each file a name which has some meaning so that when I click on 'Find' I can pull up the document quickly. Of course, I know what you're going to say – why not think about filing these documents in folders. That's my next resolution – to set up my system before the semester starts.

Kevin, second-year Chemistry student

Most of the methods for note-making discussed in this chapter can be used effectively on your laptop or desktop. The added advantage is that you can set up files and the appearance of the document on screen in advance to save time. In this way you can decide upon a template for units of study at the beginning of each semester. For example, the Cornell System, which is explained in Chapter 2.2, can be set up as a template.

Reviewing and consolidating your notes is easier on computer, and the final product will be clearer. You can change the size of the font at the press of a button so that information stands out more clearly. You can underline and mark phrases in colour. In Microsoft Word, for example, you can add post-it type notes.

Diagrams, flow charts, Venn diagrams, pyramids and tables are functions that you can utilise so that the machine draws the outline structures for you. This means that you can set up your structure in advance and concentrate upon adding the concepts and facts while listening to your lecturer. Adding branches to your diagrams if you remember other information is also done at the touch of a button and you will find that any re-scaling is done automatically for you on screen by the machine.

6 Organising your notes

Students who make the most use of their notes have given some thought about organisation and storage. These hints and tips can apply to written notes kept in files or to your electronic notes. Giving some thought to the organisation at the beginning of each year will have benefits for your strategic working. You cannot afford **not** to consider this section – it will improve:

- your use of existing time by making more time available
- your knowledge and understanding of your units of study
- your essay grades
- your examination grades.

A good storage system is one which **you** have devised, not something which someone else has imposed upon you. You just have to think about trying to retrieve information from the online help systems of different programs – it is sometimes frustrating and time-consuming because whatever way you try and search, the information does not come to the surface. This is often because you are dealing with someone else's logic and mental network of storing information, and the terminology they use to facilitate access to the information. In other words, their framework, structure and organisation is different from the way you access information. Take time to reflect upon your folders and computer filing systems. You can easily measure their effectiveness by the time it takes to find the file or the notes you need!

Retrieval of information

This section will provide some methods which are tried and trusted and make for greater efficiency. However, you may need to try out different systems or combine systems to improve upon your current way of working.

The key question when deciding how you will organise your notes is what do you need the information for? For ease of efficiency, most well-organised students arrange storage of notes to allow access for:

- background information for essay writing
- revision notes for examinations
- background information for substantial project work.

Thus, the categorisation of the information often follows the structure of the course or units to accommodate the multiple purposes to which the notes will be put. However, an alternative framework for you to consider is to collate the information by theme or topic. In this way, the logic behind your storage hinges upon content information which will be drawn from a number of sources, units, and even year of study.

Before a unit of study

If I don't take time just before each term starts to sort out my files, I know that I will never catch up, and there will be bits of paper everywhere. One term I felt I was constantly chasing my tail because I didn't organise myself before my lectures started. In the long run this meant that I actually wasted time – at a time when I could least afford to because of the pressures of essay deadlines – having to try to remember which notes go with which.

Karen, second-year Law Studies student

At the start of a semester you need to take stock and be clear about which units you will be studying. Getting this overview is not only helpful in making decisions about storage of notes but is also a good exercise in getting an overview of how your units fit together so that you start to develop your own mental map or network of information.

The essential equipment for storage of notes will depend upon whether you are fully electronic in your approach, hard copy only or a combination. The latter is often the approach which students have to adopt because of the way information is made available by academic tutors. The basic tools for the job are listed in the table opposite.

As the volume of notes increases, your ability to locate information quickly will decrease if you don't keep your files tidy. This entails clearly labelling information.

Equipment	Options
Files	**Size**: You need to decide whether you are going to combine a number of linked units or whether you prefer to keep a separate file for each unit. Postgraduate courses tend to be in greater depth, and this means that the volume of notes is greater. A4 files are the most common but may not hold sufficient information. Lever-arch files have greater capacity and are more robust. **Colour**: Some students buy different coloured files so that they can more easily locate information when under time-pressure. **Notebooks**: You may need to use this type of format if you are undertaking laboratory work or field work. Because notebooks are bound and do not contain loose sheets, they are excellent for sequential information but the disadvantage is that they lose the flexibility to insert additional information. However, part of course assessment may be the production of your notebooks as evidence. The decisions about size and colour also apply. Remember it is about accessibility of information in your busy lives.
Paper	**Types**: Lined, unlined, squared. Your choice will be highly individual. However, it may also be governed by the subject you are studying. For example, Mathematics students sometimes prefer squared because it is easier to manipulate worked examples. If you write linear notes, lined paper is better. If you prefer visual or mapping notes, unlined paper works best. **Colour**: Most students are very traditional and use white paper. However, you might like to experiment with other colours. Using cream or pastel colours can make information more accessible and prevent visual stress (which can cause headaches while reading). It is worth considering using two colours to differentiate summary sheets and the rest of your section notes.
Section markers	These are vital pieces of equipment. They will speed up retrieval of information and accessibility **if** they contain a heading.
Post-it tape flags	These supplement section markers and enable you to decide upon important information which you need to get hold of quickly. They are moveable and come in different colours so that you can categorise information more effectively. When writing essays, you may find information you need dotted around your files, and these tags can save time in locating your required information.
Pens/pencils	Your choice of writing tool is very individual. However, employing different colours can be worth considering.
Marker pens	These will be needed when you review and consolidate your notes. Colour-coding information will help it to stand out for ease of access.

7 Labelling information: quick-start retrieval

If your notes are going to be used, then you need to get at the information. Often you do not have the luxury of time to go through notes meticulously to refresh your memory. Therefore, it is essential that you start out with systems to make retrieval smooth and efficient.

You will collect notes from different sources so you need to make sure that you label and file your information carefully. Apart from the notes which you make during lectures or when conducting your background reading, you will have handouts given to you in lectures and there will be electronic information available for you to download. In order that you are not overwhelmed with paper, it is worth spreading the workload.

Let us consider what is involved and when the organisation takes place: before the lecture or at the start of a unit (**Pre**) – at the beginning of a semester; in the middle of lectures (**during**) – during a lecture or as soon after it has finished as possible; or as part of your review and consolidation procedures (**post**).

Organisation Task	Pre	During	Post
Title on spine of the file	✓		
General List of Contents for each file		✓	
General List of Contents for each section		✓	
Each section should be clearly delineated and labelled	✓		
Each set of lecture notes should be dated, numbered, clearly titled and the lecturer's name recorded		✓	
Sub-headings should be clear and bold		✓	✓
Each page should be dated, numbered and have a reference. e.g. Unit 243:7:2 to signify unit code and the number of the lecture in that series and the number of the page of your notes for that lecture. This is important not only for quick access but also if you dropped your file and had to sort out the paper!		✓	✓
Summary sheet with bullet points for each section			✓
You may wish to combine lecture notes with other course notes. E.g. a hard copy of the electronic notes provided by your department; related journal articles; related general web information			✓

It is useful to keep your own notes, lecturer's handouts on the day, downloaded notes from a departmental intranet and other Internet notes you have downloaded on a topic all together in the same section. Remember if you have clearly titled your notes you will be able to differentiate your sources if you need to use the information for an essay or a project.

It cannot be stressed enough that putting a title on your notes and numbering the pages as you go will save you time in the long run.

8 On reflection

Your notes are a source which will help you to understand and remember factual information. Taking time to manage your notes systems will have an impact upon your studies. Well-organised files will facilitate retrieval of the valuable information for a variety of uses. However, the format of your notes should be moulded to your needs. Trying out different ways of presenting your notes may help you to interact and think about your subject which will, in the long run, make a difference to your grades.

Summary of this chapter

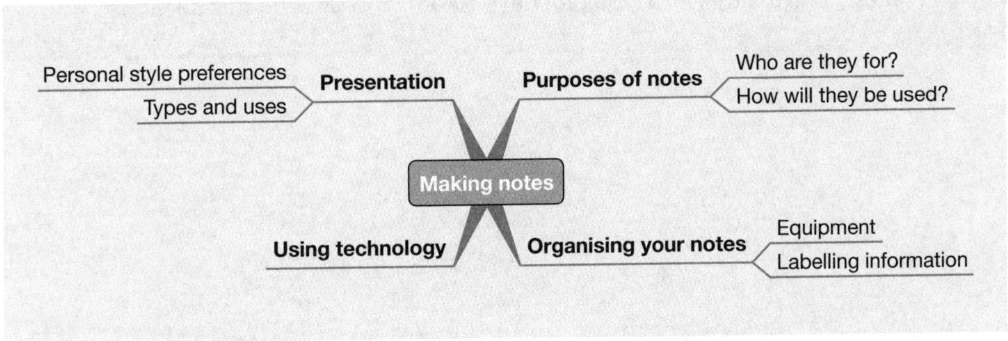

ACTIVITY 2 Update your personal development planner (PDP)

Now reflect on your current abilities and consider what you need to do to improve. You may want to transfer this information to your own institution's personal development planner scheme.

Grade your confidnce on a scale of 1–5 where 1 = poor and 5 = good.

My developing skills	Confidence level 1– 5	Plans to improve
I am aware of a wide range of note-making styles.		
I know the skills needed to make notes.		
I know how to match notes format with context/task.		

Date:______________________

Getting extra help

Go to your Students Union to find out where to go for skill development. Many universities and colleges have tutors who provide this service.

2.2 How to get the most out of lectures

If you have to take notes in a lecture, the pace, rate of delivery and framework for presenting the information are all out of your hands. The pressure is on to think on your feet, to try to make sense of the thinking which has gone on behind the scenes in the preparation of the lecture and to be able to record information at speed – in other words the ability to multi-task. Thus, it is vital that your listening skills and your note-making abilities are in tip-top condition to enable you to get the most out of lectures.

In this chapter you will:

1. assess your own interaction during lectures
2. explore the skills needed to get the most out of lectures
3. examine how to prepare for lectures to develop efficiency
4. develop keener listening skills.

USING THIS CHAPTER

Estimate your current levels of confidence. At the end of the chapter you will have the chance to re-assess these levels where you can incorporate this into your personal development planner (PDP). Mark between 1 (poor) and 5 (good) for the following:

I know the skills needed to get the most out of lectures.	I know the different types and purposes of lectures.	I can listen effectively and differentiate the information I am listening to in lectures.

Date: ________________

1 Are you a lecture sponge?

Lectures are a waste of time.

Angela, first-year student

A **sponge** learner is ready (or not so ready) to **soak up** information from tutors and lecturers. This sounds comfortable and relatively relaxing, but it is an ineffective way of learning. Did you know, for example, that if you listen to someone (for example, a lecturer), without actively making notes or participating in some other activity, you will be doing well to remember 20% of what's been said?

There are many reasons why some students do not get as much out of lectures as they should. Often this is because they have not prepared sufficiently and have inappropriate expectations of lectures.

What do you expect to get out of a lecture?

Pitching your expectations high is one of the ways you can yield good results. If you intend to interact with the information you will receive during lectures, you need to have the right mindset (see Activity 1).

ACTIVITY 1 Am I a lecture sponge?

Answer true or false to each of the statements.

	True	False
1. The lecture (or series of lectures) should teach me all I need to know on that subject/topic.		
2. I want to go into the lecture and get all the information I need for my assignment.		
3. I should not need to take notes because the information is provided as handouts or online.		
4. I do not need to think in lectures; I just need to listen carefully.		
5. Lectures should contain pictures, video clips, etc. as well as written and oral communication.		

If you have answered 'true' to most of these statements, you will find that there is a gap between your expectations and what lectures offer. This is neither the fault of your lecturer nor of you. It is simply that the rules of the lecture game do not match what you expect. Most students want value for money from the lectures but it is important to understand the purpose of lectures as a teaching tool. This will help you to get the most out of them.

How to increase your capacity during lectures

Activity 2 explores some of the problems that students have expressed about lectures. Identify your problems and look at the solution hint so that you can go immediately to the appropriate section of this chapter.

ACTIVITY 2 What do I do in lectures?

Problem	Solution
Your expectations for the purpose of the lecture are inappropriate.	Look at the purpose of lectures so that you adjust your expectations.
You are unable to cope with the volume of information because it is **all** new to you.	You need to do some pre-lecture preparations.

Problem	Solution
You quickly go into information overload and give up taking notes.	You need to do some pre-lecture preparations to ensure that you are ready for listening and understanding the information more effectively and at greater speed. You need to sharpen up your listening and selection skills.
You do not recognise or understand some of the new terminology.	You need to do some pre-lecture preparations.
You cannot follow the gist of the lecture and seem to become muddled.	You need to have a tentative information framework upon which to hang the information. You need to do some pre-lecture preparations.
The information seems very detailed and in great depth.	You need to do some pre-lecture preparations so that you have your own framework or skeleton of information before going to the lecture.
Your questions are not answered during the lecture.	This may be the result of a misunderstanding of the lecture format. Have a look at the purpose of lectures.
You are distracted easily by other students who are talking or by rustling of paper.	Either choose where you sit very carefully (if possible) or learn how to cut out extraneous and unwanted noise. Develop more effective listening skills.
The lecturer's style may not match the way you take in information.	You need to be more aware of the way academic tutors present information so that you can choose an appropriate method to take in more information and also to get the information down more effectively. Try to increase your listening skills. Try to vary the format of the presentation of your notes.
Your lecture notes are not used later on.	Match up the purpose of the lecture, the type of lecture and your presentation format so that the notes will be helpful. Develop more effective listening skills.

2 The purpose of lectures

Lectures are not the same as seminars and group tutorials. They serve a different purpose, and consequently the anticipated outcomes for students are different. Lectures last between 40 and 50 minutes. As a teaching tool, they are intended to give information to groups of students. In some ways they are cost-effective in that they can deliver information to large student cohorts. The size of the student group will depend upon the subject and the individual university. Some undergraduates are taken aback when they walk into a lecture theatre, and there are up to 500 students present. The size of the group can vary between 25 and 500.

Most departments organise a series of lectures to coincide with specific units of study. At the start of the unit, some students seem unaware of the purpose of lectures. However, this may be a case of crossed messages, and that the lecturers' intentions are not made explicit to students. For example, many lecturers do not usually expect to be interrupted by students' questions during a lecture. Some academics will tell you that they have set aside a little time at the end for questions but many will give their 'speech' and disappear. This is down to individual teaching style and delivery. However, be alert to the lecturer who sets aside time for questions. This may change your note-taking tactics during the lecture in terms of making your questions stand out in your notes as a memory jogger for later. Usually, you are expected to listen to the talk. Many lecturers use PowerPoint slides on a large screen to get across their points. Some lecturers may use an overhead projector (OHP) with transparencies (OHTs) containing information. These may be typed or handwritten. In some subjects, notably Mathematics, lecturers provide examples by writing mathematical workings at speed on a board. The traditional lecture does not contain activities – these appear more frequently in seminars.

However, there are various types of lectures, and the efficient student is aware of these types so that most use can be made of the information, format and style. This means that you may need to think on your feet quite quickly to spot the type and be flexible in your response in terms of expectations and note-taking.

Type of lecture	**Purpose**	**Outcomes**
Keynote	Keynote lecture is intended to raise issues/questions. Setting the scene and giving a broad overview.	To get you to question information and research. To inform you of the main issues.
Introductory	Introducing a series of lectures. Setting the scene and giving a broad overview.	To provide you with a framework of knowledge/ concepts upon which everything else will hinge.
Sequential	Each lecture builds upon the previous one.	An assumption of prior knowledge from previous lectures.
Focus	Takes a specific aspect of a topic and goes into detail. Provides information and detail about specific research.	To fill in or put flesh upon the framework which was provided in the introduction.
Conclusion	Sums up the key points of previous lectures. Draws all the threads together.	To give an overview which can be used in conjunction with introductory lecture notes.

Source	How to make use of it
Online information	
Department site	Check electronic information which is available. This may be in the form of PowerPoint notes or information sheets. Read this information in advance of the lecture to put you in the right frame of mind and to prepare you for key concepts and ideas.
Internet searches	Download background information to help you understand what the lecturer is getting at.
Library site	Check the subject section to find out what your subject librarian has loaded up for different courses/units.
Yourself	
	Make a list of questions which spring to mind about the topic. See if you can get the answers in the lecture. (If not, at least this is a checklist of things you need to find out.) Get your file/notes organised in advance to save time on the day (see the section on notes organisation in Chapter 2.1). Anticipate some sub-headings for your notes.

Making effective use of pre-lecture notes and downloads

In the long term, pre-lecture preparations will help you to understand new concepts and ensure that you are ready to take in new terminology because you have had to engage with the information and have had to think about it. Think about athletes. They always perform warm-up activities to ensure that their muscles are flexed beforehand and to ensure that performance is high. Pre-lecture preparations have the same main purposes and act as a warm-up for the brain or to get you into the right frame of mind to absorb the lecturer's information more efficiently and effectively. The hidden side-effects are explained in the table opposite.

Pre-lecture activity with collected or downloaded information	Purpose/use
You can go through them carefully and highlight with a coloured marker pen important information.	This will increase your understanding. This will improve your memory skills. This will help you to retrieve the information later because crucial information stands out and provides a quick-access short-cut for the brain.
You can also annotate those notes – make your own comments or questions in the margin.	This will increase your understanding. This will improve your memory skills.
You can highlight key terminology (and put a definition of meaning alongside if necessary).	By putting the definition in your own words, this will increase your understanding and memory – much more so than if you simply copy out someone else's definition.
You can scan them into your computer.	You can customise the layout so that you can make your own additional notes during the lecture alongside the lecturer's notes. (Some students prefer to customise printed lecture notes by double spacing for ease of access; or make space for your own notes parallel to the lecturer's notes.) Once again, reading and making decisions about what to do with the layout will provide valuable reinforcement.
You can scan the notes into your computer and make up your own concept map.	This is useful for those who prefer to have information in this alternative format rather than the traditional linear format. Making yourself do this activity can help you to develop your own map of the information.

Cautionary tale

I haven't got the time to do all this before each lecture. It's bad enough having to keep up with everything as it is.

Sharon, first-year History student

It is short-sighted to think that there is not enough time to do this type of pre-lecture preparation. It will save you time in the long run because you will get more out of the lecture in terms of your understanding; your notes will be of a better quality; and this in turn will boost your chances of doing a better assignment or remembering information for examinations. It boils down to ensuring that you organise your time as effectively as you can and add this element into your weekly schedules. Try out some of these activities over a semester and reflect upon your grasp of the topic and your ability to cope with the process of writing an assignment.

Supposing I did all of this beforehand. What would be the point in actually going to the lecture!

Jim, second-year English Studies student

Jim is not the only student who has made this comment. However, the point he is missing is that during lectures, tone of voice, emphasis and other body language will strengthen your understanding. Remember, some lecturers try to provoke thought by their tone of voice, and this does not come across in the impersonal notes. You can't get all of this from the two-dimensional downloads and information on screen. It is true that some lecturers are more memorable in their delivery than others but this human interface may spark off discussions with your friends, and you will not be able to participate in this further dimension to the purpose of lectures – to generate discussion and questions.

Post-lecture activities: what to do with the information after lectures

What do **you** do with your lecture notes after the lecture? Many students toss the notes into a file, often in a haphazard way. Some have a number of file pads which are used randomly for various lectures, and the notes are left there for filing at a later date. But what happens when you drop your bag, and the notes are scattered everywhere?

It is a matter of organisation but you also need to reconsider the purpose of notes which was discussed in Chapter 2.1. **If** your notes are of real value, you will need to do some work on them as soon after the lecture as you possibly can – while the information is still fresh in your mind. Your notes will be vital for assignment and examination success so why not spend some valuable time in reviewing, consolidating, tidying up the loose ends and reflecting.

- The organisation of your filing system is personal but the system has to be maintained and each set of lecture notes needs to be carefully filed away into your system. See Chapter 2.1 on note-making.
- Take time to read through your own notes to make sure they make sense to you. You may have to write in full some of the abbreviations you were forced to use in the lecture because of the speed of the lecturer's delivery. Tackling this soon after you have taken the notes means that you can draw upon recent memory of what the lecturer said to improve your notes and make them more understandable.
- Highlight key words and phrases so that they will stand out when you come back to the notes at a later date.
- If you have not had time to do sub-headings, read through a section and put a succinct title to it. Check your sub-heading titles and consider whether you need to change these so that the notes have greater cohesion and you will be able to immediately recognise the framework of the information at a later date when your memory of the lecture has faded.
- Write the key concepts in a different colour in the margin next to important information. This is termed annotating your notes.
- A4 Summary Sheet – if you can discipline yourself to do this, you will reap greater benefits. This is a bullet-point summary of the information and key points. By doing this, you will have to review, reflect and consolidate the knowledge and information and most importantly you will have to put it into your own words. This can be placed at the begin-

ning or the end of each notes section so that you can get a quick reference to what is contained in the notes to help you decide whether you need the information for an assignment at a later date. These Summary Sheets are also useful for revision purposes.

4 Lecture alerts: behind the scenes

Obviously, lecturers have their own style of delivery and quirky ways. However, there are some features that you might like to look out for in order to alert you to possible outcomes which could affect your concentration and selection of information.

Body language cues	Alert
Speaks very quickly	Need to have good listening skills. Look out for key words/information. It may simply be a sign of nervousness.
Speaks very softly at the beginning of the lecture	This may be used as a ploy to get students' attention and to calm down the 'audience'. If used for this purpose what they say at this point may not be vital.
Reads from notes	This type of lecture places greater pressure on your concentration skills because it can often be delivered in a monotone. The lecturer may be nervous or unsure of the information and needs to rely heavily on notes.
Says some things very slowly	This is a verbal method of underlining and putting information in bold. It is likely that the information is important so you need to record it in your notes.
Repeats phrases and sentences	It could be that the lecturer has lost his place in his notes! More often it is a way of emphasising important information so you need to record it in your notes.
Pauses occasionally	You have to decide if this is an individual, stylistic feature or not. It could be that the lecturer has lost his place in his notes! It may be a ploy to make a point that some students are talking during the lecture. It may be the lecturer's way of emphasising important information so you need to record it in your notes.
Turns to screen to go through slide information (be it OHT or PowerPoint)	This is the sign of an inexperienced lecturer. Sound levels will naturally drop so you need to be listening carefully.

Body language cues	Alert
Paces up and down in front of 'audience'	This type of style of lecturing is often accompanied by lack of use of notes. The lecturer knows his stuff! It can be distracting for some students, so you must ensure that your concentration levels are high.
Use of rhetorical questions	You are not expected to answer these either by shouting out the answer or raising your hand. They are used to get students to be critical or to demonstrate the current debates and issues. The lecturer then proceeds to answer his or her own question. At times they are a device to vary the delivery so that students do not fall asleep in lectures!

Environmental features	Alert
PowerPoint slides	Where are the notes? Are hard copies available in the room? Was I expected to download them myself prior to lecture?
PowerPoint slide usage	(i) As information handouts only (usually six slides per A4 page) to start off your notes. (ii) As an aide-memoire for note-taking (usually three or four 4 slides per A4 page with lines for you to personalise the information). (iii) Some slides are for information only and are not talked about by the lecturer; others are brought up on screen and additional information is given. If a lecturer uses this style, you must be alert and concentrate so that you do not lose your place!
Overhead transparencies (OHTs)	This is an alternative to PowerPoint. It probably means that there is no electronic version available for download. Each slide contains succinct information which you are expected to record in some way.
Writes information on board	You need to take down this information because it may not be contained in any other source of notes.

An awareness of these features will ensure that you get even more out of your lectures.

5 Template for note-taking

Taking notes in lectures does rely upon the expertise of the lecturer. Style of delivery and expertise varies, and this can have an impact upon your ability to keep up with the notes but more importantly the need to be flexible. This applies to all formats of note-taking.

Your note-taking should ensure that you leave spaces for the lecture's afterthoughts and revisitings. Lecturers are only human and at times suddenly remember information that should have gone with an earlier section. At other times, lecturers can be imparting information from their notes and at the end of a section, they want to bring you up-to-date information which they have just read about. This information has to be tacked on and you would need to try to place the information in the appropriate section of your notes. If you have left no room, you should ensure that you link the information by arrows or colour-coding when you are involved in the post-lecture activities.

On the other hand, one of the problems with making a note of what the lecturer has said in a linear manner is that there is less room for flexibility. A template for lecture notes could solve your problems.

The Cornell Method

This is a method which was developed over 40 years ago by Professor Walter Pauk to help his students at Cornell University (Pauk, 2000). It was intended to increase efficiency and originally consisted of six stages. It was his intention that students:

- record information from lectures
- reduce their notes
- recite the information to aid recall and memory
- reflect
- review the information to make sure they understand it
- recapitulate and make a summary.

The following table shows how you could organise your note-taking, the Cornell way. As you can see it is a template which could be prepared beforehand, using your word processor. Section A provides vital information to help you to identify your notes at a later stage. Section B is the space where you write your information during the lecture while Section C will allow you to reflect upon what you have learnt during the lecture and give you space to write up distilled and useful information. This could be essential for use in gathering information for your essay or as a start to producing effective revision notes. Of course, the active student will come away from the lecture with some questions unanswered and Section D will provide space for you to summarise the lecture to get a global or overview picture.

<table>
<tr><th colspan="2">A. Lecture title: Date: Lecturer's name: Page number</th></tr>
<tr><td>B. Space for information taken down during lecture</td><td>C. Additional notes in post-lecture phase:
key words;
key concepts;
key theorists/names.
Additional information which you have remembered from the lecturer's talk which you didn't have time to record in lecture.</td></tr>
<tr><td colspan="2">D. Follow-up:
Questions you might have
Commentary</td></tr>
</table>

Uses

Its main advantage is that it is possible to cut down on re-doing notes. Again, you have to be well prepared in advance for this way of taking notes. However, once you have got into the routine of preparing your pages in this way, you will quickly adapt and the lecture workspace (B) will not seem restricted or limited. It will also provide you with more useable notes for revision. Similarly, if you are searching through your files for information to put into your essays, you need only glance at the summary section to find out if there is anything worth using.

6 Using a laptop during lectures

Electronic notes are now part of a student's life. Writing electronic notes during lectures is down to personal preference but also to the facilities which are available in your college or university. If you have a laptop computer with wireless connections you will have access to many facilities. However, not all lecture rooms are set up in this way at the moment. To help you to decide whether electronic notes are viable for you, consider Activity 3.

ACTIVITY 3 Should I use a laptop in lectures?

Which of the following statements apply to you? Answer true or false.

	True	False
1. I prefer not to work straight onto screen.		
2. I do not feel confident working on a computer under pressure.		

	True	False
3. My keyboard skills are slow.		
4. I am not sure about basic functions of my word processor.		
5. I do not like to read information straight from the screen.		
6. I feel embarrassed using a computer in front of other people.		
7. I am worried that I might press the wrong keys and wipe all my lecture notes.		

If your answers are mainly true, you really ought to consider whether you are ready or really want to make electronic notes during lectures and seminars. You need sophisticated skills of listening, summarising and multi-tasking when coping with lectures. Making electronic notes adds another dimension to this complexity. You need to ask yourself whether using an electronic format during the lecture is the right approach for you. The crucial questions you have to ask yourself are:

- Do I have the necessary skills?
- Is this way of note-taking going to support me or be a barrier to my learning?
- Do I want to take notes in this way?

Of course, if the answer to the final question is 'no', then you will eliminate this mode of 'writing'. However, you need to make sure that in the long term you are not closing doors for more efficient ways of working both at university and beyond.

You need to have a good **speed of typing** if you are going to stand a chance of keeping up in lectures. This may seem a trite remark but spending some time in a vacation or before you embark upon your course learning how to touch-type or improving your typing speed will be time well spent. The old adage 'practice makes perfect' has never more been true than in these circumstances. The more time you set aside to practise your skills, the quicker you will become. The best case scenario is that you are able to **touch type**. This means that you can look at the slides and still type in your information. Being at this level of expertise also implies that you will not be slowed down looking for a specific key. If this happens, the lecturer will be three sentences ahead of you, and you will be constantly chasing your tail. Touch typing does not imply that you use both hands – though this is better. Many students can type at speed only using two fingers on each hand. You need to ensure that your typing speeds and your knowledge of the word processing programme are automatic so that you are not slowed down grappling with the technology!

Reviewing and consolidating your notes is easier on computer, and the final product will be clearer to read at a later date. However, a small amount of forethought can reap excellent rewards when you are under pressure to find information for an essay, for example. Thus, setting up a template on your laptop can be done in advance so that you can move around the document, placing the lecturer's information in its appropriate box or section.

7 Critical listening: ways to increase your listening skills

On average you will spend about 12–14 hours per week in lectures, depending upon your subject and your year of study. Put that way it does not seem very much. Listening to your favourite band on an MP3 player is not the same as listening to a lecture. For one thing, with the former you are in control: you have chosen the preferred tracks which you want to listen to; you know that you will enjoy them; and you are not necessarily listening to every word! It is also true to say that there is little likelihood of your being tested at the end of the tracks. Because you can listen to them over and over again, you are more likely to remember much of what you have heard – a sort of subliminal listening seems to take place. In some cases they are merely background wallpaper to other activities, and it is not crucial if your attention wanders for a time.

On the other hand, listening to a lecture requires different skills: skills which you may need to practise in order to increase your efficiency. The student who develops **active listening** skills is the one who will understand and deal with new and challenging information more effectively and will also be able to remember the information for longer periods of time before having to rehearse the information in some way (see the section on revision in Chapter 2.5).

Baseline skills

- Concentration
- Anticipation
- Questioning
- Selection/elimination
- Analysing
- Summarising

If you are questioning, selecting and summarising spoken information, you will be actively involved in the lecture. The result will be higher levels of **concentration** because you are being critical – not in the sense of negatively criticising your lecturer's voice or clothes but, more importantly, critical of what is being said. You can improve your concentration skills. It is all very well to be told not to daydream during lectures. It is natural for the mind to wander but you must make sure that you keep yourself in check. Prompting yourself with questions is a way of keeping your mind on the job in hand. Thus, if you think you are getting bored, instead of doodling, start analysing the information you are listening to.

Mental joggers – asking the right questions

- Why has it been included?
- How does it link with the rest of the information?
- Is it essential or exemplar information?
- Is this a new section?
- Does what the lecturer is saying fit in with what you have already read or is it controversial?
- What point is the lecturer trying to make?

In addition to concentration, a vital skill to use is that of anticipation because it will set off your own questions, make you listen for the answers you need, and in this process you will be selecting information and tagging some parts of the lecture as being of higher priority than other parts (selection and elimination).

What to anticipate/what to listen out for	What is its use?
Introductory statements	May indicate an overview of the lecture structure so that you can be ready to organise your sub-headings and branches of information.
Signal language	This could get you ready for lists, for example. For more specific examples see below.
Summaries/conclusions	These will help you to develop a framework of information. They can be used as a checklist when you review your notes to make sure you didn't miss anything out. They can deepen your understanding.

8 How to hone your listening skills: we hear what we want to hear

The warm-up

You can double your listening capacity by doing the pre-lecture activities. These activities will make you aware of **key terminology** and give you a broad framework of information so that you go into a lecture with some hooks upon which to put the new and sometimes challenging information. Although these activities will increase your ability to make sense of new concepts and ideas, you need to do something slightly different to ensure that you prepare yourself for **hearing the information**.

- Pick out and list key terms, terms with which you are unfamiliar and terminology which seems to be used in a very specific way in the subject. (You will be aware of this because your understanding of the meaning of the word does not make sense in the specialist texts.)
- Check your understanding by defining the terms in your own words. Then, cross-check in a subject glossary to find out if you got it right.
- Say the words aloud or better still record them onto a disk and listen to them. This way you will be prepared for hearing the terms, and your brain will not have to slow down to process the information when you are in the lecture.
- If you are working electronically, you can enlist the help of your computer if you have appropriate software. You can type in your list (or cut and paste if you are working from departmental, electronic information), and get the computer to speak the words to you so that you hear them. Voice recognition software such as Text Help has this facility and will even let you decide whether you want to hear a male or female voice!

Now you are in a better position to listen out for the key words in the lecture because your mind has heard them and is looking out for them (Activity 4).

ACTIVITY 4 Listening for key words

Here is the script of part of a lecture. Get a friend to read the text to you or scan the text into your computer and get your computer to read the information to you and see if you can pick out the key words.

The topic of the talk is 'The Dangers of the Sun'.

This is a general talk by the Health Services and is open to all and any students.

Jot down what you would anticipate you will hear about this topic:
1.
2.
3.
4.

You will find answers at the end of the chapter.

Now jot down the key words/terminology which you would anticipate:
1.
2.
3.
4.
5.
6.

You will find answers at the end of the chapter.

Text extract: 'The Dangers of the Sun'

Pick out the key words and points while you listen to this extract:

> *For many years dermatologists have warned the public about the dangers of staying in the sun without protection. Exposure to the sun can have dramatic results, apart from the treasured tanned skin. There are three points which I wish to bring to your attention in this talk. Firstly, the sun can damage the layers of the skin. The outer layer can change its appearance. The texture can become leathery with a loss of elasticity. This can result in premature ageing of the skin, causing wrinkles and brown blotches. Secondly, over-exposure can result in skin cancer. The brown blotches may be the outer indicator of cancer. They appear as moles on the skin. Next, extreme exposure to the sun increases the possibility of breaking down our natural protection from the sun's radiation. The effects of UVA and UVB are becoming more well known. Tanning shops promise their customers that they can provide 'safe' tanning. They try to convince us that UVA is a lower level of radiation and therefore less harmful. This is not true! In fact, UVA has been proved responsible for damaging the deeper layers of the skin which destroy structural proteins and thus harming the immune systems ...*

Check your notes with the answers at the end of the chapter to see if you picked out the main key words and points.

Listening for main points/ideas

This exercise will help you to improve your skills of selection and elimination. The task is best tackled as a listening exercise so get a friend to read the text to you or scan the text into your computer and get your computer to read the information to you and see if you can pick out the main points.

Text extract: 'Is a bulky diet of eucalyptus leaves the best option for the tiny Koala?'

> *Should Koalas change their diet? Are eucalyptus leaves a sensible choice in the changing environment? Is the Koalas' diet appropriate for the modern world? All these questions and more have been asked by biologists in their study of this diminutive and appealing little animal.*

The diet of the Koala is limited almost entirely to eating eucalyptus leaves. Environmental issues and the decrease in natural habitats apart, there are drawbacks and advantages to such a restricted diet. The size of the Koalas' digestive system, their metabolic structures and chemical make-up of eucalyptus leaves combine to provide a fascinating forum for discussion.

The dichotomy lies in the leaves and the digestive system. On the one hand the leaves are rich in fibre but contain high levels of lignin. Fibre is not conducive to digestion, and lignin, a woody material found in the cell walls of many plants, is indigestible. So why does the Koala have such a voracious appetite for this source of fuel? Another drawback is that the ratio of an animal's gut volume to its energy needs is dependent upon animal mass. Thus, this tiny creature does not have the capacity and its metabolic system has difficulty coping. The quality of the food is poor so this means that large quantities are needed in order to extract sufficient nutrients. So how does it manage to digest and process poor-quality food for its metabolic needs?

It would appear that the Koala has adapted its digestive system to cope with its roughage-laden diet. Scientists in New South Wales conducted a study in the early 1980s and uncovered three major factors.

Firstly, the Koala can regulate the passage of food through its system, like a rabbit. In this way it has developed a system which discriminates between different sized particles so that the smaller, more easily digested ones can be digested first while the coarser, indigestible matter is expelled almost immediately. This space-saving exercise allows the Koala to increase the rate at which the 'good' material can be put into the system.

Secondly, the Koala is a relatively slow-moving animal compared with others of a similar size so it is able to reduce the fuel it needs. It can be compared with the slow-moving, three-toed sloth.

Finally, eucalyptus leaves have hidden fuels. Although the woody, indigestible lignin is present, there is also a wealth of lipids and phenols which are rich sources of energy. However, the Koala's system cannot cope with phenols so these are excreted, leaving the lipids which provide useful carbohydrate energy in the form of starch and sugar.

So what seems an improbable system has been adapted to take account of animal size, metabolic rates and energy-saving adaptations.

See if you have picked out the main points in the answers at the end of the chapter.

Verbal cues and signals

Your listening skills can be greatly improved if you know what triggers to listen for and the significance of these signals.

Signal	What to expect
Start with	This may be signalling the introduction which will give overviews.
Lecture is divided into ...	Tells you the structure.
However, on the other hand, but, conversely, on the contrary, despite	This signals contrasting or opposing information and evidence.
In addition, in other words, put another way, also, as I said previously	This signals repetition of information or provides you with another definition or explanation.
For example, that is to say, furthermore, another example, such as	These alert you to the fact that what follows will be examples of a main point.
Especially, specifically, most importantly, I cannot stress enough	Lecturers will use these to signal emphasis so listen very carefully because they obviously think the information is vital/important.
Firstly, secondly (etc.), next, then, penultimate (last but one), ultimate, finally, in conclusion	Be ready for a number of points or lists.
Therefore, thus, because, consequently, accordingly, if ... then, as a result of this	Cause and effect.
I'll expand on this later on ... I'll give you more detail about this later in the lecture ... I'll take this point up later ...	This means that you must be on the alert to link up later information with this earlier point. You might even leave space in your notes to accommodate this.
In conclusion, let me summarise, let's recap, in short/in brief, to wrap up, the main points covered were ...	These are useful because they will help you to get the global/big picture because the lecturer has summarised the information for you.

The significance of knowing about these signals when you are listening to someone speak is that you are expecting and anticipating certain types of information to follow. This will aid your understanding and speed up you processing of the information so that ultimately your notes will be of a better quality.

Thus, by a more focussed and active approach to your listening, you will be able to make more effective notes and overcome the problem of forgetting what you have heard.

9 Recording lectures

This section explores the use of electrical and electronic devices to record and store information from lectures and seminars. Before you rush off and buy some gizmo, you need to consider its uses, the advantages and disadvantages of different devices and likely academic tutors' attitudes and responses to usage (see Activity 5).

Activity 5 Recording lectures: myth or reality?

Look at the following comments made by students and decide whether you think they are true or false.

Statements made by students If I use some sort of recording device …	True	False
It will take all the hard work out of lectures.		
It will save me time.		
It will mean I do not have to do anything.		
It will help me remember information.		
It will ensure that I understand my lectures.		
I can sell the information to other students who didn't make the lecture.		

To find out if you are correct, look at the answers at the end of the chapter. The implications for these statements are discussed in this section. Some students have been encouraged at school and sixth-form college to use dictaphone-type devices. They may have been useful and appropriate at that stage of study but you need to consider your academic demands now, and whether this type of method of recording is most suitable and appropriate to your individual needs.

Devices

There is a baffling array of gadgets available on the market. Which one you choose largely depends upon what you want to use it for:

- tape recorders
- mini-disk recorders
- mobile telephones
- PDAs (personal digital assistants).

The pros and cons of these gadgets are discussed in the table opposite.

Device	Pros	Cons	Additional features worth considering
Tape recorders	Cheap to buy. Small and portable. Tape cassettes are inexpensive.	Not very versatile. Information on tape is not easily transferred to other systems. A one-hour lecture takes an expert two hours to transcribe. Sound quality is variable and can be dependent upon where you are sitting in relation to the lecturer.	Variable speed playback enables you to slow down play-back so that you can take in information more effectively. There are different sizes of tape cassettes. If you intend to share with others you need to consider compatibility. Is there an advanced facility to 'mark' information while someone is speaking – aids retrieval later.
Mini-disk recorders	Sound quality on play-back is excellent and not reliant upon sitting at the front for best results. Fairly cheap to buy. Small and portable. Mini-disks are fairly inexpensive. Mini-disk capacity is larger than tape cassette. Navigation is easier – therefore searching for specific information is quicker and less time-consuming. Can be used for other purposes – e.g. recording music.	Attractive gadget and therefore stealable. A one-hour lecture takes an expert two hours to transcribe.	Variable speed playback option enables you to slow down play-back so that you can take in information more effectively.
Solid-state recorders	Record information onto RAM chips or cards. Easier transfer of information from one system to another. Recording time is longer than both the above. Small and portable.	A one-hour lecture takes an expert two hours to transcribe.	
Mobile telephones	You probably already have one so no additional cost.	Recording space is limited. Only use in emergencies.	Check the memory capacity. Is there an option to plug in memory cards to boost facilities?
PDA	Small and portable. Voice memo is available on more expensive models.	Expensive if you get one with the options you need for this type of activity. Limited capacity for recording speech. Need to be well organised and to back up information regularly onto another, more permanent system. Attractive gadget and therefore stealable.	Look for MP3 facility to enable you to listen to text.

A final consideration – some machines can record information in a way that is compatible with speech recognition software on your computer. However, your machine has to be set up to recognise the voice before it will download and transcribe recorded speech. This may seem like an excellent solution but the practicalities are such that ***all*** of your lecturers would have to take time out of their busy schedules to go through the voice recognition programme. However, if you have one lecturer for a lot of your time, it might be worth considering. But be ready for your lecturer to refuse, stating time pressures, etc.

Recording protocols

If you wish to record the lectures in some way, apart from cost, utility and meeting your needs, you must also bear in mind other factors. It is important that you get **permission** to use your machine. This means that you might need to e-mail lecturers before the start of their unit to ask for permission. It is also worth briefly reassuring your lecturer about the purpose to which you intend to put the recordings. Some students explain that they are auditory learners and take in information more readily if they hear it while reading handouts and notes. It might be that you need to request a temporary use of a recorder because you have broken the hand/arm with which you write. Many lecturers are uneasy about students recording their lectures. Some are openly hostile. You need to be aware of this so that you are not frustrated or upset by responses to your request. The reasons some lecturers do not want you to record their lectures often relate to copyright of intellectual property or the fact that they can no longer control how their information is used.

'What are they going to do with this information?' is a question frequently asked by lecturers. Some academic tutors are wary of giving permission because a lecture may contain off-the-cuff comments and responses which the lecturer would not want to be used for future purposes. It may be a reflection of the litigious society in which we live that lecturers are on their guard concerning recording of lectures because of the notion of 'evidence which could be used, etc.' That is not to say that this is commendable, but it is certainly understandable.

If you seek permission at the beginning of a unit, this usually means that you do not have to make the request at each lecture. Of course, if there is a stand-in lecturer, it is only polite to inform them that you have been given permission to record the lecture.

At university you will be expected to cope with the recording and the machine so that it does not interfere with the smooth-running of the lecture. Academic tutors do not expect to be given the machine so that they can turn the recording on and off. This may have been the system at school but it is different in Higher Education settings. You will need to think about the ethics of selling your recordings to other students.

Summary of this chapter

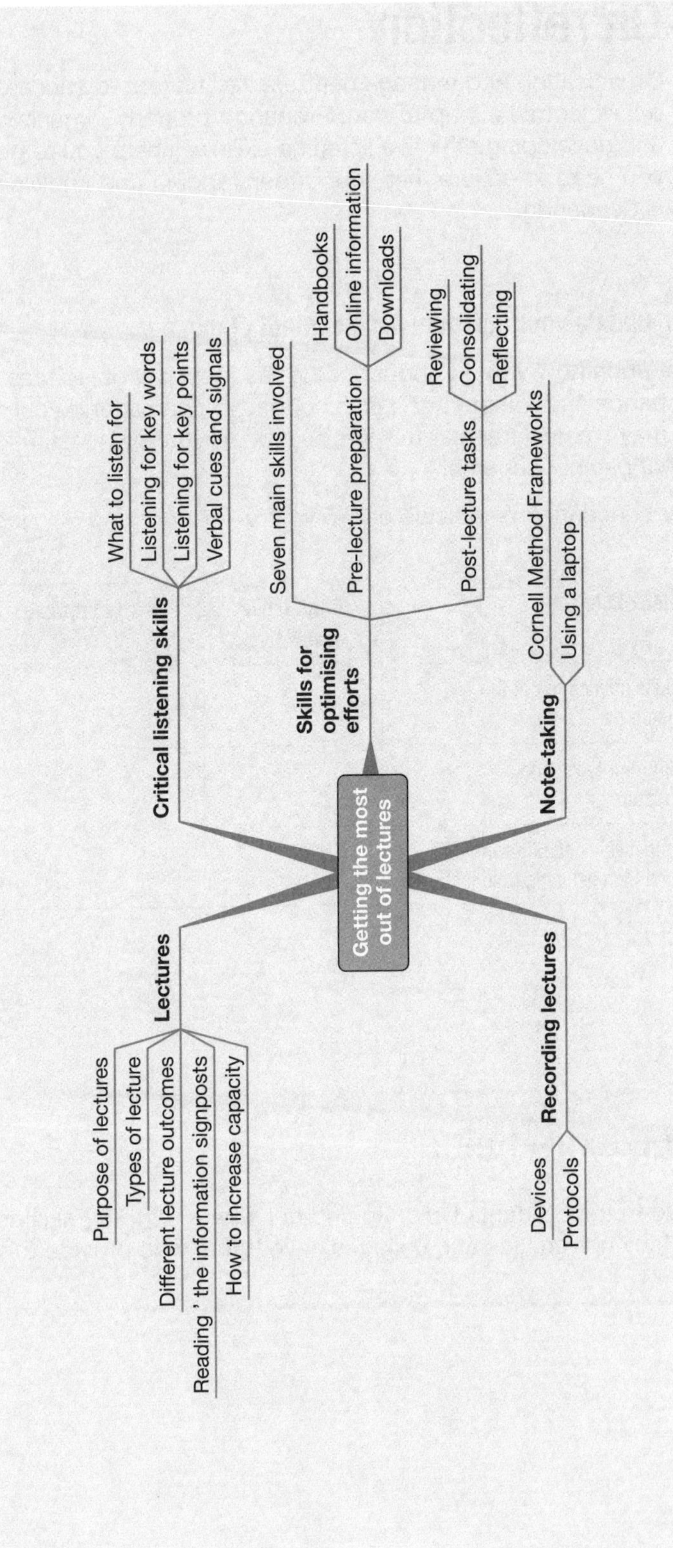

10 On reflection

Organisation and management are key factors to success. Getting the most out of lectures is up to you. Preparing properly, organising your note-taking and developing effective listening skills will help you to gain the added value you need to ensure that your understanding and knowledge of your subject is deepened.

ACTIVITY 6 Update your personal development planner

Now reflect upon how you go about getting the most out of lectures and how you intend to change and adapt your habits so that you can spend your time more effectively. You may want to transfer this information to your own institution's personal development planner scheme.

Grade your confidence on a scale of 1–5 where 1 = poor and 5 = good.

My developing skills	Confidence level: 1– 5	Plans to improve
I know the skills needed to get the most out of lectures.		
I know the different types and purposes of lectures.		
I can listen effectively and differentiate the information I am listening to in lectures.		

Date: ______________________________

Getting extra help

Go to the Students Union to find out where to go for skill development. Many universities and colleges have tutors who provide this service.

Feedback on activities

ACTIVITY 4 Listening for key words

The talk: 'The Dangers of the Sun'

Jot down what you would anticipate you will hear about this topic:
1. Problems of over-exposure
2. Skin protection and radiation
3. Skin cancer
4. Ageing process

Now jot down the key words/terminology which you would anticipate:
1. Skin cancer
2. UVA/UVB
3. Dermatologist
4. Skin layers
5. Over-exposure
6. Cancerous moles

Sample notes

Dermatologists warned about the dangers of overexposure without protection.

1. Sun damages layers of the skin, changing appearance:
   (a) texture – leathery with a loss of elasticity
   (b) result – premature ageing of the skin, causing wrinkles and brown blotches.
2. Secondly, over-exposure – skin cancer:
   (a) brown blotches indicator of cancer
   (b) appear as moles.
3. Extreme exposure – skin's natural protection from the sun's radiation destroyed:
   (a) effects of UVA and UVB more well known
   (b) tanning shops – UVA is a lower level of radiation and therefore less harmful. Not true!
      (i) UVA responsible for damaging the deeper layers of the skin
      (ii) structural proteins destroyed
      (iii) immune systems damaged.

Text extract: 'Is a bulky diet of eucalyptus leaves the best option for the tiny Koala?'

Should Koalas change their diet? Are eucalyptus leaves a sensible choice in the changing environment? Is the Koalas' diet appropriate for the modern world? All these questions and more have been asked by biologists in their study of this diminutive and appealing little animal.

Koala diet: limited – eucalyptus leaves.
+ & – to restricted diet

The size of the Koalas' digestive system, their metabolic structures and chemical make-up of eucalyptus leaves combine to provide a fascinating forum for discussion.

Leaves and the digestive system

Leaves

- rich in fibre
- fibre not easily digested by Koalas
- but high levels of indigestible, woody lignin

Digestive system

- gut volume to energy needed = animal mass
- Koala capacity = small
- eucalyptus nutrients poor so large quantity needed

System adaptations

1. Koala can regulate food in system:
   (a) differentiates types of food
   (b) expels coarser indigestible matter
   (c) left with smaller, more easily digested particles.
2. Cut down on energy requirements:
   (a) slow-moving
   (b) needs less energy
   (c) unlike other small animals
   (d) like three-toed sloth.
3. Koala extracts energy fuel carbohydrate from eucalyptus:
   (a) lipids – rich source of energy
   (b) expels phenols
   (c) gets starch and sugar for energy.

Reference

Pauk, W. (2000) *How to Study in College,* 7th edn. New York, Houghton Miffin.

2.3 Working in a real team

Working with others is always a balance between maintaining our own individuality and becoming a member of a group to which we are proud to belong. The more we join with people 'like us', the more confident we feel in being able to maintain that balance. This balance is often a result of being able to predict how each of us will behave which in turn builds up trust within a team. However, once we work with people we don't know or with those from different cultures, we are less able to comfortably predict how we will react with one another or what our expectations are. Many companies work in multicultural environments, with flatter hierarchical structures on increasingly complex issues, where you will be expected to work in very diverse teams. Being a member of such a team therefore needs more skill and you need to know the components of team building in order to make this work. Hoping to muddle along because you have had experience of working with your friends on many projects is no longer sufficient.

In this chapter you will learn how to:

1. understand what a real team is
2. identify the learning styles of your team in order to allocate key roles
3. engage with the mechanics of setting up a real team.

USING THIS CHAPTER

Estimate your current levels of confidence. At the end of the chapter you will have the chance to re-assess these levels where you can incoroprate this into your personal development planner (PDP). Mark between 1 (poor) and 5 (good) for the following.

I understand what a real team is.	I can identify the learning styles of our team in order to allocate key roles.	I can engage with the mechanics of settng up a real team.

Date: ________________

1 Introduction

We work and play together in many groupings which are brought together for a variety of purposes, such as: sports teams, informal learning groups, mentoring groups, buzz groups for creative solutions, virtual groups and project teams. We generally lump this all together as 'group work'. However, each of these groupings operate differently. This chapter will develop our understanding of working in a team project as opposed to a loose gathering of individuals; a key employability skill for your future.

The Association of Graduate Recruiters' chief executive, Carl Gilleard, talking to BBC News (2006), said that 'Employers are likely to be looking to graduates who can demonstrate softer skills such as team-working, cultural awareness, leadership and communication skills, as well as academic achievement.'

There is generally no doubt that being an effective team player and/or leader of a team is an important skill and its development starts during your studies. However, you undoubtedly have a view of group work that may not be all that positive, so let's start by revealing that position now (see Activity 1).

ACTIVITY 1 Annoying things about working with others

Below are a series of statements that students often make about group work. How would you deal with these annoying things? Answer these questions now but you may want to change your answers after reading the remainder of this chapter.

Annoying things	I would deal with this by ...
There are always free-riders in a team and their marks are boosted by those who do the work.	
Teams slow me down and that irritates me.	
I have difficulty with the topic the team has to work on and I'm afraid I'll keep the others back.	
Sometimes team members won't complete their tasks [at all, or on time].	
Sometimes teams don't divide the work up fairly.	
Sometimes you get students who just don't care about their grades, but I do.	

Check the feedback section at the end of the chapter for more information (or wait until you have read the remainder of the chapter).

2 What is a team?

A teams is a group of individuals with defined goals who work together for a particular purpose. An essential characteristic is that the individuals in a team are interdependent in order to get the job completed. However, just coming together with a group of friends does not mean that you are automatically a team. Most employers know that we have to 'work at' becoming a team and this is reflected in the significant amount of staff development that goes into team building.

Teams are able to deal with complex problems and come up with more creative solutions than individuals alone. In the workplace, teams are increasingly cross-disciplinary, drawing on the expertise of many. More than likely, your student project will be confined to those on your course, but remember, working together with different kinds of people is a preparation for future work. Good teams also enhance commitment and a feeling of community among its members.

Friendship groups and teams

We all automatically want to form a team with our friends and if you are told to form a team, you would probably do just that. The advantages of this are that you are comfortable with each other, you want to support each other and it makes you feel good. The main disadvantage of friends as teams is that your relationship is built on socialising and having fun. The project team could put a strain on that relationship as you may have to behave in a different way with a particular friend in the team than you would do socially. If someone outside your friendship group joined your team, it may also be difficult for him or her to feel accepted.

Moving from group to team

The main issue for student project groups is to move from being a group of individuals to being a team. Two management consultants, Jon Katzenbach and Douglas Smith, wrote a best-seller entitled *The Wisdom of Teams* where they looked at the difference between a group of individuals working together and high-performance teams. Their findings are summarised in Figure 1.

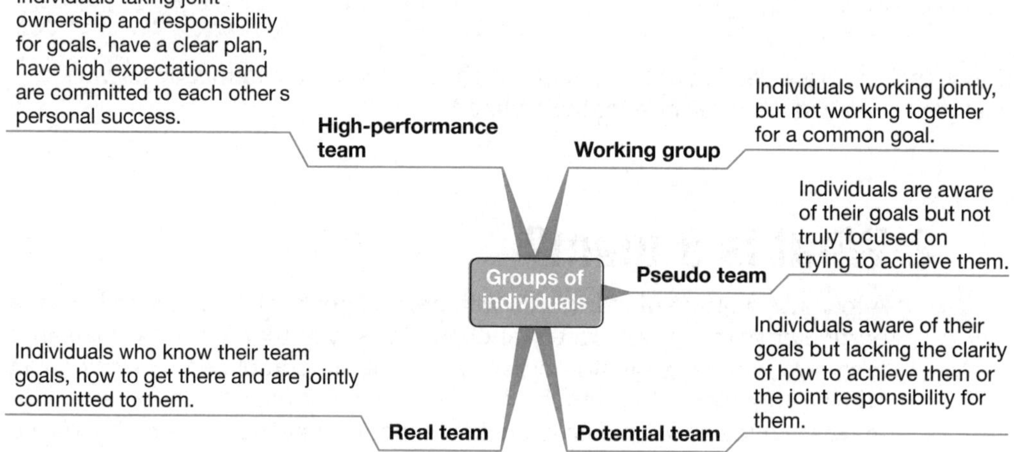

Figure 1 How individuals work together

Adapted from Katzenback and Smith (1993)

Checklist for creating a real team

Members of a team ...

- are absolutely clear of the team's goals
- allocate roles
- take joint responsibility for the goals
- plan how to achieve goals
- allocate tasks to all members
- are good time managers
- value everyone in the team
- identify and deal with hidden agendas
- trust one another to be dependable, honest, fair and objective in their dealings with each other.

Identifying team characteristics

Characteristics	Grouping*	Issues
You are working together as a group to share information, understand assignments and learn together. Each of you will take away information from the group, which will help your own understanding of a topic. The group has no accountability for its output.	Working group	As an informal grouping this can be very productive and supportive during the learning process. Recognise that you are an informal group and that you have no output as a team.
You are in a group that has been assigned a task. As a group you are responsible for the output. However, as a group you are not working collectively in order to try and achieve this. The group appears to have no interest in setting goals, working collectively and coming up with plan even though you may call yourself a team.	Pseudo team	This is a real problem grouping because you think you're team when you're not. At this level you have not developed team skills or fully understand how teams work. You need to understand the task, work collectively, identify skills within the team and be mutually accountable of the outcome.
You are in a group that has been assigned a task. You understand that as a group you are responsible for the output. You understand that you need to work together, develop a plan and be collectively accountable. You are trying to do this but it can be very frustrating because the 'team' becomes unfocused and members are not always moving together in the same direction.	Potential team	As the label for this grouping suggests there is potential here but it is not yet fully realised. By the end of year two you should at least be carrying out teamwork at the 'potential team' level. You will further develop your skills in the following year(s). Most problems with student project teams are identified with this kind of grouping (including pseudo teams). Take stock of the team skills you need to develop and make notes in your personal development planner (PDP).
You are in a group that has been assigned a task. As a group you are responsible for the output. All members of the group are committed to the project and understand that they hold themselves mutually responsible for the outcome. As a group you have identified the resources you have in your team, i.e. the skills and knowledge you can bring to the team in order to make your plan more effective. You are also aware that all team members need supporting.	Real team	If you are working at this level you understand how teams work, including the collaborative work and accountability that is needed for the output. By the end of year three you should be working on team projects at this level. Student projects working at this level should do very well. Critically reflect on the team skills you are developing. Don't forget to evaluate and evidence your developing skills in your PDP and incorporate in your CV.

Characteristics	Grouping*	Issues
You are in a group that has been assigned a task. As a group you are responsible for the output. All members of the group are committed to the project and understand that they hold themselves mutually responsible for the outcomes. As a team you know the strengths of your members and work with those strengths. In addition, you are truly interdependent and aware that each member of the team needs space and encouragement for personal development, and the team values everyone's contribution. You see the value in reflection and how it can improve your team performance.	High-performance team	This is what you are aiming for. You work with mutual interdependence that reflects the group's skill mix and personal preferences. Your language is aligned to the goals of the task and you have a strong sense of mutual responsibility for the output of the team. Team members feel fulfilled and proud to be part of this team. If you have got to this level before your final year of studies then you are doing very well, but it is a rare occurrence. Aim to be in at least one high-performance team before you finish your studies. Update your PDP with an evaluation of how your skills have developed in this area.

* Terms in this column used by Katzenbach and Smith (1993)

As you work towards being an effective team, you need to consider the various functions that teams perform in order to work well together (see Activity 2). John Adair, who is a leading authority on leadership and the first to be appointed as a professor in Leadership Studies, says that teams need to consider how they achieve the task, build/maintain the team and take care of individual needs. See Figure 2 below.

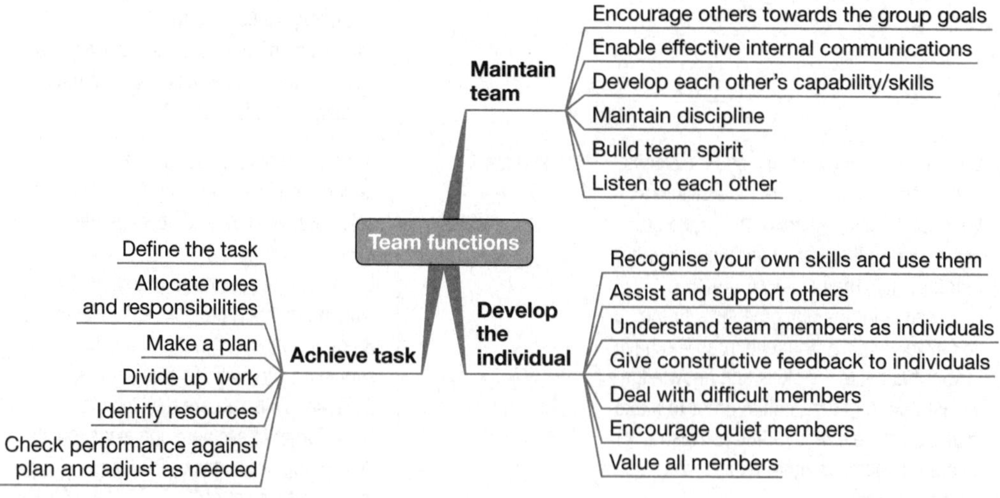

Figure 2 Team functions

Adapted from John Adair's model of how teams function (Adair, 1986)

ACTIVITY 2 Understanding team patterns – what's your view?

Each of the three areas identified by Adair (achieving the task, building the team and responding to individual needs) should to be addressed if your team is to work effectively and harmoniously. Just imagine these scenarios and identify the functions missing from John Adair's model and estimate the kind of group you think they are (working group, pseudo team, potential team, real team, high-performance team).

Check the feedback section to compare your answers.

Scenario 1

You are working with a great group – they are all your friends. You often meet in the pub as it gives a good informal atmosphere and you can enjoy the work. It is good because no one in the group nags or bosses anyone else around. You have done some reading around for this project and written a few things down and you hope that it will be useful. You assume everyone else is doing that too; after all, they all turn up and seem engaged.

Assume it is now 2 weeks before your final deadline.

	Jot down some ideas
What are the dangers for individuals working in a group like this?	
How might such a 'team' appear during the project presentation if they don't change?	
Take stock – what does the group need to do **NOW**?	
What would you have learned about team work from such a group?	
Which function(s) of the Adair model is missing in this example? What type of group do you think this is? working group I pseudo team I potential team I real team I high-performance team	

Scenario 2

You are working with a group of people – they are all your friends. You all sat down and worked out what you had to do and you think someone made a list, but you haven't seen it. A couple of your friends have become really bossy and they tell everyone else what to do, constantly adjusting and fiddling with things and even controlling what you are doing. They have told you to do something that you have no expertise or interest in and do not like how tasks are allocated. You never expected these friends of yours to be like this. You'll be glad when it is all over.

Assume it is now 2 weeks before your deadline.

	Jot down some ideas
What are the dangers for individuals working in a group like this?	
How will you all be feeling right now? Who will do those last minute tasks if you all feel fed up?	
How might such a 'team' appear during the project presentation if they don't change?	
Take stock – what does the group need to do **NOW**?	
What would you have learned about team work from such a group?	
Which function(s) of the Adair model is missing in this example? What type of group do you think this is? working group I pseudo team I potential team I real team I high-performance team	

Scenario 3

You are working with some people you know and some you don't know. Things are going well and you have even developed ground rules, appointed a group coordinator and have regular meetings. However, as time goes on problems arise as two group members aren't 'pulling their weight'; one has even stopped coming to meetings and hasn't produced anything yet. The group is getting annoyed as they see all their hard work being compromised by those who aren't contributing effectively.

Two weeks to go – what would you do from the following? Select 'yes' if you would carry out this action or 'no' if you wouldn't.

Action	Yes/No	Possible reasons
Find out if person X has a genuine reason for not doing the work		He/she may be ill, have family problems or just finding life pressures difficult at present. Depending on the answer, as a group you could give that person support or you may need to encourage him/her to seek help. Other reasons?
Ignore person X and do his/her work yourselves		It is the only way to complete the project. The tutor is only giving one mark for the completed project, so you have to. This is not ideal and it will only cause resentment. Other reasons?

Action	Yes/No	Possible reasons
Assuming there are no mitigating circumstances, then contact person X and say you need him/her to do their share – refer to ground rules and what s/he has to do to complete the project. Discuss with the person and then put it in writing – e-mail or letter – from the whole group – ensure a date for reply/action – retain a copy.		Person X realises the group is serious. Keep a record of your communication – you may need to say what you will do if you get no/little response. Other reasons?
Report person X to your tutor explaining which part of the project person X is responsible for.		This should be a last resort, but may be necessary in extreme cases. If you do this, you should tell person X and give him/her a chance to put things right. It should all be transparent and 'business-like'. Your reason?
Some of your ideas …		
Which function(s) of the Adair model is missing in this example ? What type of group do you think this is? working group | pseudo team | potential team | real team | high-performance team		

3 Getting started as a team

Before looking at the task or problem, everyone should:

- introduce themselves (often seen as ice breakers)
- agree a set of ground rules
- estimate the learning styles you have in your team as this will impact on the tasks and roles your team members are happy to do
- allocate role of coordinator.

Set your ground rules

Ground rules are vital if you want to establish an effective team. Ground rules will be the foundation for a strong working relationship based on: trust, honesty and an awareness of the expectations of each other. Social groups also have ground rules, but these tend to have developed over time and are very often unspoken. However, if someone in a social group violates these 'rules', they are often made to feel acutely aware of it. In a team, where individuals come together to start working as a team, making ground rules explicit is very important. Make sure this is the first thing you do so that when any member of the group feels things are going wrong, he/she can refer to them and remind everyone of their agreement. Be honest with the group and say what is important for you when working with them. Activity 3 helps you to consider how to establish ground rules.

ACTIVITY 3 Establishing ground rules

Develop ground rules that can be used by a team – some examples are below. List three more that would be important to you when working with a team. If you are already working in a team do this together and make sure you make a note of your rules.

Ground rules
1. Take responsibility for your own learning, actions and reactions (i.e. accept accountability).
2. Be honest and open (especially if you don't understand or agree with something).
3. Carry out your work on time.
4.
5.
6.

Determine your team profile

Teams start with a group of individuals who need to become a team. You need to recognise each other's individual differences as a resource and in order to do that it is useful to look at your individual learning styles.

Peter Honey and Alan Mumford, two British psychologists and leading experts in learning and behaviour, have developed a set of learning styles that determine whether you are: an activist, a reflector, a theorist or a pragmatist (Honey and Mumford, 1992). See the diagram below. Activity 4 asks you to identify your team's profile.

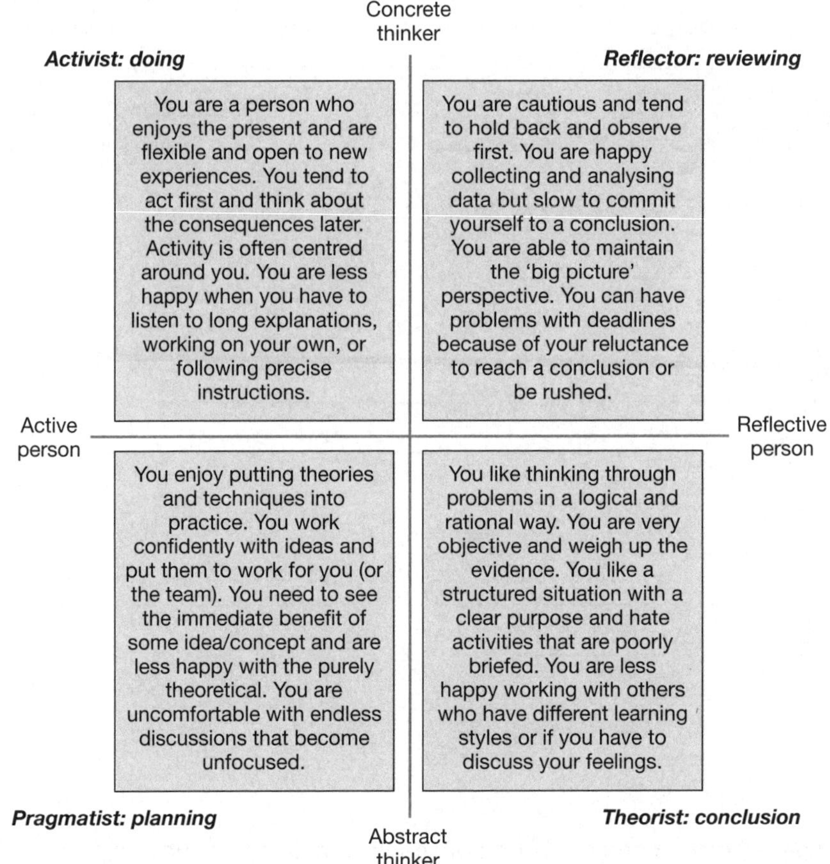

ACTIVITY 4 Identifying your team's profile

What's your team's profile? Using the diagram above identify which quadrant most describes you when working on a project. Try and do this as a team so you can identify your team's profile. If you are not working in a team currently, identify the profile that usually suits you when working in a team.

Look at the descriptions in the quadrants above. You may find you can identify yourself in several quadrants. However, rank the descriptions where it is:

1 = like me most of the time } Dominant profile
2 = like me some of the time }
3 = rarely like me
4 = never like me

Now put your rankings in the next table:

Team member	Activist	Reflector	Theorist	Pragmatist
Example: person A	**4**	**1**	**2**	**3**
Me				
Number of members ranking 1 or 2 on a given type				

In the example above, person A is predominantly a reflector/theorist. If most of the other members of your group also have this profile, you may have difficulty producing your goals on time. Knowing this in advance can alert you to the potential weakness of your team. This allows you to take corrective action early on.

According to personal rankings our team predominantly comprises:

Type	Number of members with this tendency/profile
Activists	
Reflectors	
Theorists	
Pragmatists	

Ideally, a team has a member from each of these categories, but more than likely you cannot change your team members, so use this exercise as a guide to consider how best to achieve your task with the individuals you have. Use this information to allocate roles for your team (see Section 4).

Remember as a team you still will all need to consider how you will fulfil other functions like maintaining team spirit and ensuring that everyone is valued (see Figure 2, p. 134).

4 Becoming an effective team

Now you have the basics in place, you can start planning, allocating roles and making good decisions.

Develop a plan of action

Without a plan you will not be able to work as a team. Once you have identified a coordinator/leader, you can start working on your plan. The plan does not only include a list of activities, but also protocols for the team (based on ground rules), e.g. dealing with meetings and what to do if individuals don't fulfil their tasks, etc. The designated coordinator needs to ensure there is a workable plan and **everyone** understands it and is committed to it. You can then further develop the roles of the team.

When planning:

1. Read carefully the brief given to you by your lecturer.
2. Agree what you have to do, by when and in what format(s).
3. Divide the brief into various sub-tasks.
4. Allocate team members to the various tasks.
5. Set a timetable with milestones.
6. Set out how you will handle meetings: regularity, minute taking/storing, decisions taken and actions set.
7. Establish reporting procedures and mechanisms for revising the plan, and keeping records and minutes of meetings.
8. Have a mechanism to ensure open communications with the ability to resolve conflict.
9. Plan how you will present your work.

Develop team roles

Use the information from this section and the one above to establish the kind of roles you would like in your team. You may find you have to split up along thematic lines as you may be expected to hand in work as a team, but with identifiable parts for each participant's grade. However, you do need to establish who does what and, whatever you decide, you will need to have a coordinator – someone who keeps the team 'on track' and 'on time'. There will be other roles and some people may have two roles, one on the task and another related to some element of team maintenance.

First allocate your coordinator then develop your plan (see Activity 5) and return to complete your team roles later.

ACTIVITY 5 Allocating team roles

Name	Role(s)
	Coordinator (checks milestones, group performance generally) + sub-topic task
	Record keeper + sub-topic task

Make good decisions

Decision-making can be difficult in teams. You may be more of a risk-taker than others, look at evidence selectively, have certain prejudices (often unknown to yourself) and be swayed, or not, by group pressure. All these lead to a flawed decision outcome.

There are various ways for teams to come to an agreement and make a decision:

1. **Consensus** – this agreement means alignment of the team as a whole with the goals set. Those who may have disagreed are prepared to cooperate for the success of the team and not take up defensive positions.
2. **Unanimous** – here everyone has to agree before a decision is taken.
3. **Majority** – this can be, for example, if 51% agree then the decision is taken, but this can split your team.

Ideally you want to have a consensus decision which means you are all prepared to accept the decision made. A fairly simple technique you can use as a team to air the issues during the decision-making process is the *Six Thinking Hats* proposed by a leading authority on creative thinking, Edward de Bono (1985).

Each 'hat' looks at an issue from a particular point of view. This can also reduce confrontation as people are working within the confines of their 'hat'. You don't physically have to wear different hats, but they are used to symbolise a different viewpoint. It is more objective if you adopt a hat that does not directly correspond to your own position:

- **White Hat** – with this hat you focus on information, reports and any data that are available. It is an objective position.
- **Red Hat** – with this hat you make a decision based on your opinion, intuition and feelings. It is a subjective position.
- **Black Hat** – this is a pessimistic and critical review of the decisions being taken. You focus on what may not work with this decision and what could go wrong. You are essentially looking for the weak points and the team should be able to address and counter these. This position will help you make more reliable decisions. It is an objective position.
- **Yellow Hat** – this is an optimistic viewpoint, and helps you see all the benefits and value of a decision.
- **Green Hat** – this is the hat for creativity and intuition. This position is very important when the team feels it can't move forward. Sometimes you need to harness this creativity and take risks.
- **Blue Hat** – this is the overview position or the 'meta-hat'. The team coordinator or a person chairing your meetings may want to have this hat. The person wearing this hat should know when to call on the other hats in order to come to a decision.

Once the team has heard all the views from the different hat perspectives a decision is made.

NOTE Only take time to use a technique like this for important decisions.

ACTIVITY 6 Being your own troubleshooter when teams go wrong

It is usual to go to your tutor when things go wrong in your team. This is invariably around someone not fulfilling their part, you feeling that you are doing too much or being left out. It is easy to turn to someone else, but before you do that, try troubleshooting your own problems. In the table below there is a list of things that can go wrong. You may want to add your own as well and consider how you could put things right.

If you are expected to reflect on your team work as part of your project then do reflect on how you sorted your own problems out. This can only gain you marks for initiative and being an independent learner.

Tick what might be going wrong in your team and think how to remedy it. ▶

What's happening in the team?	**Tick**	**Possible remedies** (and make cross-references to places in this chapter that could help)
Not clarifying what your task or objective is		
Not checking on progress		
Not checking on time		
Not clarifying or recording what has been decided		
Not clarifying who is going to do what		
Not clarifying what has to be done by when		
Not establishing procedures for handling meetings		
Not keeping to agreed procedures		
Not listening to each other		
Allowing individuals to dominate and others to withdraw		
[*some are*] Not turning up for meetings		
[*some are*] Not doing the work allocated		
[*some are*] Not doing the work allocated very well		
[*some are*] Not recognising the feelings of members of the team		
[*some are*] Not contributing equally to the progress of the team		

Keeping your team going

Teams can work well and then go wrong. Make sure you keep communication channels open as your team develops, so you can keep it working well. Bruce Tuckman (Tuckman and Jensen, 1965) showed us that teams go through a repetitive cycle of:

- **forming** – characterised by dependence on the coordinator, but little consensus on the aims
- **storming** – where members take up positions, establish themselves within the group, form sub-groups and challenge other team members
- ***norming*** – where agreements are met and adhered to, members feel they have their role and can make decisions, and the coordinator can work without major challenges
- **performing** – where the team knows what it has to do, and all members are committed and feel accountable for the outcome.

You may find you cycle serveral times through storming, norming and performing as your project develops. Be aware of these cycles, see them as part of the process and find a way to deal with it. If you feel inclined to seek help from your tutor, check to see if you are just in a storming phase which you need to work your way out of as a team.

Working in a diverse team

There are various aspects of working in a diverse team and this section is just a brief discussion of some of the issues. We live with diversity across our lives: different types of people, different abilities, different subject disciplines and different cultures. Diverse teams make the working with diversity

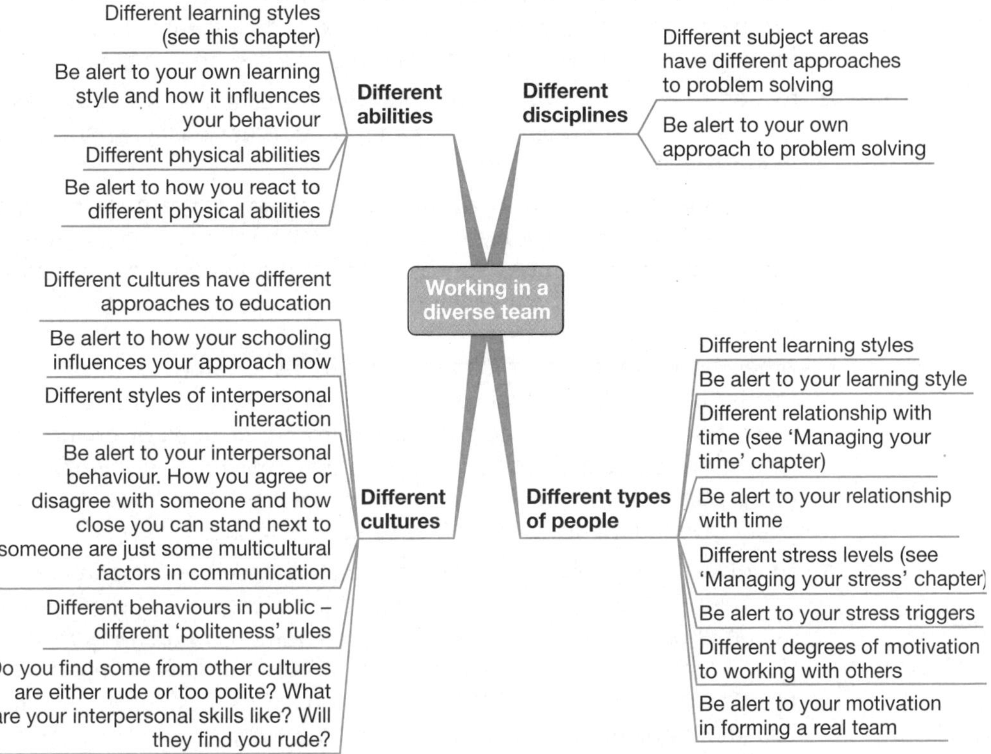

Figure 3 Working in a diverse team

more formal and it is this aspect of team working that requires more attention as we have to work harder at creating the trust necessary for effective team work.

Figure 3 on the previous page outlines some of the issues to consider.

5 Tools of the trade

While students on campus and living close can easily work face to face, not all students are full time or living close enough to do this. Forming a virtual team for those off-campus students is the only way to progress this. Although it is easier to make decisions face to face, virtual teams will gain experience of working together in an approach to teamwork that is becoming more common in the workplace.

Both virtual and face-to-face teams should be using technology. The virtual teams will be using it to communicate and store information, while the face-to-face group will probably limit it to file storage with the odd e-mail and mobile call. Virtual groups should ensure that the technology they use offers a mix of synchronous and asynchronous communication possibilities.

There are various pieces of technology that can help groups keep on track:

- **Mobile phone (synchronous communication)**: Only use your phone for the cancellation of meetings. This is too awkward for arranging meetings because you are just talking to one person at a time.
- **E-mail (asynchronous communication)**: Make sure you have each other's e-mail address. You can keep in contact easily, share documents and arrange meetings.
- **Using electronic group facilities: 'a must' for virtual groups**: Many institutions now have portals or similar software where you can set up your own groups. You can use this to keep in touch, upload key documents and generally use for team administration. Also, if you are a team who either study part time or live far away from each other, you can use an online group facility to store all your documents. If you are a virtual group, you will also want to check if your institution has software for online chatroom facilities or online conferencing software so you can have real-time conversations (synchronous). If your institution does not have these facilities, you could investigate using MSN Messenger.
- **Developing a good filing system**: You will have your documents on your own PC, but you also need a joint filing system for all the team's documents and this can be done using some online group facilities at your institution. Also, remember to organise your files to reflect your team's plan and keep well-labelled versions of your documents so that you know which document you are working with.

NOTE Make sure you back up all your documents regularly. 'I couldn't hand my work in because I had a computer crash' is becoming an increasingly lame excuse and your tutor will view it like that. Be responsible and back up your work as you go.

Checklist for a copper-bottomed approach to team work

1. Commitment: you all take joint responsibility for the success of the team and be inclusive to all.
2. Objectives: you take time to make the objectives and goals for the team clear to all.
3. Purpose: in order to keep the team motivated you all need to be clear why you are involved with this team and have clarity of purpose.
4. Plan: you need to plan how to solve the problem set you by breaking the task down into sub-tasks AND establishing how you work together as a team.
5. Expectations: as a team state what your expectations are and work towards a set of high expectations.
6. Roles: make sure you allocate roles to your team members so that you can act on your plan. Recognise individual differences when allocating roles.

6 On reflection

Through this chapter you should be able to articulate the essentials of working in a real team, reflect on your experience of working in student project teams and know what you need to do to improve the next team. At an interview for a work placement or once you leave your studies, you may be asked how well you work in groups. Now you have started to reflect on and articulate your skills, it will make this kind of question a lot easier for you to answer.

Go back to Activity 1, 'Annoying things about working with others', and see if you would now answer them differently. You should have developed some more awareness of how you would deal with these potentially annoying aspects of working with others.

Take time to reflect on your experience in project teams and the skills you feel you need to develop to make yourself a more effective team member. You may want to transfer this information to your own institution's personal development planner scheme.

ACTIVITY 7 Update your personal development planner

Having read this chapter, gauge your confidence again. How does this compare with your confidence levels at the start of the chapter? What can you do to improve? You can incorporate this into your own personal development planner. Add anything else you feel appropriate.

Grade your confidence on a scale of 1–5 where 1 = poor and 5 = good.

My team work skills plan	Confidence level 1–5	Plans to improve
I understand what a real team is and I am developing my skills to achieve this. *Section 2*		
I have identified my learning styles and know how it can affect team performance. *Section 3*		
I know the mechanics of setting up a real team and put those steps in place when I work in a team. *Sections 3, 4, 5*		
I understand that a major challenge is working in a diverse group. My team is aware of the issues involved and alert to possible problems. *Sections 2, 3, 4, 5*		

Date: ____________

Getting extra help

- Your institution or course probably offer team building training. Take advantage of this and take time to reflect on what you are learning.
- See the references at the end of the chapter.
- A general web search on 'team building' or 'working in teams' will bring up a host of information for you to choose from.

Feedback on the activities

ACTIVITY 1 Annoying things about working with others

Annoying things	deal with this by ...
There are always free-riders in a team and their marks are boosted by those who do the work.	Start with ground rules for your team. Agree what you will do in advance if someone doesn't do their share. If the situation persists you let your tutor know (rationally, not in a whingeing manner) of what you have done and that it has not improved.
Teams slow me down and that irritates me.	Listen to what other team members are saying rather than assuming they can't contribute. Recognise the different types of contribution they bring. If I am better at the technical side, I am happy to share this with the team as we are all interdependent.
I have difficulty with the topic the team has to work on and I'm afraid I'll keep the others back	I will let the team know of my worries and offer to do some things that I know I am good at.
Sometimes team members won't complete their tasks [at all, or on time].	Check if our ground rules are being flouted. Enforce our rules and if this does not improve inform our tutor. State the measures taken in order to improve this ourselves.
Sometimes teams don't divide the work up fairly.	The team may be working as sub-groups within the team. This has to be stopped. This issue has to be talked about so that everyone feels they are being heard and valued.
Sometimes you get students who just don't care about their grades, but I do.	The team needs to be convinced that they are interdependent and let others down if they don't work. This is part of the ground rules and if it cannot be solved by the group, it needs to be discussed with the tutor.

ACTIVITY 2 Understanding team patterns – what's your view?

Scenario 1

Type of group

This is more of a 'working group', i.e. a group of people who are not really pulling together as well as they could. These individuals are probably working informally as a 'working group' without realising it and possibly see themselves as a team. They have ▶

assumed that since they all worked well together before, it would be successful. However, as a team they have to work differently and very often working with friends is not a good idea as old and established ways of getting along may not be appropriate for this task.

Adair group functions

The group lacks a focus on the task and they aren't building their team although it is working at a very social level (maintenance). The group needs to redefine itself as a team.

Scenario 2

Type of group

The group is more of a 'pseudo' to 'pseudo team'. You started out identifying your goals but you don't seemed to have shared that. Why didn't you ask to work on the identified goals, rather than just moaning that you haven't seen them? Some of your friends realise they need to behave differently if they want to get the job done, but seem to be doing this in a unilateral way. It appears they have taken the lead instinctively, without discussion, which makes them appear bossy. If this group wants to stay together as a group of friends **and** a team, it needs to openly discuss how they can achieve the task set and the different roles it will have to adopt in order to do that.

Adair group functions

This group is basically lacking the team building function. Some of you are trying to achieve the task while others are still operating as a social group. This group needs to think of itself as a team and of ways to bring everyone together on task and be mutually dependent.

Scenario 3

Type of group

This group is more of a 'pseudo' to 'potential team' and with a little effort and the development of interdependence and joint responsibility for the goals you could be a 'real team'. It may be that this team didn't fully discuss the task and identify the resources within the group at the very beginning. Management theory refers to the importance of frank discussions within a group so that all are in agreement (aligned) with what has to be done, how it has to be done and who has to do it. Remember a 'real team' has shared responsibility and is moving in one direction towards the goal.

Adair group functions

This group appears to be achieving most of the Adair functions but not as effectively as it could. As the group develops, it may need to reassess some of its earlier decisions as to the needs of individuals in the team and how the team spirit should be maintained. Keep lines of communication open so that problems can be ironed out before they become obstacles to achieving the task.

ACTIVITY 6 Being your own troubleshooter when teams go wrong

What's happening in the team?	Tick	Possible remedies (*and make cross-references to places in this chapter that could help*)
Not clarifying what your task or objective is		You haven't gone through the planning process. See Section 4.
Not checking on progress		You haven't developed a mechanism for checking how things are going. You can't leave everything to your coordinator. Go back to your planning document and put something in there that you can all sign up to. This is very important.
Not checking on time		As above. It is part of your progress checking mechanism.
Not clarifying or recording what has been decided		Include as part of your planning mechanisms for recording your decisions. See Sections 4 and 5.
Not clarifying who is going to do what		You don't seem to have allocated roles, see Section 4, and in order to do that you need to understand the learning styles of your group, see Section 3.
Not clarifying what has to be done by when		This means as part of your planning you have not established a timetable with milestones.
Not establishing procedures for handling meetings		Again this is part of your planning process, see Section 4. Devise an electronic method for storing your decisions/actions from meetings, see Section 5.
Not keeping to agreed procedures		Check you have your ground rules in place, Section 3, and how you deal with individuals who flout them, Section 4.
Not listening to each other		If you remember, being a real team means collaborating and appreciating all in your team. Look again at the team functions from John Adair, Section 2.
Allowing individuals to dominate and others to withdraw		See above and this relates again to the functions in a team.
[*some are*] Not turning up for meetings		Your ground rules and procedures for making them work should be applied here. This is why it is important to set these up **before** things go wrong. See Sections 3 and 4.

What's happening in the team?	Tick	Possible remedies (*and make cross-references to places in this chapter that could help*)
[*some are*] Not doing the work allocated		As above. However, you may want to check that this person really did agree to do this work. If it really is a problem, you may need to reallocate tasks. Be flexible enough to do this.
[*some are*] Not doing the work allocated very well		It is quite likely that you will get some highflyers in your team and others that are struggling. If you feel the work some do is not up to standard, bring the team together and work out a way of resolving this. Should someone else do that aspect, does he/she need some quick coaching? Find out the problem.
[*some are*] Not recognising the feelings of members of the team		This relates back to the 'develop the individual' aspect of John Adair's model. Every member of your team is important and every team member needs to recognise this.
[*some are*] Not contributing equally to the progress of the team		First check why this is happening. Maybe those concerned feel they are contributing well. Be honest and clarify the situation. Again, with a good plan and clear milestones you should be able to go back and identify where things are going wrong. You may need to make adjustments.

References

Adair, J. (1986) *Effective Team Building*. Aldershot, Gower.

De Bono, E. (1999) *Six Thinking Hats*. London, Penguin.

BBC News (2006) 'Graduate demand outstrips skills', 7 February available at: **http://news.bbc.co.uk/** and search on the title of the article.

Honey, P. and Mumford, A. (1992) *The Manual of Learning Styles*. Maidenhead, Peter Honey.

Katzenbach, J. R. and Smith, D. K. (1993) *The Wisdom of Teams*. New York, HarperBusiness.

Tuckman, B. W., and Jensen, M. A. C. (1977) 'Stages of small group development revisited', *Group and Organizational Studies*, 2, 419–27.

2.4 Presenting your work

Being able to present your work well as a student, and later on in your job, is an invaluable skill. You have probably sat through countless talks already and looked at many posters, so you instinctively know the kind of presentation that bores you. Now is your opportunity to articulate your instincts and hone your presentation skills for both posters and talks.

In this chapter you will learn how to:

1. prepare information for posters
2. design posters for visual clarity and coherence
3. design slides for clarity
4. recognise what makes a good and bad oral presentation
5. know how classic mistakes in oral presentations affect your audience and how to avoid them.

USING THIS CHAPTER

Estimate your current levels of confidence. At the end of the chapter you will have the chance to re-assess these levels where you can incorporate this into your personal development planner (PDP). Mark between 1 (poor) and 5 (good) for the following:

I can understand the key elements of poster design.	I can understand key elements of slide design.	I can understand the characteristics of effective oral presentations.

Date: ________________

1 Introduction

Being able to give a good and clear presentation to a public audience is a skill that you and your future employer will value greatly. Prospective employers invariably ask for your experience in using these key skills during interviews. You need to be able to articulate what makes a good and poor presentation and offer evidence for your knowledge. So, when you are asked to give a talk or produce a poster as part of your studies, recognise the importance of developing the skills of delivery as well as conveying the content.

Posters and oral presentations are forms of presentation that enable you to develop your confidence in different ways. Posters check your ability to succinctly present information, and present it in an attractive and message-focused way, while oral presentations allow for more information and a more in-depth delivery. In both modes you will probably find yourself taking questions and explaining your ideas.

2 Poster presentations

Assessed coursework can take the form of a poster presentation. This can be, for example, an individual piece of research, a group project or a visual essay where you present the ideas of a particular topic. Whatever the content of your poster, a poster is a visual presentation format and as with any other form of communication, it should 'tell a story'.

Before you do anything, start with a checklist:

Checklist: clarify what is expected from your poster assignment

1. The purpose of the poster and the intended audience.
2. The size of the poster required.
3. Any specifications for the production, e.g. does it have to be through particular software, can you produce it by hand, or use a cut and paste method?
4. Expectations regarding display, e.g. do you need to print it out or display via a PC/laptop?
5. Printing quality, i.e. can you print out in draft form as this is much cheaper?
6. The presentation, e.g. in a conference setting with your posters set up around a room or as part of an oral presentation.
7. The assessment criteria.

Information regarding the checklist is discussed in this section.

Planning what you want to say

Identify your audience

Establish who your audience is. Your tutor should give you guidance here. Don't just assume that you are writing for your tutor because there is a tendency to think he or she knows this material already and you don't need to explain it in such detail. So, it is be better to assume your audience is an intelligent 14-year-old.

NOTE Researchers are now asked by some Research Councils to write an abstract of their research that could be understood by an intelligent 14-year-old.

Identify your message

The key to any poster is deciding **what** your message is. In order to do this you need to distil the key points of your work on to some rough paper and arrange the order of your 'story'.

If you are reporting on work from your individual research project or a group project it is good to write a short section at the beginning (approximately 200 words) which outlines:

- why you did this research (gives a context)
- how you did it (method)
- issues it raised (there may be some interesting things to solve on the way)
- key findings/conclusion/recommendation.

This is similar to an 'abstract', which is found at the beginning of a journal article in order to prepare the reader for the content of the paper. Once you have the abstract, you have the key ideas for your poster and your introduction.

If you have not carried out any data-gathering research, you may be asked to present a poster on a topic. This is something like a visual essay and you will also need to start by jotting down a summary of your reading by:

- stating the importance of this topic (gives context)
- listing the key points/issues/positions (either as theoretical positions, key researchers, key solutions, etc.)
- offer critical reflection on what you have read and a concluding remark.

Once you have summarised what you have found, you have the key ideas for your poster and they can be part of your poster introduction.

Secondly, your poster must have a very clear message. The information in your abstract or introduction can be further developed in the boxes on your poster (see 'Designing your poster' below).

How we read a poster

A poster is not a jumble of things that can be read in any order (unless you are using the poster as a form of art). Generally, we read a poster from the top left and work our way down to the bottom right, as with any page we read. However, you can break this rule if your route through the poster is clear and logical.

Coherence (progression of ideas) is important in any written document and a poster is no different. Make sure your start and end-points are obvious. More creative subjects may want to flout this rule and offer a more visually demanding display. If this is the case, you need to decide if your reader needs to come away with key pieces of information and how you will visually identify them.

Remember, readers will probably spend no more than about 5 minutes reading your poster. In that time you have to convey your message through words and images. Identify key pieces of information (see 'Identify your message' above).

Designing your poster

Layout

A fairly transparent way to design your poster is to allocate text and picture boxes to the size of paper you have. Your first decision is the size (A1?) and the orientation (portrait or landscape?) of your poster. Figures 1–3 show different layouts.

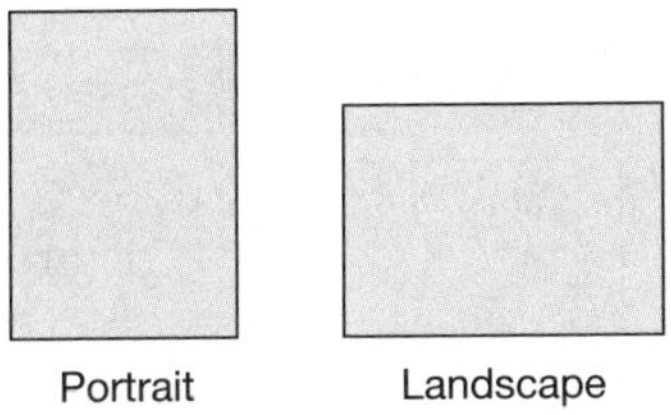

Portrait
Landscape

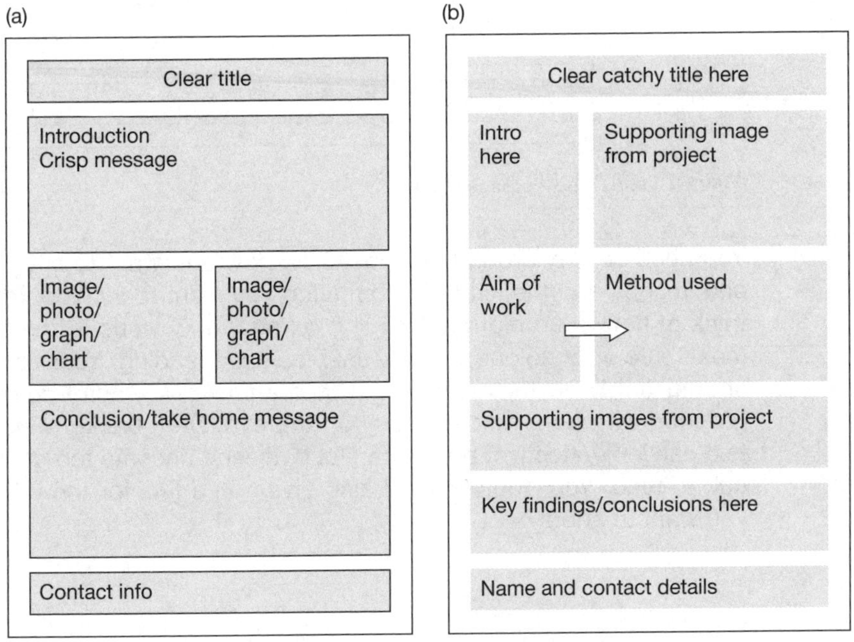

(a)
Clear title
Introduction
Crisp message
Image/
photo/
graph/
chart
Image/
photo/
graph/
chart
Conclusion/take home message
Contact info
(b)
Clear catchy title here
Intro
here
Supporting image
from project
Aim of
work
Method used
Supporting images from project
Key findings/conclusions here
Name and contact details

Figure 1 Portrait: mixed column solutions. (a) Predominantly single column with lined boxes (b) Predominantly double column with or without lined boxes

Clear precise meaningful title
Intro
More detail
Conclusions/
findings
Image/
graph
Image/
graph
Image
or
graph
Image
or
graph
Future work
Contact details

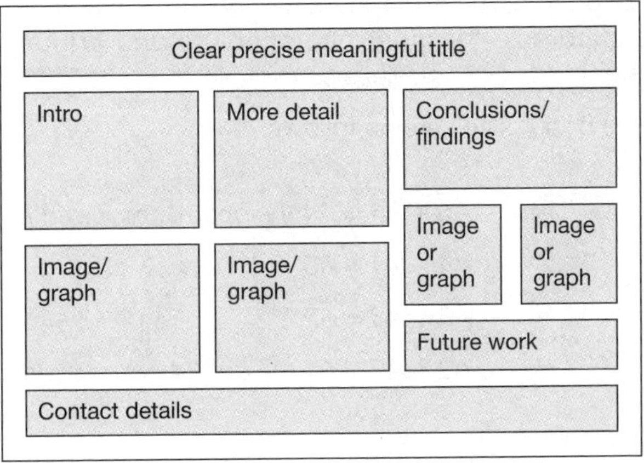

Figure 2 Landscape: a more visual poster

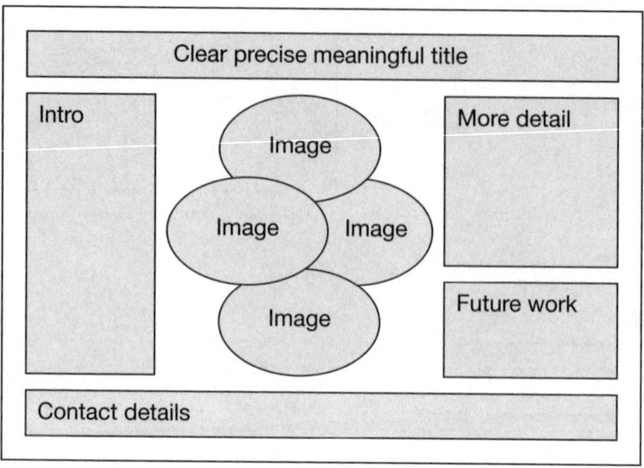

Figure 3 Landscape – collage effect[1]

You need to play around with ideas on how you want to set out your text and images and the kind of information you want to include. Remember to think of how your information will flow, so it is obvious to the reader. Also, make sure your colour scheme enables easy reading. Your colour scheme should enhance the message, not dominate it. Pastel-coloured backgrounds with dark text are easy on the eye. Dark backgrounds with light text can look effective, but be careful it doesn't become too garish and difficult to read. Your topic should also give you a feel for the colour scheme you want to adopt.

Poster size

Paper sizes are standardised and the ISO (international standards office) paper sizes we use are labelled as 'A' size papers ranging from A7 to A0; the smaller the number the larger the paper size. The paper size we use most often is A4. Most student writing blocks are A4 size and it is also the standard size for most photocopiers and printers. The usual size for a poster is A1.

Some paper sizes are as follows:

A5 + A5 = A4 (height 29 cm × width 21 cm)

A4 + A4 = A3

A3 + A3 = A2

A2 + A2 = A1 (height 84 cm × width 59 cm)

[1] Acknowledgement: thanks to Adam Warren from the University of Southampton for the inspiration of poster making through these diagrams.

Text: size of font and choice of font

Remember people will be standing some distance away from your poster, so make your text easy to read from about 1.5 metres. You may want to use fancy fonts, but be careful – simple, clear and well-proportioned fonts are better. Try to use a point range between 20–35, but the size you choose will depend on the font as some can appear clumsy when too big.

Some of the options you have are:

Typeface: serif or sans serif?

The basic choice is between serif and sans serif fonts.

Many studies have shown that sans serif and a wide letter look are easier to read.

Times New Roman is a serif font but with a rather narrow letter look. This generally rates poorly on readability tests. This is also now considered rather 'old fashioned'.

Garamond is also a serif font but the letters look a lot wider and this makes it easier to read. If you prefer to use a serif font, this is probably better than Times.

Arial is a sans serif font and the letters combine a narrow look with an uncluttered letter shape.

Verdana, on the other hand, is also a sans serif font, but the letters have a wider look which makes it easier to read.

Font size

It will depend on the typeface you use, but as a guide: the main title at approximately 100 points, sub-headings 50 points and the main text 25 points.

Emphasis

You may want to emphasise key points. Below are some possibilities. However, only use two, at the most, in one poster. You can:

- use bold, italics, underline or capitals
- change the text colour
- put text in a graphic or box.

Alignment

The human eye can detect very quickly if text is not aligned and this can make it look unprofessional. It is like wearing clothes that are not ironed. Make sure your text does align and if you have a list ensure that all the first words in your list start the same, i.e. don't use a mixture of capitals and lower case.

Line length

Line lengths that are too long or too short interfere with the speed of reading. A good average line-length to work with is approximately 39 characters long.

Graphics

Select graphics that enhance your text. Some stray images will look very odd.

Checklist: do's and dont's

- **Don't** have lots of different typefaces.
- **Don't** use lots of different point sizes
- **Don't** use your emphasis features for a large block of text.
- **Do** have a consistent layout
- **Do** include white space around your text as this gives contrast to text and rests your eyes.
- **Do** print a draft copy to check before the final print.

Don't use an unusual font as the printer may not recognise it.

Tools to use

You can prepare a poster by freehand drawing, writing text in a word processor, printing and then cutting and pasting onto your paper or using a software package. Check with your tutor how he or she wants you to prepare your poster. Part of your assignment may in fact be the use of a particular piece of software.

Microsoft PowerPoint is a natural choice for most as it is already part of Microsoft Office. As a UK student (of recent years) you will probably have used this software for school coursework. Before you start you need to set up the page size and orientation you want to use. To do this in PowerPoint for an A1 poster, open a new file and click **File > Page Setup > Custom**, select a **Width** of 60 cm and a **Height** of 84 cm, and choose either portrait or landscape orientation.

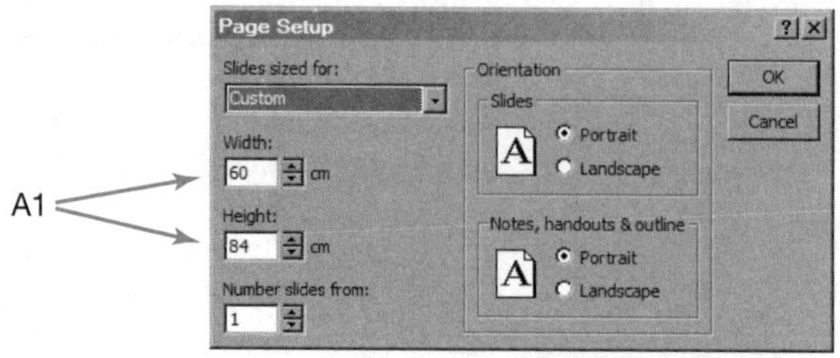

You can then save your PowerPoint file onto a CD or memory stick and take it to someone who can print it the size and weight of paper you require. Try and get an A3 (twice as big as A4) draft copy of your poster to check the layout and colour scheme before printing at A1 size.

NOTE If you have had no experience of PowerPoint, check to see if your institution is running any ICT sessions or tutorials.

Displaying your poster

There are several ways of displaying your poster:

- on a display board
- hanging from nylon thread (need heavier weight paper for this or mounted on card)
- sticky tape on a lecture room wall.

NOTE If you are going to present your paper outside your institution, you may need to have it laminated (your institution should have facilities for this). You will also require a cardboard roll to transport it safely to your venue.

Checklist for your poster

There is nothing worse than hanging up your poster only to find an obvious spelling mistake. Poster language must be correct. You (or better still someone else) need to:

1. check your message for clarity
2. reduce the number of words and still keep it clear
3. check for spelling mistakes
4. check your images support your text
5. check the order of information for cohesion
6. get a draft A3 copy to check layout and colour.

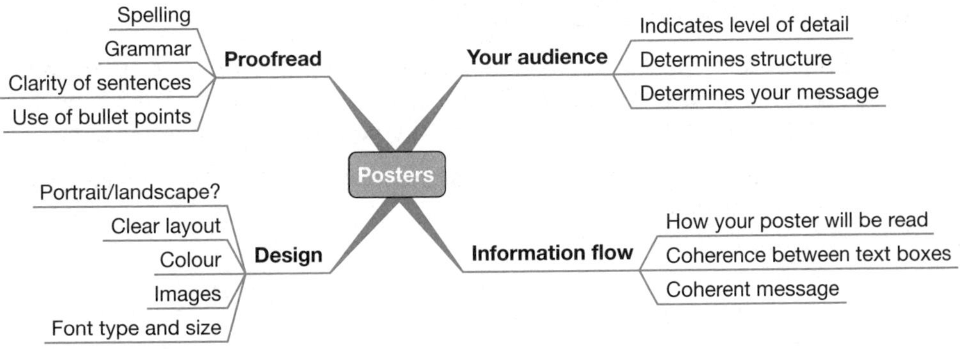

Figure 4 Poster summary

Talking about your poster

Although your poster sits there for all to read, you will probably be close by and may be asked some questions. You should practice explaining in a simple way what your work was about, why you did it, any problems you had to overcome on the way, and the outcomes and conclusions. If your poster is an 'ideas poster' on a topic, you need to be able to explain the central message and issues of the topic presented in your poster. Your poster may be the visual aid for an oral presentation in preference to slides.

See Section 3 for some information on oral presentations.

Having your poster assessed

Your tutors will tell you how they are going to assess your work. Some of the things that they may look for are listed below:

Criteria	Description
Knowledge	The knowledge presented is accurate, relevant to the title, key points clearly evident.
Structure	The poster has a clear beginning and end. The text boxes have clearly defined pieces of information.
Language and images	Language is clear, concise and easy to understand. It is appropriate for the intended audience. No spelling or grammatical errors. The images enhance the text.
Amount of information	There is enough information to inform the audience of the topic and not too much to require lengthy reading.
General impression	The poster is visually attractive. The content presents new information or information from a different angle. It has some novel/interesting things to say.

3 Oral presentations

Giving a talk can mean standing up alone or with a group and presenting your ideas, or your project work. You can use visual aids like slides or, if you are presenting a small paper in a seminar context, have no visual aids.

Before you start you need to consult the following checklist as this will influence what you do.

Checklist: identifying what is expected in your oral presentation

1. The topic – identify and present the key issues.
2. The talk – group or individual.
3. The purpose of the talk and the intended audience.
4. The length of time you have to talk.
5. The length of time for questions.
6. The method of presentation, e.g. overhead projector, via a computer, with no visual aids at all.
7. The handouts – are you expected to provide them, if so how many?
8. The room layout: where will you stand, where can you put your papers? If you are a group, how will you arrange yourself in the space?
9. The running order for presentations – are you one of many that afternoon?
10. The rehearsal – use to decide who says what in a group talk.
11. The assessment criteria – address them in the preparation.

The oral presentation assignment

Once you have provided answers from the checklist above, you can start preparing your talk.

Organising what to include

The amount of detail you put into your talk will be determined by the purpose and the audience, but your talk must always have a **beginning**, a **middle** and an **end**.

If you are presenting on an individual or group project you need to:

- contextualise the project – lead in
- state how you carried out the project
- mention problems you may have experienced
- state your findings and conclusions.

If you are presenting an idea you need to:

- contextualise the issues
- state where you researched the issues (a broad brush approach to show where you have your evidence)
- discuss controversial issues
- state any conclusions.

NOTE A common mistake with many student presentations is that the talk fails to have a proper introduction that contextualises and introduces the audience to the topic. Many students jump straight into the fine detail of their work. **Don't do this**, as the audience has to work hard to 'catch up' in order to understand you. You have to assume that your audience may not know as much about the topic as you and providing an introduction is a key element in a talk.

Timing

Check how long you have for your 'slot' and confirm if this includes question and feedback time afterwards. As a rule of thumb work on the following for a 30-minute slot:

- 15–20 minutes talking
- 10 minutes questions and/or feedback

Again, as a rule of thumb, if you assume one slide per minute then you should have a **maximum** of 20 slides for a 20-minute talk.

The method of presentation

The most common ways of giving a presentation are as follows:

- via a computer using presentation software
- using an overhead projector (OHP)
- with no visual aids at all.

When using an **overhead project** or you will need transparent slides to either write on, with a marker pen, or print to from your computer. You can use a presentation package, like Microsoft PowerPoint, and print directly onto OHP slides. It is not recommended that slides are handwritten as this can appear messy, unless you have particularly clear handwriting. Graphics would also have to be hand drawn and that is not a good idea.

When using a piece of software you can **present via your computer**. This gives a clearer presentation and enables you to add graphics easily, include colour and use hyperlinks if necessary. If part of your work was to produce a website, then this would be vital.

Giving a talk with **no visual aids** is quite difficult. The traditional example of this is reading a paper in a tutorial. This can be very tedious. If you were expected to use this mode of delivery, it would be wise to put your key ideas on cards and talk around the ideas, rather than reading directly from your paper.

Slide design

As with posters, the design of your slides is important. Your audience will not want to read a lot of text from your slides. You are not there to read from your slides; that is pointless and tedious. Your slides are there as visual aids to set the scene for the topic you are talking about and give a visual anchor around which you can talk. Therefore, the more visual you can make your slides the better – as long as it doesn't look like a comic! We all remember:

- images
- diagrams that show connections/processes
- key words and phrases (especially if they are repeated often enough).

We don't remember dense text or bullet points very well.

Software like PowerPoint have built in slide designs, but there are only a few that are really usable and not too fussy. We have all seen those designs too often and this can create boredom in the audience before you start. So, avoid the template designs in the software and create your own, if you can (Figure 5).

Try using more images than text, but make sure your images are related to your work.

Your slides should be clear and uncluttered in order to be understood. Select a font that is easy to read, and be guided by the suggested font sizes in PowerPoint (point size 32 for main bullets and 28 for sub-bullets).

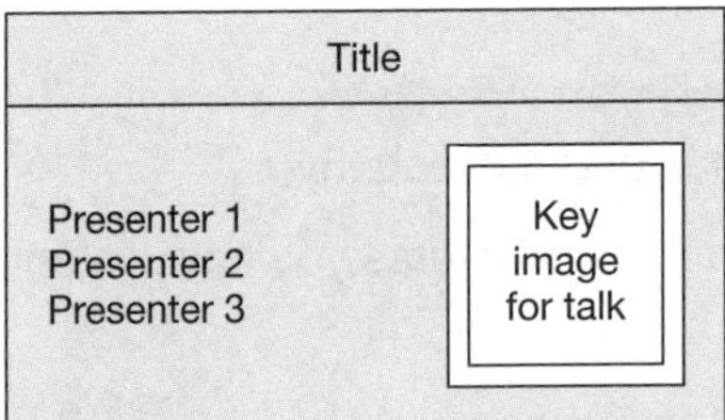

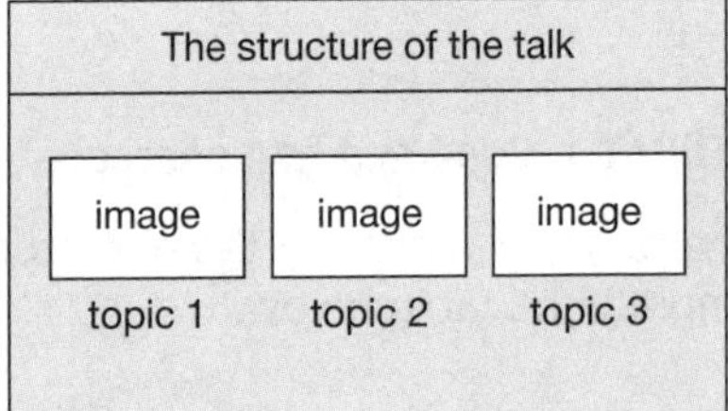

Body of talk: topic 1 [mixture of images and text]

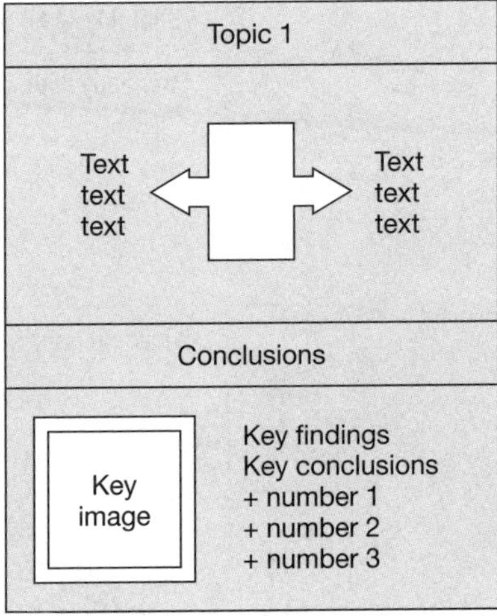

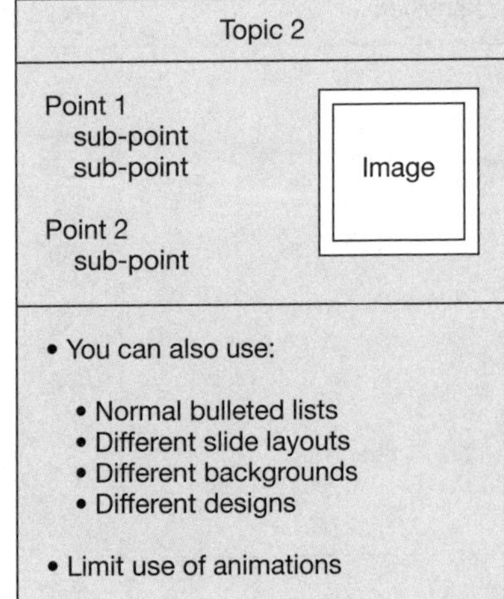

Figure 5 Slide designs

Take as many digital photographs as you can of your work while you are doing it so you can include them in your presentation. This can be, for example, your team, the equipment you used, the results (if visual) and simplified graphs. This will really bring your presentation to life.

What audiences remember

Your audience will only hear what you have to say once; they have no opportunity to go back and check. What you say at each point should be clear. We all remember how things 'fit together' better than a list of things. If you can show how things are connected (via diagrams), how processes work (flow diagrams) and how things look (images, pictures) then this will make your presentation memorable. Identify your 'take-home message' and make sure you say this at the end in a clear voice with visual support.

Characteristics of oral presentations

Activity 1 will look at our experience of listening to and/or giving a talk.

ACTIVITY 1 Good and bad characteristics in oral presentations

For a moment, consider the numerous talks and lectures you have listened to and complete the table below.

Characteristics of talks you have enjoyed ...	Characteristics of talks that bored you ...	Your strong and weak points when giving an oral presentation
		I'm happy with ...
		I'd like to improve ...

Were any of your own strong and weak points in the feedback section at the back? Check to see the effect they can have on an audience.

Dealing with nerves

Many people get nervous when they have to speak in front of others, even if they have been presenting for years. You may think your lecturers are fine at giving talks, but invariably the first few lectures of a semester cause a few 'butterflies' even to long-standing performers. Having some nerves is good as this gets the adrenaline flowing and keeps you alert and on top of the subject. You may find that you are nervous at the beginning of the talk, until you get into the swing of it, and then you are fine. This is very common. Problems only occur when your performance nerves overtake you.

Some of the things you may be nervous about are:

- an overwhelming feeling of being watched
- feeling that others will think you're stupid
- forgetting what you want to say
- losing your thread and getting muddled.

Some of the signs that tell you that you're nervous are:

- shaking
- forgetting certain words
- stuttering
- sweating
- your voice becomes higher than normal
- you speak too quickly
- being tongue-tied.

You may be able to recognise some of these characteristics when you give a talk, and the effect can be distressing.

Dealing with performance nerves

The first thing you need to do is take back control, and you do this by increasing your confidence in your own ability by being well prepared and in control of the topic you are presenting. Rehearse your talk so that you practice the words and phrases you are going to use and assess how long your talk will last so that it is within your time limit. Most student project presentations are approximately 15–20 minutes, but if you are presenting as part of a group you may only have 5 minutes for your part. Never go over your time limit. When you rehearse, you should identify areas that don't flow, where you are unsure of the point, or where you've included something that you are now unhappy with. A rehearsal will also identify the key sentences you need to link between slides.

The next thing you need to do is deal with your emotions. As stated before, some nerves are good, but not too many. Your aim is to calm yourself down so that you can think and speak clearly. Try visualising a speaker you admire. Identify why you admire that speaker and try to visualise yourself presenting like him or her. You need to do this regularly so that it becomes a habit and when you stand up, there you are 'in character'. If that doesn't work for you, deep breathing is often recommended in order to lower your heart rate and reduce your nerves. Finally, reflect honestly with a friend on your performances. You may feel, for example, that you were hesitating a lot, but more than likely the audience didn't notice it. Your perceptions of your performance are therefore often different from the audience's. Essentially, you have to find out what works for you, and it is important to be proactive in achieving that.

Activity 2 helps you to recognise if you have performance nerves.

ACTIVITY 2 Recognising if you have performance nerves

Indicate for yourself: 1 = rarely me , 2 = sometimes me , 3 = always me.

Characteristics of performance nerves	This is me: 1–3	What I plan to do
An overwhelming feeling of being watched		
Feeling that others will think you're stupid		
Fear of forgetting what you want to say		
Fear of losing your thread and getting muddled		

Check the feedback section at the end of the chapter.

Delivering your talk confidently

First, remind yourself that giving a talk is not the same as writing an essay that you then read out. Reading aloud from a script will result in poor marks for the 'communication skills' aspect your assessment (see feedback for Activity 1 on p. 173). So, writing an essay or long-hand notes and then reading it is not an option! What you will need is some form of notes – perhaps 'prompt cards', unless you are confident enough to rely on PowerPoint slides or transparencies to act as prompts for you.

When written text is read aloud it always sounds monotonous, and it is easier to read it than to listen to it! Free speech is much more interesting, and it does not matter about the odd 'um' or 'err' – that's natural and allows some 'processing time' for your audience.

The key features that you need to consider during the delivery of a talk are your:

- voice and pace – vocal formatting
- engagement with the audience
- manner of handling of questions.

Voice and pace

In Activity 1 you may have identified some voice characteristics that illustrate a poor talk. Being alert to your voice and pace are key attributes to public speaking. Check out Figure 6 below and, when you rehearse your talk, check your voice and pace characteristics.

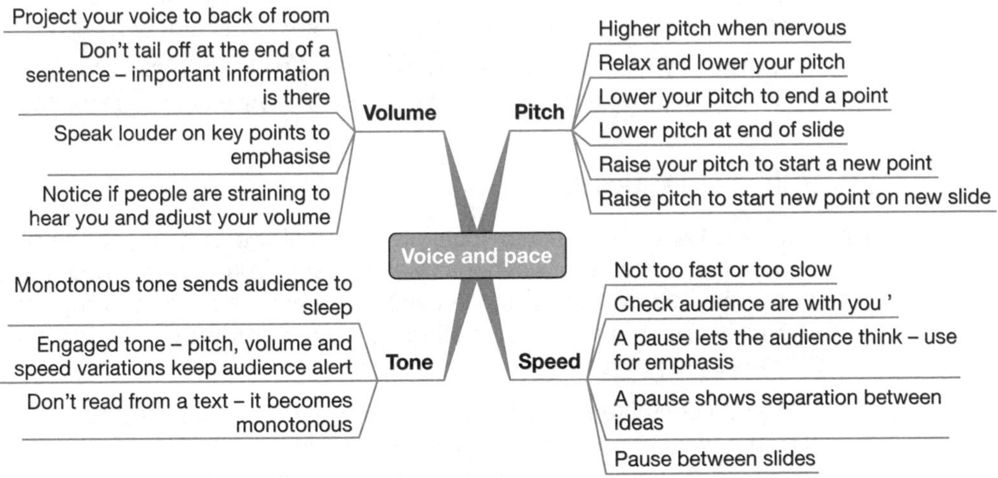

Figure 6 Voice and pace summary

NOTE Use language markers, e.g. and now … the next point … in contrast … in conclusion … and finally … plus voice tone to indicate a change or a new point. This can be done by raising your voice, speaking more slowly and pausing slightly before moving on, which helps the audience to follow the flow of your talk. Don't use clichés or empty, worn-out phrases.

Engagement with the audience

For those of you in the process of developing your oral presentation skills, you can tend to focus on yourself as the speaker and forget about the audience. This is a cardinal mistake. Once you accept that the audience is there and you want to engage with them, then your talk will become an interactive event and you will enjoy it. To engage your audience therefore you should:

- stand for 8 seconds at the beginning of your talk looking at the audience. Just scan across the room and don't look at anyone in particular – this cues the audience that you are ready to speak
- introduce yourself while scanning the audience
- start positively and not with an apology because something didn't work – your audience are only interested in what you have to say now
- look and sound interested in your talk and the audience
- tell your audience the structure of your talk
- maintain the right pace and use voice features mentioned above
- thank the audience for listening and invite questions.

NOTE If you read from a paper you will not be able to engage with the audience as you will lose eye contact, start to mumble into your paper, be monotonous and read too fast. If you find that slides are not enough and you feel quite nervous, use notes on a card, or a paper with large print – around verdana point size 16. Add notes to tell yourself to look at the audience, pause or stress a point.

Handling questions

This is always harder for the individual presenter. However, you need to prepare as well as you can for questions. Make a list of your key messages and look at the questions that could be asked for each. If you are in a group, you should answer questions relating to your contribution to the talk. Question areas to prepare for include the following:

- Why you chose to research the topic using a particular method.
- Did the work of a key author influence you in any way?
- How did you arrive at your conclusions (possibly the choice of statistics used)?
- What difficulties did you find during your research and how did you overcome them?
- If you did this work again, what changes would you make?

NOTE If you get questions you can't answer, be honest. It is always obvious when a speaker tries to invent an answer. You can always thank the questioner for that question, as it will move your thinking on.

Planning a talk

Whether you are planning your talk for yourself or with a group, the key features remain the same. However, group presenters have the added task of deciding how each presenter contributes to a coherent talk (see Chapter 2.3, 'Working in a real team').

ACTIVITY 3 Oral presentation: time check

If you are involved in preparing for a presentation use Activity 3 to check your progress.

14 preparation time check tasks	To do	Doing now	Done
In the weeks or days before the talk			
1. **Understand your research topic** and ensure you know enough background to feel confident with your particular angle on it. This will also give you confidence in question time.			
2. **Structure your talk** by identifying key messages and points for development within those sections. If you are presenting as a group you will divide the sections between you. Make sure you have a beginning (stating what you will do), a middle (develop your arguments) and an end (present a conclusion). Remember, group presentations need to allocate responsibilities.			
3. Decide on the **visual style** you will use and prepare your slides well. Make sure they are uncluttered and easy to read.			
4. **Decide on a title** for your talk. Try and make it short but informative. Use the 'Baked Beans' approach – 'it says what it is' – you can always have a fun strap line (like a sub-heading), but it must be catchy.			
5. **Write brief notes** on to 'prompt cards' to help make sure that you cover the ground you intend to, and in the right order.			
6. **Practise** giving your talk and timing it – either to friends, or between yourselves.			
7. **Check the room layout for the talk** and make sure that you know where you will stand or sit, where your audience will be, and the equipment you will use.			
8. Identify your '**take-home message**' and how you are going to deliver it.			
9. **Assessment criteria**: do you think your talk will meet the assessment criteria. If not, what changes do you need to make?			
On the day of the talk			
1. **Re-read your prompt notes** and any supporting material, such as handouts you may have prepared for the audience, to make sure you 'get on-message'.			
2. **Get to the venue early and check the equipment**, if you can.			
3. Remind yourself of the simple but vital **rules for delivering your talk confidently** (voice, pace, audience, questions).			
4. **Support each other** in a group presentation. Identify where you will all stand, and how you will link between speakers.			
5. **Relax, breathe deeply** to keep those nerves in check (see above) and remember that your audience is on your side!			
You're on! Go for it!			

4 On reflection

This chapter has looked at only two aspects of presenting your work: posters and oral presentations. Essays, reports, making and producing things and portfolios are just examples of other ways you can present your work. In all of these, be clear what is expected of you, how it should be presented and what your message is. You should also pay attention to the coherence of your message, with regards to the general look and feel of the product. When you present your work you should feel proud of the content and how it looks.

ACTIVITY 4 Update your personal development planner

Having read this chapter, gauge your confidence again – how does this compare with your confidence levels at the start of the chapter? What can you do to improve? You can incorporate this into your own personal development planner and of course add anything else you feel appropriate.

Grade your confidence on a scale of 1–5 where 1 = poor and 5 = good.

My presentation skills development plan	Confidence level 1–5	Plans to improve
I can condense information relevant for poster presentation.		
I can design a good poster using the key elements of design.		
I can identify key messages when giving a talk.		
I am gaining confidence in recognising and reflecting on my strengths and weaknesses when giving a talk.		
I understand the principles of slide design.		
I can engage the audience when I give a talk.		
I know how to deal with questions.		

Date:______________________

Getting extra help

- Check your institution as most universities have web pages giving you support for a range of study skills. These are usually there to provide brief tips.
- The website *Mind Tools*. There is a wide range of self-help tips on this site. The material is directed towards business people, but advice is suitable for anyone wishing to develop their skills in these areas. See **www.mindtools.com/CommSkll/PresentationPlanningChecklist.htm.**
- If you are expected to use ICT and a presentation software you are unsure of, check your institution. Your options should be a paper, virtual or hands-on tutorial.
- Look for books on 'public speaking'.

Feedback on activities

ACTIVITY 1 Good and bad characteristics in oral presentations

Some of the key factors that determine the quality of a presentation are shown in the following table:

Characteristic	Effect on the audience	Solution
Little or no eye contact	'Hello' we are here as well!	Make every effort to look at your audience. Look around and try not to look at just one person. If you look at one person all the time it becomes embarrassing and the new focus of attention for the audience.
Mumbling	What is he/she talking about? After trying to understand for a while, the audience will give up.	Practice your talk beforehand and either record it, or get a friend to listen. You need to project your voice. Always talk to the back of the room rather than those at the front.
Monotonous voice	A monotonous voice becomes a drone and the audience can't work out what is important in your talk. If this goes on for too long they start to daydream, go to sleep or just wish they were somewhere else. Avoid the EGO effect (eyes glaze over).	The message in a piece of written text is delivered via headings, sub-headings and paragraphs. Your voice has to format your text for you. You can use **pitch**, **loudness** and **pauses** to create effect. Use these to show movement between ideas and emphasise important points.

Characteristic	Effect on the audience	Solution
Reading from the paper	Your audience feels bored. If you read from the paper, first you tend not to look at the audience very much and, second, your reading speed will be faster than free speech.	Read from cards if you feel you have to read something. Make the font large as it is difficult to read large font quickly. Also put notes on your card telling you what to do, e.g. 'look at audience', 'make reference to diagram on visual', etc.
Little or no structure	Your audience feels 'what is this all about?' Audiences are very forgiving at the beginning of a talk and usually assume it will get better. But if after 5 minutes it is not clear how you are going to structure your talk, they will get annoyed and only have you to focus on instead of the content.	Remember, if you get lost in a book, you can flick back through the pages. You can't do that when listening to a talk, so you must provide visual and oral help to reinforce the structure. Pause between sections and speak louder at the start of a new section. See these as vocal formatting techniques.
Too much information	Oh no, not another graph I can't read or another slide full of tightly packed bullet points. The audience can only take very tightly packed information for a few minutes, then there is overload and they switch off.	Identify your key messages for your talk and expound them. Better to present too little rather than too much. What is the 'take-home message' from your talk? Make sure they at least remember that.
Bad visuals	Your audience feels annoyed. Poor graphs, small images, tightly packed text all add up to 'noise'. The audience can't read it so why use it?	If you are using graphs, create a visual of the trend for your presentation. If you want them to see detail, give it as a handout and talk around it.

ACTIVITY 2 Recognising if you have performance nerves

Characteristics of performance nerves	What you can do
An overwhelming feeling of being watched	Once you engage with your audience and start looking at them, you should start to reduce this feeling. Try and think how you feel when you are having a conversation. If you don't look at people, this feeling could intensify.
Feeling that others will think you're stupid	This is a confidence issue. Make sure you practise your talk, know how to explain difficult things and be comfortable with the order and content of your slides.
Forgetting what you want to say	This is also part of a lack of confidence and something that you fear when you get stressed. If you practise you should have the key phrases and concepts ready for use.
Losing your thread and getting muddled	This happens when you feel stressed. You need to start by feeling positive about your talk. You have practised, you may not say everything in an ideal way, but no one will notice. If your structure is clear, you can't get muddled.

2.5 Excelling in exams

Examination success is the final hurdle. Examination marks often form part of your overall mark and thus count towards your final degree. Success depends upon knowing what is expected, good organisation, appropriate notes and effective memory techniques. This chapter will help you to explore what works and why. It will increase your skills and productiveness.

In this chapter you will:

1. examine the purpose of revision
2. explore new and effective techniques for efficient revision
3. learn about memory strategies
4. learn how to organise yourself during the examination.

USING THIS CHAPTER

Estimate your current levels of confidence. At the end of the chapter you will have the chance to re-assess these levels where you can incorporate this into your personal development planner (PDP). Mark between 1 (poor) and 5 (good) for the following:

I can manage and organise the whole revision process effectively.	I can recognise which revision notes system to use for different purposes.	I understand how to control pressure and stress.	I understand the characteristics of productive memory strategies.	I can use effective strategies during the examination.

Date: _______________

1 Introduction

What are the most common reasons why students do not get the marks they anticipate?

Some students dread examinations while others will admit that they enjoy the adrenaline rush. However, many students are at some time disappointed with their grades. Unexpected failure or low marks do not always mean that the student has not revised or that they do not understand the subject. A survey of tutors and examiners highlighted a number of common problems (see Activity 1).

ACTIVITY 1 Where do I stand?

Reflect upon your previous examination performance. What do you think could be improved? Look at the table opposite and be honest with yourself. In the right-hand column there are suggestions for methods to improve your performance, and cross-references to some relevant sections in the book.

This chapter will take you through the solutions so that you can increase your performance and get better grades.

Problem	Has this happened to you? Answer yes or no	Solution
Failure to answer the question set.		BUG Technique (see Chapter 4.1)
Misinterpreted the question.		BUG Technique (see Chapter 4.1)
Answered the wrong number of questions.		Get to know what is expected of you (see Sections 3 and 4).
Insufficient examples to support ideas/arguments.		Get to know what is expected of you. Improve your revision mapping techniques.
Insufficient knowledge.		Get to know what is expected of you. Distil information into manageable revision notes.
Illegible handwriting.		Practise writing at speed to maintain legibility.
Incoherent writing – long, rambling sentences which do not make sense to the reader.		Concept maps to connect information more effectively will have an impact upon your written communication and organisation.
Not all the questions answered. This may have occurred because you have run out of time or spent too long on the early questions.		Be strict and stick to time allocations worked out prior to the examination during revision. Memory recall strategies and techniques need to be strengthened. Practise recalling information under timed conditions.
Forgot the information on the day.		Relaxation techniques. Have a good night's sleep. Do not drink large amounts of alcohol and caffeine before the examination.
Course materials not referred to sufficiently.		Get to know what is expected of you. Listen out for tips and guidance during lectures. More effective revision notes. Increase your memory techniques.
Irritating errors – spelling mistakes, weak and incomplete sentences, silly errors in calculations, etc.		Leave some time at the end of the examination to check through your work for irritating errors.

2 What is revision?

Perhaps this question is jumping the gun, and the first question should really be 'Why have examinations?' Examinations and revision are closely interlinked. Examinations are a way of finding out what you have understood from your course. Many lecturers refer to 'learning outcomes', and examinations are a method of testing your grasp of those outcomes. Contrary to popular belief, examinations are not a fiendish method, devised by your tutors, to trick you!

The answer to the question 'What is revision?' may seem obvious, but it is important to make sure that you understand the purpose of revision so that you optimise your efforts. In its literal sense revision means 'seeing again', and this is what you will be doing when you go over your notes and look back on the information you have gathered over your units and modules. However, if you want to be an effective reviser, revision is much more than reading your notes. You need to develop an active approach. This will ensure that you get better grades. So what makes a successful reviser?

- Preparation
- Organisation
- Memory and recall

Activity 2 asks you to identify your problems with revision.

ACTIVITY 2 Common difficulties with revision

Which of these apply to you?	Tick ✓
1. I am often frustrated at examination times.	
2. I am often **very** nervous at examination times.	
3. I often find that I can't sleep properly at examination times.	
4. I seem to spend a lot of time revising and not getting the good results.	
5. I am not sure if my techniques are the most efficient.	
6. I mainly leave revision until it is almost too late.	
7. I put off my revision and find myself looking for other things to keep myself occupied.	
8. I have vast amounts of notes to help me revise.	

Check the feedback section at the end of the chapter to find out how to start changing your working patterns.

3 Productive revision

Be prepared

Most students come to university with some ideas about how to go about revising for examinations. However, the strategies you have used in the past may have been effective for the type of examinations you did then, but are not necessarily the most efficient now. Preparation is not only about drawing up a timetable and arranging your files and books on your work space! Activity 3 asks you to reflect upon how you have tackled revision in the past; you should analyse what worked well (you got good results) and what didn't work well (you got poor results).

ACTIVITY 3 Productive working habits

Which of these revision techniques worked well for you and which didn't?

	Yes/No
1. Writing out my notes again and again helped me to remember facts and information.	
2. Reducing information into shorter notes helped me to remember facts and information.	
3. Memorising essay answers.	
4. Writing out sample essay answers under timed conditions.	
5. Using concept maps, mind mapping or diagrams helped me to remember facts and information.	
6. Putting important information on to audio tapes and playing this over and over again.	
7. Revising with friends.	
8. Using colour (coloured highlighters, for example) to help me to summarise and understand key points and to remember facts and information.	
9. Reading my lecture notes (without any other activity).	
10. Writing out essay plans from past questions.	
11. Spending long periods revising a week before.	
12. Using memory triggers to help me remember.	
13. Using key words as the basis for understanding.	
14. Any other method you have used.	

In certain circumstances, these are all useful techniques either on their own or, more appropriately, in combination. However, you now need to consider their role and value in the context of study at university level. Think about why and when certain techniques worked well for you and why others did not, and develop your own approach.

4 Countdown not meltdown

Be organised

Preparation, organisation and memory recall are the essential elements of good revision. It is important that you have a clear revision strategy leading up to examinations so that you do not experience 'meltdown' or excessive anxiety during your examinations. This section explores:

- how to develop the right 'mindset'
- the tricks of the trade, i.e. the best strategies for maximising time and results
- dealing with examination nerves
- last-minute countdown.

The right 'mindset'

Preparing for examinations is not just about learning and memorising facts and information so that you can regurgitate them in a timed examination. It is also about:

- knowledge of what is expected of you by your tutors
- consideration of the assessment criteria
- selection of important theories, ideas and evidence
- realistic self-expectations
- development of efficient note-making systems
- development of organisational strategies
- increasing your memory capacity
- ability to 'crack the code' of the examination questions
- getting a buzz from understanding your subject.

Knowing what to expect and, equally importantly, what is expected of you are vital parts of the revision process. These two factors should drive your preparations and inform your strategies. See Activity 4.

ACTIVITY 4 Knowing what to expect

This table will get you actively involved with your revision right from the start of your unit/module. Use it as an memory aid and keep it prominently displayed at your workstation (wherever you do most of your studying) as a constant reminder. If you are studying for Joint Honours or have examinations set by more than one department, it is vital that you check each department's rules and regulations. Do not assume that they are the same.

What to expect	Source of information	Fill in your answers in this column
List the number and title of papers/ examinations I have to take this semester	Course handbooks. Departmental online information. Examination office – some of the larger institutions have a central office to deal with the organisation of examinations and have a section on the college/university website.	
What am I allowed to take into the examination room? (e.g. calculators, statutes for law tests, course notes)	Course handbooks. Departmental online information. Check with the unit tutor.	
What will be provided for me in the examination room? (e.g. periodic tables, molecular models, scientific calculators, law statutes)	Course handbooks. Departmental online information.	
What do I need to take into the examination room? (e.g. pens, pencils, coloured highlighter pens, etc.)	Examination officers (either departmental or institutional) will let you know the regulations.	
What type of questions can I expect in the various papers?	Past papers: take care that there are no changes for your year. Course handbooks. Departmental online information.	
How many sections are there in each paper?	Past papers: take care that there are no changes for your year. Course handbooks. Departmental online information.	
How many questions do I have to answer?	Past papers: take care that there are no changes for your year. Course handbooks. Departmental online information.	
Where are the instructions on each paper?	Past Papers. Course handbooks. Departmental online information.	
What is the length of the examination paper?	Past papers: take care that there are no changes for your year. Course handbooks. Departmental online information.	
What is the marking allocation for the questions in the paper?	Course handbooks. Departmental online information. Check with the unit tutor.	
What are the assessment criteria for the unit/module?	Course handbooks. Departmental online information. Cross-check with learning outcomes.	
What are the expected 'learning outcomes' for this unit/module?	Course handbooks. Departmental online information. Lecture notes from your tutor – some tutors display these at the beginning of units or lectures.	

As you can see, a lot of information can be gathered from your course handbooks. The library is another source of information. Many departments deposit past papers in the library (often in a reference section) and more and more are available electronically. Collecting photocopies of past papers of the relevant examinations that you will be taking is essential.

Hot Tip

Much of this information can be gathered before you start your new academic year because you will have discussed with your tutor which units/modules you will be taking. So before you dash off on holiday, why not get this information and store it in a safe place, clearly marked. October is always a hectic time, and you will be bombarded with a lot of information at the start of your courses. Consequently, many students do not feel they have time to collect information for events that will not take place for months! This is short-sighted. The other advantage of getting the information before you are plunged into a new academic year is that libraries, in particular, are less busy at the end of June and early July and you will be able to gather your information more quickly.

What type of examinations will I have to take?

Your tutors use many different ways to test your knowledge and understanding. Some subjects traditionally use essay questions, while others have always used multiple-choice questions. You may find that for some units paper 1 might utilise multiple-choice-type questions and paper 2 relies upon essay responses. Knowing a little about the different types of questions can inform your revision strategies because the different test types tap into different skills and memory techniques. These are summarised in the table opposite.

Some people have the knack of remembering vast amounts of facts and being able to regurgitate them quickly. These people can score highly on multiple-choice questions. There are others who need time to mull over information and gather their thoughts together. Without lots of timed practice, they will not score well on multiple-choice questions. In an ideal world it would be good if you could choose the type of examination format which suits you best. The reality is that the type of assessment and the ways in which examinations are traditionally set, as yet, do not reflect different learning styles. Besides, the variety of methods for assessing students test different skills, as you can see from the table opposite. Sometimes your tutors want to find out if you have remembered important facts. This could be the case with the viva that medical students have to take: a sort of oral, fast-paced test of factual information. Multiple-choice questions also enable your tutors to test this type of knowledge. However, most examinations will demonstrate your understanding of the subject and your ability to draw out relevant information to answer the question which is posed. In other words, the ability to handle information which you have stored in your memory.

Type of examination question	Definition	Skills needed
Multiple choice	A statement followed by a choice of answers which are often short and succinct. They test your knowledge of facts.	Good memory for facts. Quick memory recall. Reading accuracy and fluency.
Short answers	These questions require you to write brief paragraph answers and test your knowledge of facts.	Good sentence writing. Succinctness and summary skills. Selection of information.
Essays	These are the same as your course assignments and require you to write coherently and convincingly. They test not only facts but your interpretation of them.	Cracking the code (question analysis). Summary skills. Selection of information. Paragraph/sentence writing. Good grammar and punctuation.
Open book	This type of examination allows you to take in course texts and notes. Some students are duped into thinking they do not test memory.	Selection of information. Location of information. Linking and mapping information.
Take-home tests	Students are given three or four essay titles and have to prepare for these in advance. They do not know which question they will have allocated to them until they enter the examination.	Good memory. Selection of information. Summary skills. Organising thoughts in coherent written format.
Problem-solving/case studies	Some departments prefer to set these types of examination questions. Students are expected to marshal facts and put them into real-life, imaginary settings.	Cracking the code (question analysis). Selection skills. Linking and mapping information.
Practice tests	Medical and Health Professional students, for example, are often tested on their practical ability to apply knowledge.	Application of knowledge and understanding. Good memory. Speed of recall and assembly of information.

How organised are you?

The key to success in many circumstances is organisation – not just in your studies but also in the way you run your life. However, organisation pervades every aspect of revision. It relates to your physical environment – for example, where you keep your revision notes, how you categorise your information – as well as the information you have to remember. A well-organised student also has better control of his or her inner self and is thus able to deal with concentration, motivation, stamina and examination nerves.

When should I start my revision?

It is never too soon to start the revision process. Many students leave it too late to do a proper job. Have you ever said: 'If only I'd started earlier with my revision'? Revision is an activity which should be ticking over quietly throughout your unit or module, reaching a crescendo of activity in the weeks and days before the examination. Many students put themselves under unnecessary pressure in the last few weeks before the examination by trying to make their revision notes at the same time as learning and committing information to memory. It is no wonder that the brain and memory are overloaded and less effective! Try to pace yourself and start the revision process at the beginning of your units instead of at the end.

Overview of the revision process

The table opposite provides you with guidelines for pacing yourself and maximising your efforts. Once you get into the 'Before, During and After' routine you will find that you can improve your grades in examinations.

Before (the start of your unit)	**During** (while your lectures and the unit is taking place)	**After** (at the end of your unit in the time before the start of examinations)
1. Collect all the necessary past papers and store them in the appropriate revision file. It is useful to analyse the examination questions so that you can get an overview of the topics which are set and those which come up frequently.	5. After a series of lectures and seminars on a particular topic/theme, gather together all your information from different sources. These could be handouts, electronic information provided by tutors, your own lecture notes and notes you have made for background reading (possibly in preparation for an assignment).	8. Read through your revision notes and information to ensure that they still make sense and that you understand what you have gathered together in (6).
2. Purchase some special files in which to keep your revision notes – these are different from your course and lecture notes as you will see later in this chapter.	6. Distil all this information into dedicated revision notes. (Note-making techniques are explained in Chapter 2.1.)	9. If you have gaps or your notes do not seem to make sense, you will need to go back to the original notes and information to improve your revision notes.
3. Section off your revision files with clearly labelled dividers. You will need to cross-reference these sections with the examination themes and topics.	7. It is a good idea to sub-divide your topic information into the following sections: • key words • concept map • list of important facts/theories • key theorists • selection of quotations	10. Begin the memory stage of your revision – memory techniques are explained later in the chapter.

Before (the start of your unit)	**During** (while your lectures and the unit is taking place)	**After** (at the end of your unit in the time before the start of examinations)
4. This is for those who like to use technology to help them with revision. Set up a separate folder on your computer for revision. Divide the folder into files which match the topics/themes that are to be assessed. Perhaps you could code the files with an 'R' for revision to make sure that they do not get muddled with on-going coursework and lecture notes.		11. Practise recall of information under timed conditions. Various techniques are explained later in the chapter.

The multi-dimensional revision map

For some students, revision is like a journey. To reach your destination in good time, it is worth investing in accurate maps. You need to keep in mind your journey's end, even at the start of your revision. On a journey there are times when you have to plot and plan out the whole journey and for this you need to see all the road networks and how they link together. At other times you need to focus in on the minute details of street plans. Thus, in the examination there will be occasions when you will need to have the big picture of a topic to help you to make decisions about which elements or networks are applicable to the question. At other times, when working on your essay answer, you will be dealing with individual facts. You need to be able to manipulate both the whole and the parts to answer questions effectively. These are the mental acrobatics you will have to employ when you are in the examination room. Good revision will help you to be in control of your map and to know when to switch from the big picture to the fine details. However, what makes examinations so special is that they put you under timed pressures.

Time-controlled conditions put an added dimension to the revision process. Not only are you expected to be able to recall factual information accurately, to manipulate this information to meet the demands of specific questions and to assemble information from different mental storage areas, but you also have to do this under the pressure of time. Think of each topic as a big map. The way you organise the storage of facts and figures, theories and quotations will determine how quickly you can assemble the relevant information for a given task or question. However, it does hinge upon good networks which are adaptable and can provide you with quick routes to get you to where you want to be. The better organised your information is, the smoother, and therefore quicker, it will be to map out your information effectively.

What is your filing/storage system like?

Use different coloured files to gather and store your revision notes for each of your examinations. Believe it or not this simple start to your organisation will reduce stress in the final countdown to your examinations. You will have all the relevant information at your fingertips and will not have to waste time searching through lecture notes and various topics to carry out your memory routines. Keep your revision CDs or coloured floppy disks in a pouch or zipped transparent folder by topic/section.

It is a good idea to stick to one system for organising each section of your files. As suggested in the chart above, you will need:

- key words with your definitions
- list of important facts/theories
- key theorists
- selection of quotations
- concept maps.

Suggestions for building up these sections in your files is given in Section 5, 'Tricks of the trade', below.

Once your storage framework is in place, using either separate files or computer folders and files, you can start gathering and distilling information in readiness for storing it in your memory systems.

5 Tricks of the trade: good revision notes

This section provides you with ideas for techniques for formatting your notes. It also explores ways in which you can produce more effective revision notes which in turn will increase your memory capacity and strengthen your knowledge and understanding of the subject.

Examinations can help you to consolidate your knowledge and bring together lots of different strands from your unit. During revision time you may find that the 'penny will drop' for you on some topic that you found puzzling during the semester. Making effective revision notes will help in this process and will ultimately give you an indication of what you understand and where the gaps are in your knowledge. In Activity 5 you are asked to identify and analyse your personal preferences for revision notes.

ACTIVITY 5 My revision notes techniques

Have a look at the different types of notes systems presented in the table opposite. Decide upon your personal preferences for using the different types. Then analyse and evaluate whether they have been of real help in remembering information for examinations.

Note types	Preferences 1 = frequently used 2 = not often used	Memory lubricators Ask yourself if the note type has helped you remember information for examinations
Lists		
Linear notes in bullet points		
Diagrams (some subjects lend themselves more to this than others)		
Notes in prose format (sentences/paragraphs)		
Concept maps		
Flash cards		
Posters		
Ceiling maps		
Audio notes		
Grids/tables		
Time lines (not only useful for History students but when you have to know about the progress or development of a innovation, etc.)		
Other (see Chapter 2.1 'Making notes', for ideas)		

What sort of notes you produce and how you distil a whole series of lecture notes into revision notes is to some extent personal preference. There are a variety of ways of producing effective notes which you may want to consider. It is vital, however, that whatever system you choose it provides **you** with **useful notes** and is an **efficient** use of your time and effort.

Hot Tip

Remember revision should not be a passive activity. Making your revision notes, by whatever technique or combination of techniques you choose, is only a means to an end: effective tools for memory stimulation and ultimately obtaining better examination grades. However, these notes are merely one part of the whole process. Sitting back and admiring your notes will not get your desired outcomes. It is the interaction between your mind, the information (subject context), memory stimulators and your examination systems which gets results.

If you always do the same things to revise, how do you know if they are really working. Could you be more efficient? Could you have remembered the information if it had been presented to you in a different format? It is just as important to evaluate what you did linked to your results. The type of information you are dealing with will also have a bearing upon your success or otherwise. For example, trying to remember the intricacies of the respiratory system, with its high level of difficult subject terminology, might be best approached using labelled diagrams rather than linear, bullet-point notes.

How good are you at customising your notes for revision purposes?

ACTIVITY 6 Customising your notes

Grade your effectiveness judged against past examination performance, where 1= very useful; 2 = useful; 3 = just adequate; 4 = not effective.

Revision notes	Allocate grade
1. I only use the notes I made for an assignment/essay on this topic.	
2. I only use my lecture notes.	
3. I put all my notes from different sources together in a file.	
4. I only use my lecturer's handouts and downloaded electronic information from the departmental intranet.	
5. I make a new set of notes from all my sources.	
6. I do not have revision notes.	

If you only use one source of notes, you have to be confident that they are comprehensive. Remember that notes made for another purpose, e.g. for an assignment/essay, may not be right for the job of revision. If you gather all your notes from different sources into one file or section, you must be careful that there is not repetition of information. This can cause a drag on your time and sap your energy and memory.

If you make a new set of notes having gone through all your sources, do you end up with more or less notes? In these circumstances, more is not necessarily good as you will see. Besides, if your revision notes are greater than your other notes, you need to ask yourself whether the increased volume helps or hinders memory.

Some students find that they have amassed a lot of lecture notes and notes made from books and articles for a specific assignment. It may seem rather daunting to try to consolidate these a couple of weeks before the examinations! It may be an impossible task and as a result you are immediately put off doing what is a very important aspect of revision that involves not only memory techniques but understanding.

If you have organised your lecture notes carefully, at the end of each topic/unit you might find it useful to make revision notes while things are fresh in your mind. It is often a good idea to place your revision notes at the beginning of the section and identify them in a different colour so that they stand out when you come to the final stages of revision in the build up to the examinations. Many students use different coloured paper for this or a range of coloured pens or coloured fonts.

You can customise your revision notes in many ways. Broadly speaking, you can start by drawing up a big route map (concept mapping notes) or you can draw small, detailed maps (information notes). You must decide which is the best way for you to work. There is no right or wrong way, simply personal preference.

How to customise your revision notes

If you want to provide the best support for your memory and retrieval systems so that they can work at speed under pressurised, timed conditions, you need to categorise and compartmentalise information into different maps.

Revision maps

At different times in your examination you will need to draw upon different parts of information to show off your knowledge and understanding to the examiners. There will be occasions when you need to use the **subject terminology** correctly and with confidence. For this you will need to have **key words** with your definitions at your finger tips. Sometimes you will gain marks for factual detail which is accurate. You will be drawing upon your store of **important facts/theories**. If you want to demonstrate the depth of your knowledge and understanding you will need to be familiar with key **theorists**, **leading figures** or **important innovations**. Being able to draw from a selection of **snappy and relevant quotations** is impressive. At other times your examiners want to find out how well you really understand the topics/subjects and will set questions whereby you will be expected to select and assemble information to bring out the connections. **Revision** or **concept maps** enable you to perform in this way.

During the course of your lectures and seminars it is always good to have an eye out for creating your revision maps.

Key words/subject terminology

Whether you set up a dedicated file in your revision folder on your computer or whether you prefer to work using paper and pen, it is vital that you have an ongoing list of key terminology. In some subjects, such as Nursing and Medicine, there are many words which look very similar but have totally different meanings. Thus, it is vital that not only do you list the key words but that you know what they mean. Copying a definition out of a dictionary will not aid memory recall. The definitions need to be in your own words so that you can understand them. This will give you confidence and speed when using the terminology under pressure in examinations.

A simple two-column table is the most effective way of gathering the information as you go along and is clear and easy to read when you get to the memory stage of revision (see Activity 7).

ACTIVITY 7 Key word map notes

Choose one of the topics/units which will be examined. Start to fill in the table. Keep this in your revision file.

Key word/phrase	Your brief definition (If unsure of this, check the accuracy with a knowledgeable friend)

As part of the ongoing nature of revision, this is a two-stage process:

- **Stage one**: Collect the most important key words and terminology as you go along throughout the lectures and seminars. This will be a random activity.
- **Stage two**: Can the lists be regrouped in any way? This might help you go look again at the terminology to make decisions about how to mentally map the information. Some students use colour at the regrouping stage so that they are preparing for memory storage and map connections later on.

Factual information

If your revision notes are to be of any use, you must distil the information you have. As soon as you have come to a natural pause or finishing point with one of your units, you need to distil your information into manageable revision notes. Summarising notes or handouts into **'distilled' notes** (key words, phrases) should take up no more than two sides of A4 for each topic.

If you look at some of your notes from different sources, you will find that some of the information is repeated, though in different words.

1. Read through all your notes/sources of information on a topic.
2. Identify the parts where repetition has occurred.
3. Shorten this information into your own words.
4. Pick out the key points first, followed by examples or subsidiary information.

You will have to choose a revision notes system which is suitable for your information, so try out different systems. The type of format you use will depend upon personal preferences to some extent but is often triggered by the type of information with which you are dealing.

Which note format do you prefer?

Here is some information in two frequently used formats: mind-mapping and linear. Look at both and see which one makes sense to you.

An example of linear/branch notes

Family: family perspectives[1]

Feminist perspective

- Black feminists
- Radical feminists
- Feminist Marxists
- Liberal feminists
- Marxist feminists
- Common themes:
  - patriarchal institution
  - familial ideology

[1] With grateful thanks to David Bown, Sociology lecturer, for supplying these helpful mind-maps and branch notes.

- power structures
- women's experiences
- division of labour

New Right perspective

- Promotes traditional family
- Opposition to lone-parent families
- Boys suffer from absent fathers
- Dysfunctional families in underclass

Functionalist perspective

- Loss of functions theory:
  - Talcott Parsons: two 'basic and irreducible' functions
  - George Murdock: four universal residual functions
- Multiple functions family:
  - Ronald Fletcher: 'multifunctional family'
  - Eugene Litwak: 'non-bureaucratic functions'
- William Goode: movement to nuclear family
- Dysfunctions:
  - Vogel and Bell: emotional scapegoats

Marxist perspective

- Michelle Barrett: docile workforce
- Christopher Lasch: haven in a heartless world
- Reproduction of labour

Interpretive studies

- Studies of ordinary family life
- Meanings of family life

An example of mind-map notes

As you can see in Figure 1, information in mind-map notes is categorised by colour (or shade) rather than as a separate linear branch. The five main headings are in bold so that they stand out as the main branches or stems from the central theme.

An example of a table/grid format for recording: theories/famous people/innovations/inventions

Depending upon your subject and your topic, you can gain marks in examinations by showing off your knowledge about how development and progress has been made. For Education students, it is important to be

Figure 1 An example of mind-map notes

aware of the educational system and how it has evolved to become an inclusive education system. You would need to know key names and dates; you would have to be able to state ideas and theories as well as solutions. Law students have to be aware of the Criminal Justice System, its development to today's system, and who the key players were and are. Engineering students may need to know about processes: who invented such systems and what is involved, or the theory upon which the system is based. Psychology students may have to have knowledge of the measurement of intelligence and would need to know the different theories of what makes up intelligence.

This type of information is often given along the way during lectures and in the course of your background reading. It is as well to keep a separate section in your revision file to keep this type of information all together. Using grids and tables is often one of the most efficient methods of gathering this type of information. It enables you to memorise the facts but also to obtain an overview of information from which to compare and contrast (see Acitivites 8 and 9).

ACTIVITY 8 Key theories and people map notes (1)

The table below is part of a worked example to demonstrate how you can record this type of information.

Theory	Definition	Named person(s)	My comments
One general intelligence	'g' factor: general ability to reason. Many common abilities classified under this. To do with neural processing speeds. Linguistic, logic and spatial skills.	Cattell Spearman	Cattell – Introduced 'fluid' and 'crystallised' intelligence. 'Fluid' – is memory dependent and deteriorates with age. Abstract reasoning and problem-solving abilities. 'Crystallised' – increases with age; attributes can be taught. Performance on culturally loaded tasks. Spearman – developed factor analysis.
Three stratum	Built upon Cattell and Spearman's foundations. Incorporates reaction time.	Carroll	Three layers. Hierarchical layers. Notion of quicker the reaction time, the higher the IQ.
Multiple	Humans have combinations of different types of intelligence. Not limited to single/one general theory.	Gardner	Reaction to 'g' factor and its components. Multiple – started with seven and then identified nine types of intelligence, e.g. musical, interpersonal, intrapersonal, mathematical, logical, linguistic, spatial, kinaesthetic, naturalistic.
Triarchic	Componential theory of analysis of intelligence.	Sternberg	Opposed Gardner. His categories are analytic (academic) and practical.

The development of thinking relating to the notion of intelligence and comparisons and differences can be drawn out of this table. Thus, the basic framework of information is given together with personal commentary. These notes are the foundations for a compare and contrast type of essay; yet the information could be used more generally as background information to a debate about nature versus nurture.

ACTIVITY 9 Key theories and people map notes (2)

Now try this out for yourself with one of your units by using of the two grids provided.

Theory	Definition	Named person(s)	My comments

Name a theory or concept related to the chosen topic	Who supports this theory or concept?	Who opposes this theory or concept and why?

Relevant quotations

During the examination, if you can give a punchy and relevant quotation to back up and strengthen what you are writing about and the point you are trying to make, you can gain some valuable extra marks. However, you have to balance up whether (a) you have the time to search them out and learn them, and (b) you have the memory capacity to remember quotations. Writing an inaccurate or irrelevant quotation is just as bad, if not worse, than not quoting at all. Your choice of quotation is also crucial because it must be linked to an important point or a unique saying/idea. Thus, it is vital that you remember the accurate quotation but also that you know what point it is making.

Hot Tip

Taking into account the above advice, it is better to learn short quotations or phrases which will do the job you want. You should be on the look out for these while you are conducting your research reading and while you are going through various handouts. It is worth alerting your consciousness to pick up on these when they are given in lectures. Often they are throw-away remarks but can be used most effectively in examinations.

Revision/concept maps

No revision notes section should be without an A4 or A3 revision/concept map of the whole unit. These maps are invaluable for ensuring that you make the connections with all your information. These will help you to obtain a greater depth of understanding of your subject. They are most useful to help you forge links between ideas in a theme or topic.

These maps tend to be fairly complicated, depending upon your topic. Figure 2 gives an example of a simplified map to show you how the general ideas are linked together.

Having a concept map at the beginning of each section of your revision notes can fuel your final countdown. You can also use it to test yourself in the final stages of the revision process.

Poster displays

These are similar to concept maps but on a larger scale. The best type of poster display for revision purposes is on an A3 size paper. This size allows you to incorporate visual information which could stimulate memory later on. Posters should be kept in a prominent position.

> *I always put one on my ceiling above my bed so that when I'm lying in bed forcing myself to get up, I gaze up and see the poster. It's sort of like a subliminal thing to help me remember.*

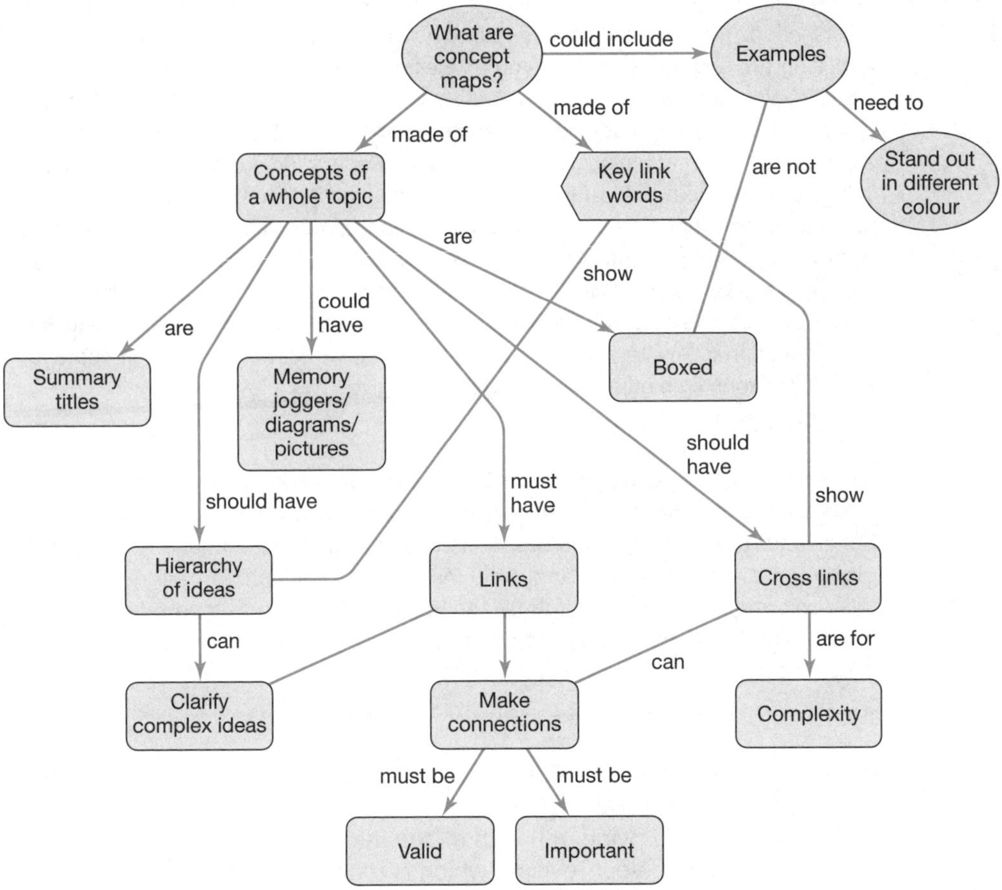

What are concept maps?
could include
Examples
need to
Stand out in different colour
are not
made of
Concepts of a whole topic
made of
Key link words
are
show
are
Summary titles
could have
Memory joggers/ diagrams/ pictures
Boxed
should have
should have
Hierarchy of ideas
must have
Links
show
Cross links
can
Clarify complex ideas
Make connections
can
are for
Complexity
must be
Valid
must be
Important

Figure 2 A simplified revision/concept map

Adapted from: **www.mc.maricopa.edu/dept/d43/glg/Study_Aids/concept_maps/conceptmaps.html**

Hot Tip

Strategic revision

Look back at Activity 4, 'Knowing what to expect', where you were asked to find out what your examination papers will be like. You can make good use of past papers in many ways. Obviously, your tutors would like you to learn everything connected with the unit. However, you need to be ready for the format of the examination. You have to apportion time properly and be ready for the way in which the tutors word the questions. You will not have much time to figure out what a question is getting at and what information is required under the pressure of the actual examination. Therefore, your preparations should cover all eventualities of which you have control.

Time allocations

If your paper consists of essay-type answers, then it is important to work out how much time you should spend on each question so that you can pace yourself in the examination. You will need to take into account allowing yourself reading time and choosing the best questions for you as well as allocating some time for checking your answers. Some papers do not allow you to do any working for the first ten minutes. This ensures that students read the paper through and start to make decisions about which questions to answer. Some departments assume that students will do this and do not ring-fence or protect any time within the examination. Make sure you know what happens in your subject so that you can calculate the amount of time you have for actually writing your responses. If your paper is a mixed response type (one short section, with short answers or multiple-choice type, followed by a couple of essay-type responses), you also need to consider matching time allocation to maximum marks per question. It would be foolish to spend a lot of your precious time on a question which only gives you a few marks.

Question spotting

Many students look at papers which have been set over the previous two or three years so that they can get a feel not only for the topics which come up (patterns) but also for the wording of the questions (manipulation of information). For example, you may have learnt all about the Industrial Revolution and the question on this topic requires you to weigh up the impact of this upon a certain sector of people. This could have an effect upon the way you make up your revision notes in readiness for memory learning and recall.

If you have managed to work through all the 'Tricks of the trade' section, you will now have a well-organised revision file which is properly compartmentalised. It will provide you with all the information you need to move on to the next stage in your revision which is making sure that you can memorise all that is contained in your file sections.

6 Memory stimulators

However effective we are at preparing and organising revision and gaining an understanding of the material, we have to commit it to memory for an examination. The more thoroughly we understand a topic, the more easily we can deal with unexpected and/or complex examination questions. So, it is important not to rely totally on pure memory recall or rote learning (learning chunks of information by heart). We need to develop strategies to help us remember.

Why do some people seem to have good memories and others struggle to remember what day it is? Perhaps those with good memories have developed strategies for remembering, and they have worked out ways of remembering which suit them best. **Rote learning** may have worked in the past for some examinations but at university this is not a sensible strategy because of the volume of information you will have to deal with and because you are overloading your memory without understanding the subject. This type of learning uses up a lot of brain capacity, and, in particular, memory capacity. The problem with this is that it leaves little spare capacity for other activities which go on during an examination. It is difficult to remember isolated strings of information, but when you have found a way to connect them, then you have a deeper understanding of the material (concept maps will support this), and this is makes it easier for you to recall the information you need.

Wouldn't it be wonderful to cast your eyes over a page of information and automatically be able to remember everything on the page? There are very few people who have got photographic memories to enable them to do this. Most students have to work at developing memory capacity and, as one gets older, it is neccesary to keep the memory lubricated by constant practice. Many students have a negative view of their memory ability. You will be surprised how much you can do if you use the right stimulators. There are different types of memory, and knowing how the memory operates can help you make strategic choices to get the most out of the time and effort you put into memorisation at revision times.

How the memory works

The brain is like a living computer. It relies upon hard disk storage (long-term memory), portable storage facilities (short-term or working memory) and a robust operating system. The operating system has to be able to make decisions about where to go for information and to ensure that linkages and connections are made smoothly between the different parts of the system.

The memory system needs you stimulate it effectively. Using the computer analogy, Figure 3 illustrates the various stages of memory interaction.

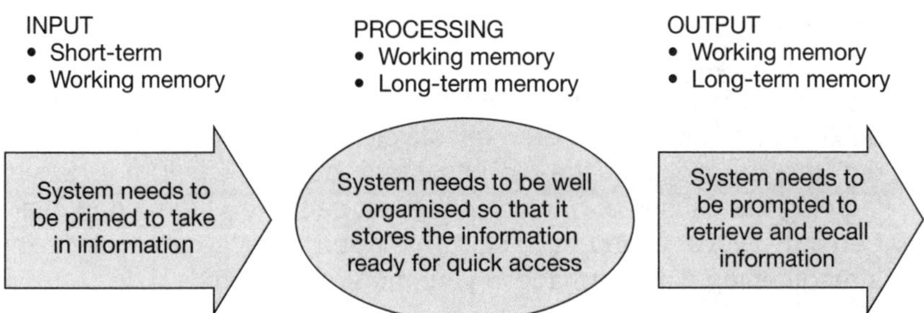

Figure 3 The stages of memory interaction

This system has to be finely balanced to get the most out of it. If you overload one part of the system, then you reduce the effective working and processing of other parts of the system. Just like a computer, this reduction will lead to sluggish operation and retrieval. Many of you will, at one time or another, have complained bitterly that your computer takes forever to load up stored information. Some have said that it is possible to go away and make a cup of coffee while the computer chugs on and displays the irritating hour-glass to let you know that it is loading and retrieving your information from within its filing and operating systems. Rote learning, mentioned previously, clogs up your systems. It saps a lot of the energy from your processor and output systems. Consequently, if you are taking in further information, such as reading a part of an examination question, the balance of your system is skewed and everything starts to slow down – just what you do not want in timed, pressurised conditions.

For optimum working the memory system needs:

- motivation
- minimal stress distracters
- concentration surges.

Therefore give your memory system a chance to work well by ensuring that you are in control of your stress levels, cut out unwanted distractions, and utilise memory joggers to provide the concentration surges and lubrication for your memory system.

What sort of memory strategies (joggers) do you use?

Think about how you remember. Answer the following questions:

- What was your first day at school like? (episode)
- What is your home postal code? (fact)
- Where did you have your last lecture? (episode)
- How do you open a document on the computer? (procedure)
- What is a key concept in your favourite topic? (knowledge)

Our long-term memory is organised so we can remember facts, episodes, knowledge and procedures. These use different aspects of our memory. In addition, how facts and knowledge are remembered (written text, diagram, mind-map, etc.) could reflect your ability to recall that information. Certain subjects can be remembered effectively by drawing and labelling diagrams, e.g. the intricacies of the blood system, but this would not be suitable for learning the causes of poverty in the last century, where a grid chart may be better. However, if you have set up revision files you are well on the way to strengthening better storage in your memory system.

You may find yourself better at remembering some types of things than others. Can you identify your memory strengths and weaknesses? See Activity 10.

Check the feedback section at the end of the chapter to see a sample of two topics and the strategies appropriate for each topic.

These strategies help you to prime your memory input system so that you give it the best chance to work. They will also provide effective organisation systems for storage during the processing stage.

ACTIVITY 10 Memory strategies/joggers

List two topics you will be studying (select quite different types of topics):

TOPIC A ________________________________

TOPIC B ________________________________

Memory strategies	**Topic A**	**Topic B**
Mind-mapping, diagrams and flow charts		
Associations – making links with the information (concept map)		
Writing out information		
Remembering information in lists – rearranging the order of the list so that the first letters of each word on the list make up something silly or amusing – a memorable mnemonic		
Using shapes and colour		
Saying the information – to yourself or out aloud		
Poster display – similar to a concept map but incorporating visual clues as well		
Customised fridge magnet displays		
Chunking or grouping information		
Devising a story about the facts		
Flash cards		
Anything else you have found useful		

Of course, controlling your environment will also ensure that you give the whole system the best chance to operate. Distractions will weaken the effectiveness of the memory system so it is imperative that you evaluate what distracts you and how you are going to eliminate these (see Activity 11).

ACTIVITY 11 Controlling distractions

	Your answer	Ideal? Better to ...?
Where do you revise?		
Is it noisy?		
What about comfort factors?		
Do you take regular breaks?		
Do you set realistic targets for what you can memorise in a specified time?		
Do you prefer to revise alone or with friends/both?		
Do you need to spread out your notes?		
Do you walk around when you are memorising information?		
What is likely to distract you?		
What time of day do you prefer to revise/study?		

Bursts of concentration are better than setting aside long periods to revise. Research suggests that we can only sustain **productive** concentration levels for 40 minutes at a time. The memory retains more when you concentrate for short periods of time. If you have set aside a three-hour chunk of time for specific revision and memory learning, make sure that you split it up into small 15-minute chunks and then take a brief break – stretch your legs, make a drink (preferably not containing caffeine or alcohol) and do some relaxation exercise.

How do you prepare for timed conditions? The output stage

If I had plenty of time, I could recall loads of information.

Emma, second-year Environmental Science student

I can produce a really good essay which flows if I had more time.

Andrew, first-year History student

Most of us would agree with these students at some time during examinations. However, the trick is to ensure that you are prepared for the real circumstances and that you can trigger your brain to recall information from the different storage areas at speed. It is no good having all the information to answer a question if you do not show it off in the examination itself. It is well worth reminding yourself of the time you have apportioned for each examination response (see 'Hot Tip: Strategic revision', p. 197).

Once again you need to give your memory the best chance for success and this will mean a two-staged attack.

Stage 1: Getting the information to stick in your long-term memory

The memory is better lubricated when it has small chunks of information to deal with initially. So break down your facts etc. into bite-sized portions. Go over them regularly to imprint them and then see what you can remember. Gradually put the chunks together so that your memory makes the connections and so that you can recall larger and larger sections.

Stage 2: Retrieving or recalling the information at speed

The knack in examinations is bringing the information out of the depths of your memory. This means that you must set aside time to rehearse this. Practising recall of facts and timing yourself is important. On the day not only will you have to do this but in response to a specifically-worded question, you might have to pull out parts of one of the storage drawers or files in your long-term memory and combine these with others. This slows the process down so you need to make sure that your speed and accuracy of recall is good. Many students practise recalling information at speed by getting hold of previous examination papers and timing themselves with specific questions. Try out a number of strategies in Activity 12.

ACTIVITY 12 Recall speed strategies

Try out some of these strategies. Remember that your subject matter may determine which ones are the best.

Recall speed strategy	Recall time	How to improve ...
Labelling a diagram		
Drawing a cycle of information		
Listing main facts/events		
Drawing and labelling how things work (e.g. for procedures)		
Constructing an essay plan for specified questions (e.g. for take-home examinations; questions from past papers)		
Writing out prepared essay questions		

7 Controlling the pressure

The mind and body function well on a certain amount of stress. Levels of adrenaline can keep you ready for action which is needed during the examination. Certain levels of stress can keep you on your toes, more alert and ready for action. Stress also means that your motivation is stimulated so that you have a positive attitude to your revision. However, too much anxiety and adrenaline can be counter-productive. To keep a check on your levels, go back to Chapter 1.1, 'Managing your stress'. This provides excellent advice and guidance. Learn to recognise your stress levels and carry out some of the solutions which are contained in Chapter 1.1. Here are some reminders for you:

Stress-busting techniques

1. **Exercise**. This will help the physiological aspect of stress and the release of endorphins will give you a feeling of euphoria as well as help your heart. It is also ideal for getting rid of anger and frustrations. If you want to choose only one stress-busting technique, then choose this one. It is important not to remain static while you are revising. Many students walk around while using their memory strategies.
2. **Relax**. When you are feeling stressed out it is difficult to unwind. You may find you have to make a big effort to do this. It may be better to go classes such as yoga or tai-chi. Exercising also helps you to relax. If you want to develop your own relaxation techniques then try deep breathing or meditation. While you are revising, make sure that your shoulders, neck and hands, in particular, do not tense up. Regularly do some relaxation exercises for these areas while you are sitting. See if relaxation tapes can help you to unwind.
3. **Eat well**. Avoid junk food and too much alcohol – both of these can sap your energy and make you feel low. During revision time, some students drink excessive amounts of caffeine which can be found in coffee, tea and cola-type drinks. There is the popular idea that drinking coffee will keep you awake so that you can revise all through the night before your examination. Whilst this liquid intake may keep you awake, it has an adverse effect upon your memory capacity and functioning.

   I kept myself awake all night with mugs of coffee so that I could learn and memorise my notes the night before my exam. The coffee certainly kept me awake but I had a memory blank in the exam and felt exhausted. I did worse in that exam so I'm not going to do that again.

   Peter, second-year Chemistry student

   Of course, if you have paced yourself in the weeks before examinations, you should not need to take these drastic measures.

E-day pressure countdown

Examination day or e-day has finally arrived. This is another source of stress and anxiety. Remember that anxiety can cut down on your memory's performance so carry out the following countdown checklist to give yourself the best possible chance in the examination.

Checklist: e-day countdown

- Make sure you get a good night's sleep the night before the examination.
- Think positively: your hard work in the build-up to the day will pay off.
- Avoid groups of 'friends' who want to talk about what they have learned. This can be a source of worry. Panic rises when you listen to what they have done because it is different from you. If you have carried out the stages of revision set out in this chapter, you will be well prepared. Anyway, who is to say that your friends are right?
- After the examination it is better if you avoid groups of 'friends' who want to talk about what they did in the examination and what they wrote. This is another source of anxiety. There is nothing you can do to change what you wrote in the examination. Besides, who is to say that your friends are right?

8 Last-minute countdown

Rushing around at the last minute or on the day of the examination places you under unnecessary pressure. Go through this routine. It will keep you calm and positive as e-day approaches.

- Double-check the day, place and time of your examination.
- Check that you have a good pen and at least one spare ready for use.
- Check that the other equipment you can take into the examination is in good working order.
- If you are allowed to take in notes or a textbook, make sure that you have followed the regulations. Some departments require you to erase all your supplementary notes on textbooks so that they are 'clean' for the examination.
- Minimise your personal belongings – money and mobile telephone.
- Switch off your mobile telephone before entering the examination room.

9 The examination: 10-point plan

Stress can be minimised by getting into routines which take your mind off your anxiety levels. This section looks at what to do at the beginning of the examination, during the examination and at the end.

The beginning

1. Remind yourself of your worked time allocations. If necessary, jot these down on your answer booklet in pencil.

2. Read through all the questions carefully.

3. Categorise the questions:
   (a) the ones you can do
   (b) questions for which you have some of the information
   (c) questions which you cannot answer
4. Decide on the order in which you will answer the questions. Start off with the ones you are most confident about and which will give you a chance of gaining the most marks.

During

5. Now take each question in turn.
6. Read the question carefully and do the BUG technique (see Chapter 4.1, Section 4) to work out exactly what information you need to include and how to handle the information.
7. For essay questions, do a framework plan or a mind map. This means that you download all the relevant information before you start writing. This will take pressure off your memory and enable you to produce a more coherent and cohesive response.
8. Remember your reader – get to the point and then expand upon it.

After

9. Try not to do a post-mortem of your performance.
10. Do **not** check with others about what they did. Remember, if it is different from what you did, who is to say that they were correct?

10 Special examination arrangements

Some students can be granted special arrangements for examinations. These students will need some sort of proof of entitlement. Usually, this is provided when eligible students have applied for the Disabled Students' Allowance (DSA). In these circumstances, the student's needs are known well in advance and are unlikely to change over time. There may be occasions when something unexpected happens which could affect examination performance: for example, breaking a hand or arm; family bereavement etc. Your institution can respond to both of these circumstances but it needs to know as far in advance as possible to organise the best arrangements for you.

What are special arrangements?

There are a variety of types of arrangements:

- additional time
- separate room
- a reader
- a scribe

- an amanuensis (reader and scribe)
- a computer.

If you think you are eligible, you need to discuss how special arrangements can be organised. Your personal tutor, the Disability Officer or the Dyslexia Coordinator are usually the best sources of information.

NOTE Do **not** leave this to the last moment or you may be told that nothing can be organised at short notice.

11 On reflection

This chapter has focused upon revision and examinations. You have been taken through suggestions, advice and guidance for ways to tackle the whole process. Some sections may have challenged the way you currently work and you may find that your skill levels and working habits have changed. It is vital that you constantly reappraise the way that you go about your revision and preparation for examinations to make sure that you maximise your efforts to gain the best marks and grades.

Summary of this chapter

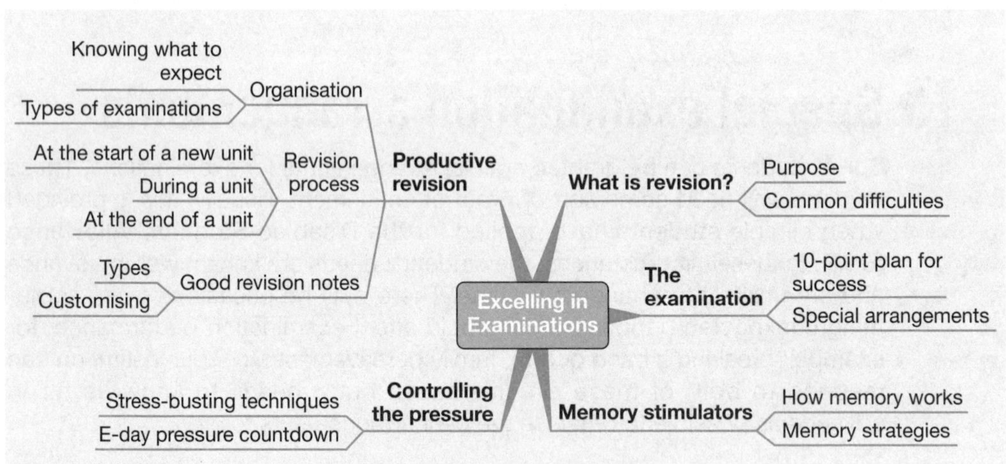

ACTIVITY 13 Update your personal development planner

Now reflect on your current abilities and consider what you need to do to improve. You may want to transfer this information to your own institution's personal development planner scheme.

Grade your confidence on a scale of 1–5 where 1 = poor and 5 = good.

My developing skills	Confidence level 1–5	Plans to improve
I can manage and organise the whole revision process effectively.		
I can recognise which revision notes systems to use for different purposes.		
I understand how to control pressure and stress.		
I understand the characteristics of productive memory strategies.		
I can use effective strategies during the examination.		

Date: ____________________

Getting extra help

- Go to the Students Union to find out where to go for skill development. Many universities and colleges have tutors who provide this service.
- Some departments organise special revision sessions. Check to see if these are available.
- Revision buddies: some students find that getting together with others on the course is a useful and interactive method of revising. To get the most out of this, you need to plan this with your friends so that you all are at the same stage of revision when you meet. It is frustrating if you have worked on a section but the others haven't.

> The following books will help you to improve your examination technique:
>
> Buzan, T. (2006) *The Ultimate Book of Mindmaps*. Harper Thorsons.
>
> Buzan, T. (2006) *Brilliant Memory: Unlock the Power of your Mind*. BBC Active.

Feedback on activities

ACTIVITY 2 Common difficulties with revision

Which of these apply to you?

	Tick ✓
1. I am often frustrated at examination times.	
2. I am often **very** nervous at examination times.	
3. I often find that I can't sleep properly at examination times.	
4. I seem to spend a lot of time revising and not getting the good results.	
5. I am not sure if my techniques are the most efficient.	
6. I mainly leave revision until it is almost too late.	
7. I put off my revision and find myself looking for other things to keep myself occupied.	
8. I have vast amounts of notes to help me revise.	

If you have ticked one of these then it is time to start thinking about how to improve your revision strategies.

If you ticked '1'

You have not perfected an efficient system of revision. Your memory strategies may not be the most effective. You need to try out different techniques. (Read this chapter carefully to identify where you could make improvements.)

If you ticked '2'

Most people are nervous at examination times. However, if you are excessively nervous, you may need to learn how to control your examination nerves more effectively (see Section 7, 'Controlling the pressure').

If you ticked '3'

This may be a sign of your growing anxiety. It is also an indication that you may not be using the most productive strategies for revision (see Section 3,'Productive revision', Section 5 'Tricks of the Trade', Section 6, 'Memory stimulators' and Section 7, 'Controlling the pressure').

If you ticked '4'

Your revision may be without a proper focus and plan of campaign. You may not know how to prepare for revision. You need to try out different techniques (see Section 4, 'Countdown not meltdown'; Section 5, 'Tricks of the Trade' and Section 6, 'Memory stimulators').

If you ticked '5'

You are stuck in a rut and no one has told you how to revise properly. You need to try out different techniques (see Section 3, 'Productive revision' and Section 5, 'Tricks of the trade').

If you ticked '6'

Your time management is in need of an overhaul (Section 4, 'Countdown not meltdown' and Chapter 1.2, 'Managing your time').

If you ticked '7'

This is often a sign of procrastination. Of course, it may be that revision has been an unpleasant experience in the past. It may be that you are dithering because you don't have a plan of campaign or you don't know how to revise.

If you ticked '8'

Having large files of notes is not necessarily appropriate for revision. It takes time to search through lots of information to find what you need. This may be time you do not have. For some students, a thick volume of revision notes is like a security blanket. However, you need to ask yourself if your notes are time-efficient. Remember that it is quality not quantity which matters! You need to explore ways in which you can distil your information (see Section 5, 'Tricks of the trade').

REMEMBER! If you always do what you have always done,

You will always get what you have always got.

Now is the time to take stock of your revision habits.

ACTIVITY 10 Memory strategies/joggers

List two topics you will be studying (select quite different types of topics):

TOPIC A The cardiovascular system

TOPIC B Handover procedures on the hospital ward

Memory strategies	Topic A	Topic B	Uses and relevance
Mind-mapping, diagrams and flow charts	✓	✓	Topic A: Labelling a photocopied diagram. Topic B: Numbered flow chart helps to remember procedure.
Associations – making links with the information (revision/concept map)	✓		Topic A is interconnected while B is more sequential.
Writing out information	✓	✓	Write out either the diagram or flow chart to help make mental links.
Remembering information in lists – rearranging the order of the list so that the first letters of each word on the list make up something silly or amusing – a memorable mnemonic			Not relevant for B – correct order is essential.
Using shapes and colour	✓		Topic A lends itself more readily to colour associations for flow of blood etc.
Saying the information – to yourself or out aloud	✓	✓	Useful to reinforce most information.
Poster display			
Customised fridge magnet displays	✓		Pictures of different parts of they system more easily displayed than text.
Chunking or grouping information		✓	Topic B procedures can be grouped.
Devising a story about the facts Flash cards	✓		Photocopied pictures of parts of system and definitions of terminology can reinforce memory.

3 Optimise your reading

In this part you can explore an essential skill which is embedded in many of the activities of university life, namely reading. Learning new approaches to reading can save you time and effort, and can increase your grades. Reading is also vital for stimulating your thinking, which is a key component for success. This section will provide guidance to help you become a 'SMART' reader. Here, SMART stands for:

Skill **M**anagement in **A**cademic work *through* **R**easoning *and* **T**hinking.

The chapters on reading will constantly draw your attention to how you can develop your reading skills. As a successful or SMART reader, you will able to use your skills to extract information from a text with ease, see Chapter 3.1, 'Reading efficiently' and Chapter 3.2 'Finding your way around text'. As an effective reader you can also maximise your opportunities by interacting with texts, thinking about them and using them to help you to solve problems through reasoning, see Chapter 3.3, 'Reading critically'. This means that you can choose the best reading strategies to manage your own reading environment, see Chapteer 3.4, 'Managing your reading'.

3.1 Reading efficiently

Reading efficiency is vital when you are at university because there will be many demands upon your time. It is vital, therefore, that you increase your reading effectiveness. Learning how to be an expert reader relies upon using reading skills properly and developing flexible reading habits.

In this chapter you will:

1. find out how effective your current reading habits are
2. explore what type of reading is expected at university
3. examine what skills are needed to become an expert reader
4. learn how to improve your reading efficiency
5. learn how to skim texts and increase your speed of reading
6. learn how to become an interactive reader.

USING THIS CHAPTER

Estimate your current levels of confidence. At the end of the chapter you will have the chance to re-assess these levels where you can incorporate this into your personal development planner (PDP). Mark between 1 (poor) and 5 (good) for the following:

I can analyse my reading skills and know my strengths and weaknesses.	I know what skills make the difference between novice and expert readers.	I know what skills are needed to make my reading more efficient.	I can interact with text and I use strategies to be an active reader.

Date: ______________

1 How do you approach reading?

In order to increase your reading potential, it is worthwhile assessing how you go about reading for study purposes. Activity 1 will help you to make the most of the different sections on reading.

ACTIVITY 1 What type of reader am I?

Number	Reading characteristic	Yes	No
1	I tend to read very little beyond what is actually required for a written assignment.		
2	I put my efforts into trying to memorise what I have read and the facts on the page.		
3	I try to relate and connect what I'm reading with ideas I have come across in other topics.		
4	When I read an article or book, I try to find out exactly what the author means.		
5	Often I find myself questioning what I read and what the author has said.		
6	When I read I concentrate on learning just those bits of information that I need to pass the assignment.		

Number	Reading characteristic	Yes	No
7	When I am reading, I stop from time to time and stand back to reflect on what I'm trying to learn from it.		
8	When I read, I examine the details carefully to see how they fit in with what is being said.		
9	I like books that challenge my ideas and thoughts and provide explanations that go beyond the lectures and seminars.		
10	I like books that give definite facts and information that can be easily understood.		
11	If I choose a journal article I read it from the start to the finish.		
12	I make notes while I am reading		

This table is based upon the ASSIST approaches to studying by Noel Entwistle (Entwistle and Tait, 1996). He differentiated between 'surface' or superficial and 'deep' or critical approaches to study. Your general approach to reading will reflect how you tackle not only this type of activity but will also have an impact upon how you go about other aspects of study. At university your tutors are looking for students who can interact with texts. This means that they want students who adopt a 'deep' as opposed to a 'surface' approach to reading and study.

Check the feedback section at the end of the chapter to find out your personal reading profile.

2 Reading beyond the school environment

Reading is one of the core skills needed beyond the school environment. Take a look at the reading lists for any courses, and you will see that academic tutors place great value on reading. In an initial lecture while I was at university, Professor Ruth Strang, an eminent linguist, said:

> *Reading proficiency is the royal road to knowledge; it is essential to success in all academic subjects. It is an entrance into almost all vocations.*

Professor Strang implies that reading is not only an essential skill which has to be used for all aspects of studying but that it can open doors to future professional success. In addition, it is an important tool to aid thinking.

Reading for academic and research purposes is very different from leisure reading. Curling up on the settee with a good book is a different experience from grappling with a journal article about cutting-edge research in your subject. With the former the choice of reading is your own and is not dictated by the course demands! Later, in Chapter 3.2, 'Finding your way around a text', you will have the opportunity to examine in more detail the different strategies you can develop to change your reading habits and to consider how to manage a variety of reading experiences. It is important that you develop and improve your skills for reading academically so that you are more efficient and can pick out relevant information more effectively. All your tutors will emphasise the need to **read critically**. What they are referring to is that they want you to consider what you are reading and weigh up what is being said. They want you to compare and evaluate what different writers have written about a topic or subject. You will be expected to form your own opinions through your reading.

To be successful you are expected to:

- select carefully from a range of reading materials both in print and electronic form
- select sections of text relevant to your task or activity
- evaluate what you are reading.

These skills will ensure that your performance is optimised but will also ensure that you can make efficient and effective use of your time. How you develop these critical reading skills is explained in the section 'Critical reading'. At college, university and at work you will be expected to get things done within tight schedules and time limits. This means that you need to develop your reading strategies so that your reading decisions and choices enable you to get the best results.

What's the difference between a novice/ inexperienced reader and an expert reader?

Expert readers are **flexible**. They employ a number of strategies and make educated decisions in the process of reading any type of text. Research by Palincsar and Brown (1984) with high school students showed that expert readers seem to be able to generate internal questions which enable them to read with understanding; to monitor their comprehension of the texts; and to evaluate and critically analyse the information on the page or on screen. Frustratingly for the inexperienced reader, these experts seem to do all of this in an effortless way. The reason is that they have internalised the complex processes so that they do not have to think about the skills and strategies they are using and about how they go about this task (Nicolson and Fawcett, 1990). In fact, many of these readers work on automatic pilot, and their brain seemed to be wired up for effective reading. Reading efficiency involves numerous aspects which the student reader needs to take account of.

3 The reading toolkit

There are three layers which should be in your reading toolkit to ensure that you can become an expert reader:

- the basic toolkit
- text ingredients
- writing communities.

Fluent, expert readers have all the above components at their fingertips. The ability to cope with texts starts with the nuts and bolts of the job: you need to have an understanding of how language is put together and how sentences work (the basic toolkit). Then you need to know about how paragraphs hang together so that you understand what the writer is getting at (text ingredients). Finally, we are all part of a writing community (writing communities). For example, the Engineering community, the Psychology community, the Archaeology community, etc. These different communities have a different way of presenting information, and it is important to know the shorthand formats used by these writers.

Most students arrive at university with some reading skills. Every student has his/her own reading habits – some good, some not so good. Like drivers who go on to advanced driving courses, the bad habits have to be eradicated, but breaking our habits is difficult at first. However, it can be productive in the long term. Identify and reflect on your reading skills in Activity 2.

ACTIVITY 2 What are your reading skills?

The following quiz will help you to reflect upon the skills you bring to your course. It will also help you identify if you have any gaps which need to be plugged. Before you come to university or as soon as you arrive, it is a good idea to do this quiz to find out what you need to do to prepare for reading academically.

Basic toolkit	Do you ...	Yes	No
	1. Know the rules of sentence structure?		
	2. Know the rules of punctuation?		
	3. Know how words are formed (the systems for word structures, e.g. simulate, simulator, assimilation)?		
Essay ingredients			
	4. Know the rules governing the structure of a paragraph?		
	5. Know about text organisation, e.g. contents, introduction, paragraphs, conclusion, etc.?		
	6. Recognise the 'glue' words which make the links in texts e.g. however, on the other hand, moreover etc.?		

Writing communities	Do you ...	Yes	No
	7. Recognise different styles of writing?		
	8. Recognise different text layouts, e.g. reports, journal articles, prose?		
	9. Recognise different language forms, e.g. figurative language, jargon, technical language?		
	10. Recognise text complexity, e.g. ambiguity and conflicting messages?		
	11. Identify writers' styles?		

Check the feedback section at the end of the chapter to find out your current level of reading skills.

4 Steps to proficiency

If you want to become a critical reader then you might like to think about how that happens. There are eight stages which highlight a person's growing expertise. However, it is not always straightforward. Once you have reached a level of skill, you may find that a new reading challenge means that you have to retrace your steps on the ladder to success and reapply some of the earlier techniques. Expert readers are constantly adjusting and readjusting to new situations, almost intuitively. Thus, they frequently reappraise their starting points. This is called a meta-cognitive or reflective approach to your reading whereby you become aware of how you tackle new and different reading experiences, making appropriate choices for how you go about the reading task. For example, if you are starting to study a subject for the first time, you will need to build up knowledge. Consequently, your choice of reading matter will be affected.

Theories about how we learn are often referred to as hierarchies, and are like steps to mastery (Bloom, 1956). This is rather like building a house. A strong and firm foundation results in a solid structure (Figure 1).

All readers start by **acquiring (1)** basic literacy skills. They need time to practise these skills and build up **fluency (2)**. Next comes a period when the reader is gaining confidence in using the skills in different reading contexts. Thus, young children will try out reading skills so that they can **generalise (3)** the skills and use them in any context. Now that the skills are in place there is a period of consolidation when the reader does not necessarily take on new reading challenges but is able to cope with many types of texts. This is the stage when the reader is **maintaining (4)** the skills and not learning new

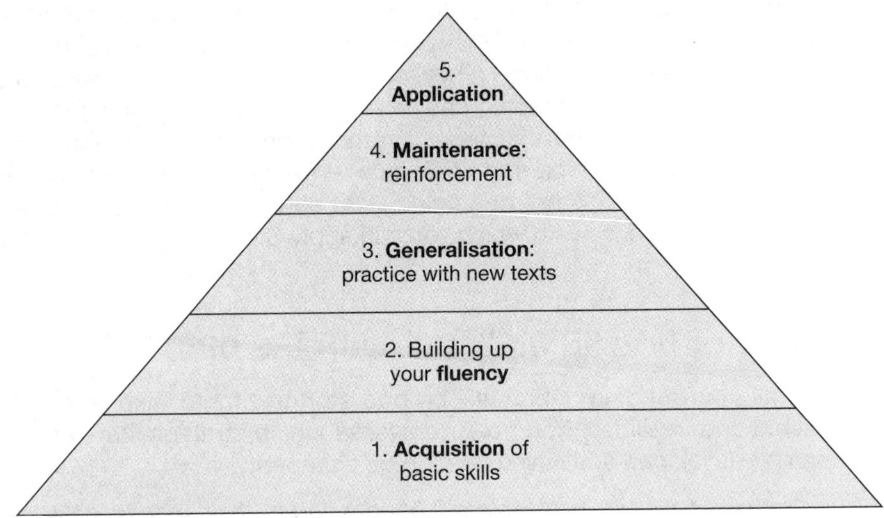

Figure 1 Steps to building up your skills

skills. The final stage in this progress is to be able to apply your literacy knowledge and skills to new contexts. At the **application (5)** stage you are able to use your skills flexibly and utilise strategies to get the most out of your reading experiences.

If your ultimate goal is to be a **critical reader**, you need all the building blocks to be in place to ensure efficiency and accuracy. The table above shows you how readers can move from novice to expert.

Reading stage	Essential building blocks to critical reading	Reading skill level
1	To build up knowledge of the topic/subject so that you understand the ideas and concepts.	Basic Novice
2	To build up your understanding of special terminology and how it is used by writers in your field.	Basic Novice
3	To be aware of the style of writing used by experts in your field.	Intermediate Novice
4	To weigh up what different writers say about a topic/subject.	Intermediate
5	To reflect upon what you have read.	Intermediate
6	To pull together different people's ideas and concepts into a cohesive framework of information and ideas – i.e. to synthesise information.	Advanced Expert
7	To evaluate the credibility of the text source.	Advanced Expert
8	To develop your own ideas from what you have read – i.e. to think critically about the ideas in the various texts.	Advanced Expert

Of course, university students, no matter which year of study they are in, need to remember that they may have to constantly reappraise where they are on this scale. When given a new assignment, you need to gauge whether your starting point for reading choices is at the 'I need to understand what they are all talking about' (Stage 1) rather than 'I am confident that I can understand the technical terminology and frameworks of ideas/concepts' (Stages 2 and 3). This will determine what sort of books you read, and the degree of confidence with which you can apply Stages 4–7.

Don't throw the baby out with the bathwater!

Not all your reading habits will be bad so it is vital to take stock of your assets and liabilities. You need to assess which strategies are useful and can be developed and which need to be changed.

> *Humans have the invaluable gift of adapting to their specific environment, and we appear to exploit all the opportunities offered for adaptation, via learning.*
>
> Nicolson and Fawcett (2001, p. 142)

However, you will need to adapt your strategies to the diverse demands placed upon you during different years of study. Therefore, you need to consider the life-cycle of studying. This refers to the different reading demands which are placed on you according to your year of study, and the knowledge you bring to a unit of study. For example, if you are new to a subject, you will have different reading demands compared with students who have been studying the same subject for three years or more. This is because you have become accustomed to the subject terminology and the style of writing. Then again, as you pick up new units of study you may need to change gear to a more basic level of reading before attempting the more critical stages. Effective and successful readers are aware of the need to reappraise their own capacity in order to approach the reading task efficiently. In other words, some reading skills are dynamic, and you have to take a proactive approach to assessing what is needed for the reading task in hand.

Do you need to improve your reading efficiency?

You are expected to do a considerable amount of reading at college or university. However, you do not have all the time in the world to conduct your reading. Therefore, it is essential that you are an efficient reader. See Activity 3 to identify your reading strategies.

ACTIVITY 3 What reading strategies do you use?

Look at these questions to find out more about the way you tackle background reading, reading for assignments, reading for literature reviews and reading to increase knowledge and understanding.

Answer 'yes' or 'no' to the following questions:

	Reading strategy	Yes	No
1	Do you read a chapter or journal article from start to finish and have a fuzzy /vague idea of what was said?		
2	Does it take you longer to complete the reading for your course, compared with your peers?		
3	Do you find that the chapters or books or articles seem to go above your head?		
4	Do you read word by word?		
5	Do you 'say' the words silently to yourself in your head as you read?		
6	Do you find you have to read and reread sections?		
7	Do you try to avoid reading complicated/advanced texts and articles?		
8	Do you vary the pace of your reading?		

No doubt you will have developed strategies for coping with reading tasks. Some of these strategies may not be efficient and may need to be examined so that new solutions can be considered. If you answered 'yes' to any of these statements, you might like to think how you can be flexible and change your strategies.

Check the feedback section at the end of the chapter to find out solutions.

Hot Tip

To help you to be more efficient and effective as an academic reader, you might need to consider one or all of the following:

1. Increasing your reading speed.
2. Finding your way around texts – i.e. gaining knowledge of how the text for your subject is put together – the hidden rules for writing in your subject which are often referred to as academic writing style. These vary according to the subject you are studying. It is important that you become part of the academic community in which you are studying. One way of doing this is to learn the correct style of communication (see Chapter 3.2, 'Finding your way around a text').
3. Making decisions about suitability of text (see Chapter 3.4, 'Managing your reading').

5 Increasing your reading speed

Urban myths about reading

If I read more slowly it will help me to understand difficult concepts and texts which seem inaccessible because of the way they are written.

Mary, first-year Engineering student

Sometimes reading slowly can impair your understanding. Slow readers are more likely to miss the point or get bogged down with minute detail.

If I read a chapter/article/section of text over and over again I will be able to understand the concepts.

Kate, second-year Chemistry student

Perhaps you are tackling a text which is too difficult initially for you or perhaps you have no clear idea of what it is that you want to get out of the text and are simply reading as a large sponge!

How fast do you read?

- Did you know that the average university student can read at 250 words per minute?
- Did you know that efficient readers can skim a block of words in less than a quarter of a second?

Try Activity 4.

ACTIVITY 4 The speed test

- Choose a passage to read which is unfamiliar to you. You may wish to use one of your recommended course books.
- Time yourself for 10 minutes.
- Count how many words your have read in this time.
- Divide your total by 10.
- Your answer will tell you how many words per minute you can read comfortably.

If it is less than 150 words per minute you need to work on this skill.

Of course, you must remember that personal reading speeds vary according to the complexity of the text and its novelty for you. If you pick up a chapter in a children's textbook about your subject, your reading speed will be high because of your own level of knowledge in relation to the complexity (or otherwise) of the text. However, if you read a cutting-edge journal article which goes into great detail about the intricacies of a new theory, your reading speed will naturally slow down to cope with the complicated sentence structures and very specific use of key technical terminology.

Increasing reading speed

Train yourself to ...	**Try this ...**
Read faster	The more you practise reading quickly, the better you can become. Try to increase your rate by choosing texts which are easy to start with.
Increase the amount of information your reading brain can take in. You can 'see' words out of the corner of your eyes. This is how you use your 'peripheral' vision.	Try reading a phrase at a time rather than individual words. With practice, you can increase the length of phrases you read at speed.
Read more quickly to improve comprehension.	Read a difficult section quickly twice. This is better than reading it slowly once!
Improve the flow of reading.	Avoid backtracking when reading. Backtracking is when your read and reread a few words or a section. This interrupts the speed at which you understand information.
Recognise the 'look' of new terminology.	Practise reading lists of key subject words. Time this activity – allow 5 minutes per day when encountering new terminology.
Avoid 'sounding out' words in your head as you read.	Give your eyes and brain practice at just looking at the words. Try to get your eyes to move forward and time yourself to see how quickly you can get to the end of the line or the next full stop.

Speed readers can read both vertically and horizontally because they are absorbing information visually and letting their brain take in many pieces of evidence at the same time. Many now appreciate the value of power walking for making the body more efficient. 'Power browsing' is the equivalent in reading and can help you to 'digest' the main themes of a book in 10 minutes! There are many websites which you can visit which will help you to improve and increase your reading speed. Some sites provide free trials of materials for a week, e.g. **www.speed-read-now.com** or **www.mindtools.com/speedrd.html**. You can also purchase software which gives exercises to increase your reading rates, e.g. **www.acereader.com**. Tony Buzan's books give many tips and practical hints, e.g. *Speed Reading* (Buzan, 2006).

6 How to get a quick overview (or skimming text)

Skimming is a particular style of reading. It is a way of gathering as much information as possible from text in the shortest time possible. Skimming is primarily a **visual activity** and is used for getting the gist or impression of a chapter/section of text. You are not reading the whole page in the usual way, and your eyes do not move from left to right along the line as they do when reading a whole text.

How to skim text

Skimming (Figure 2) is one of those reading strategies which takes confidence, and many novice readers have little expertise with the skill. It is rather like letting go of the sides of the swimming pool when you are a novice swimmer! Many people read in their head – in other words they say the words silently to themselves. This process often helps readers to remember and understand what they are reading. However, with skimming the brain takes in the information in a different way. It uses only the visual clues to gather up the text on the page.

Expert skimmers tend to look for key words, nouns (these inform the reader what the content and information is), verbs (these give the reader clues about the relationship between the nouns) and link words in that order to help them get a quick overview. Examples of link words are: however, thus, on the other hand, etc. They are the glue of the text and help to stick the text together in a specific manner, depending upon the viewpoint or arguments which the writer wishes to put across.

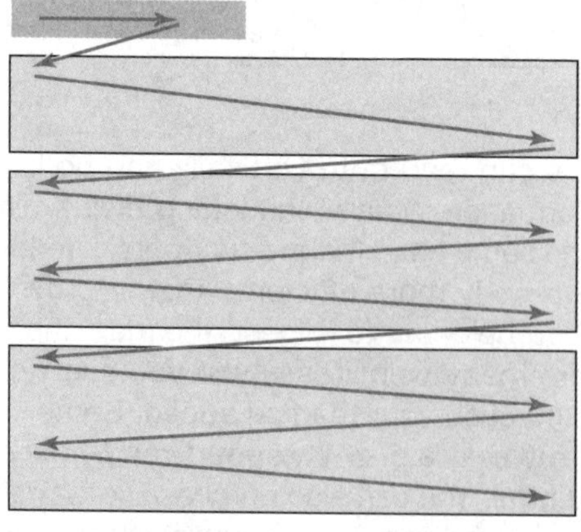

Figure 2 Example of eye movements during skimming

Skimming is useful to help you make decisions about whether a text is useful for your assignment. It also vital for those learners who like to have the big picture so that they can fit all the fine details into a framework. Skimming can be used on a book, a chapter or even a section of text.

The expert skimmer

Let's look at the way an expert skimmer operates.

> ***Skin re-growth***
> *There are specific age cycles with human skin. Between the ages of 15 and 25, apart from the odd blemish, the skin has a youthful look to it. It can take a beating with too much sun, alcohol and convenience food and still look good. This is because the cell growth is rapid during these ages and can occur on a 19-day cycle.*

This reader has picked out the shaded words and sent this information to the brain via a visual fast-track route. Notice that some of the 'glue' words help to make the highlighted information make sense: 'between', 'too much', 'still' and 'because'.

Try this for yourself with a passage from a newspaper. Choose a topic in which you have some interest and try to stop yourself from reading the words silently to yourself.

On-screen skimming

Of course, computers can speed up and support the skimming idea. You can make technology work for you by using the 'Find' facility with texts. In this way you can get the software to search for key words with a piece of text. Try it out with an electronic journal article. Copy and paste a section from the article and place it in a Word document. Now go to '**Edit**' on the top tool bar and then go to '**Find**'. You will get a dialogue box, and you can ask it to find specified key words. Thus, you can find out if the text is going to be of use for a specific assignment, for example.

7 Are you an interactive reader?

One of the skills which differentiates the expert from the novice reader is the degree to which the reader interacts with the text. Have you ever considered **doing** things to ensure that your reading is effective and that you become more efficient in the process? Expert readers prepare their mind to receive information and to select information from text before they even get to the reading materials.

Before reading – ask yourself some questions

Before you launch into reading a chapter or section or journal article, you may need to remind yourself to **preview and predict**. Try out Activity 5. The more you make this part of your reading routine, the more you will get out of your reading.

ACTIVITY 5 Priming the brain to read

Try out this activity to increase your preview and prediction skills.

Choose a chapter or a journal article which your tutor has set for essential reading to try this out.

Chapter/article title: **Why am I reading this?** (Cross-reference to Chapter 3.3, 'Reading critically')	**List what I have to find out.**	**What do I already know?** (Will this text fill in my gaps of knowledge/ understanding?)	**Is this the most appropriate text for this purpose?** (Cross-reference to Chapter 3.4, 'Managing your reading')
Prompt: • Because I need to build up my knowledge of the subject? • Because I need to find out very specific information for an essay? • Other:	**Prompt**: • Check with your tutor's instructions • Check instructions in handbooks about a specified task. • Other:	**Prompt**: List brief details of facts etc. which you already have	**Prompt**: Go back to your reason for reading the text in the first place to answer this one. Do not be blinkered. Is this the only text or are there others I need to consult?

During reading – mark up your texts

If you want to keep your concentration levels high, then mark up texts while you are reading them. This activity ensures that you are thinking about and interacting with the message contained in the text in front of you. Many students find that it is useful **to colour-code information** because this helps them to categorise information. To do this most effectively you will need to photocopy sections of text which you think are most relevant and crucial to your work. As you are reading you will have to make decisions about what sort of information it is in order to code it. This means that you will be interacting more with the text rather than being a surface reader who applies a superficial approach and allows the information to flow over the brain without being grabbed and processed in some way.

Decisions about colour coding can only be made effectively if you know your purpose for reading and what it is that you are looking for (see Activity 5 above). For example, you may want to code the main ideas in one colour in a section or paragraph and the evidence or examples or subsidiary information in another colour.

- You may want to pick out key references and names and use codes to categorise these.
- Some students find that they like to code the author's opinions in one colour and the inferred information in another.

As you can see there are many ways in which you can be creative to make you question what you are reading and to help you make more effective notes.

8 Developing reading strategies

There are many ways of becoming more interactive with your texts. A popular method is the SQ3R method. It stands for:

- **S**urvey
- **Q**uestion
- **R**ead
- **R**ecall
- **R**eview.

First of all you need to get a taste of the chapter/article you have chosen to read so you will need to skim the text to see if it is suitable for your purpose (**survey**).

Next, ask yourself why you are reading the text and what you want to get out of it so that you read with a specific focus. Your comprehension improves if your mind is actively searching for answers to questions (**question**).

Then, read carefully, breaking up your reading into small sections, looking for main ideas (**read**).

After this, mentally go through the ideas you have just read and pick out the main points. Check that you can answer your initial questions. Check that you have assimilated and gathered the information you need (**recall**).

Finally, look back to see if the passage has answered everything you wanted. How much can you remember (**review**)?

Once you learn to read, that's the end of it

The important thing to remember is that reading is a dynamic process and that your skills develop throughout life. The skills and strategies needed by 5-year-olds when reading are different from those of first-year undergraduates. Similarly, reading success at university is dependent upon the realisation that different skills are needed at different times on the course. You are constantly developing new skills and strategies. You will be presented with new reading challenges throughout your study, and this will call for the need to assess what is needed and to reappraise how you go about the reading aspect of study. Thus, it is vital that you revisit some of the questionnaires and quizzes at different times and in different years.

Horses for courses

The way you tackle the reading for an activity or task hinges upon:

- the type of activity it is – e.g. finding out about some new subject concepts or reading notes for revision
- the requirements of the assignment/task – e.g. giving a critique of one specified journal article draws upon different skills from analysing the role of Disraeli in his political leadership
- what knowledge and expertise **you** bring to the reading task.

It is vital, therefore, that you recognise the purpose of your reading activity and what it is **you** want to get from the text. Remember you do not often read a newspaper from the front page to the last. If you want the sports results and news, you will go to that section or you will search quickly for that information and skip the rest.

9 On reflection

Reading skills at college or university level are complex. Experts are constantly reappraising their skill level and making necessary adjustments to cope with the type of reading activity and its demands. Knowing the skills you need and your current level of expertise is a sure way to becoming a successful and efficient reader.

Summary of this chapter

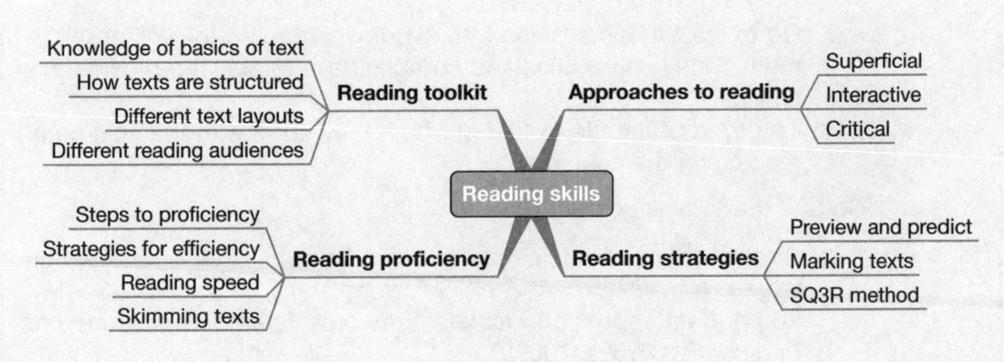

ACTIVITY 6 Update your personal development planner

Becoming an expert reader involves an awareness that reading is not a passive activity. Expert readers draw upon a range of skills to ensure that they are efficient. They do this by adopting a flexible approach to the way they tackle texts and, most importantly, they make a conscious effort to prompt the brain to interact with texts so that they are tapping into critical reading skills to get the most out of the information in front of them. Expert readers employ strategies to ensure that their reading time is time well spent.

Now reflect upon how you go about reading tasks and how you intend to change and adapt your reading habits so that you can spend your time more effectively. You may want to transfer this information to your own institution's personal development planner scheme.

Grade your confidence on a scale of 1–5 where 1 = poor and 5 = good.

My developing skills	Confidence level 1–5	Plans to improve
I can analyse my reading skills and know my strengths and weaknesses.		
I know what skills make the difference between novice and expert readers.		
I know what skills are needed to make my reading more efficient.		
I can interact with text and I use strategies to be an active reader.		

Date: ___________________

Getting extra help

- Go to the Students Union to find out where to go for skill development. Many universities and colleges have tutors who provide this service.
- Talk to your friends to find out how they cope with the volume of reading for the course.

Consult the following:

- Books which will help you to learn or revise how punctuation works, e.g. *Oxford A–Z of Grammar and Punctuation* (Seeley, 2004). *Eats shoots and leaves: The Zero Tolerance Approach to Punctuation* (Truss, 2005).
- A book on basic grammar and punctuation, e.g. *English Words: History and Structure* (Stockwell and Minkova, 2001)
- A book to help you to increase your reading speed is Tony Buzan's book *Speed Reading: Accelerate your speed and understanding for success*. It gives many tips and practical hints.

Feedback on activities

ACTIVITY 1 What type of reader am I?

What is your reading profile: are you a surface or deep reader?

If you have answered 'yes' to all or most of questions: 1, 2, 6, 10, 11, 12:

You are adopting a **surface approach** to your reading. You are organising your learning in order to be able to remember facts and figures to use in written assignments or dissertation work.

If you have ticked 'yes' for 1:

You may be missing out on some important information which can help you to understand your subject. You may have chosen this strategy because you are not a confident reader. Chapter 3.2, 'Finding your way around a text', will help increase your skills. However, this approach may be the result of poor time management. In this case, go to Chapter 1.2, 'Managing your time' and Chapter 3.4, 'Managing your reading'.

If you have ticked 'yes' for 2, 6 and 12:

You need to learn how to be a critical reader so that you do not concentrate solely on the specifics of a text and to increase your reading horizons. Chapter 3.3 on 'Critical Reading' will help you to augment your skills.

If you have ticked 'yes' for 10 and 11:

You need to increase your reading skills and strategies so that you can read more efficiently. Read all the sections in this chapter.

If you have answered 'yes' to all or most of questions: 3, 4, 5, 7, 8 and 9:

You are adopting a **deep approach** to your reading. You are thinking critically about the information you read and trying to make sense of it in the wider context of your studies. This approach to learning and studying shows initiative and understanding. Nevertheless, you can increase your efficiency by looking in particular at the Chapters 3.3, 'Reading critically' and 3.4, 'Managing your reading'.

ACTIVITY 2 What are your reading skills?

Basic toolkit	Do you ...	Yes	No
	1. Know the rules of sentence structure?		
	2. Know the rules of punctuation?		
	3. Know how words are formed (the systems for word structures, e.g. simulate, simulator, assimilation)?		
Essay ingredients			
	4. Know the rules governing the structure of a paragraph?		
	5. Know about text organisation, e.g. contents, i ntroduction, paragraphs, conclusion, etc.?		
	6. Recognise the 'glue' words which make the links in texts e.g. however, on the other hand, moreover etc.?		
Writing communities			
	7. Recognise different styles of writing?		
	8. Recognise different text layouts, e.g. reports, journal articles, prose?		
	9. Recognise different language forms, e.g. figurative language, jargon, technical language?		
	10. Recognise text complexity, e.g. ambiguity and conflicting messages?		
	11. Identify writers' styles?		

If you have ticked 'no' to 1 and 2:

You may have difficulty understanding and getting the gist of what you are reading. Your reading could be slowed down while you try to figure out what you have read. Punctuation can be a subtle indicator of the author's underlying or hidden meaning. Think about how your understanding changes when the author makes compound words by using a hyphen, e.g. notice the difference in meaning when the hyphen is added: (a) a little used boat and (b) a little-used boat. The first suggests a small boat which has been used whereas the second tells us that the boat has hardly been used. If you are not aware of these changes in meaning by the use of punctuation, you may be missing out on subtle nuances of the author's message. There are many books which will help you to learn or revise how punctuation works, e.g. *Oxford A–Z of Grammar and Punctuation* by John Seely; and *Eats Shoots and Leaves: The Zero Tolerance Approach to Punctuation* by Lynne Truss.

If you have ticked 'no' to 3:

If you know the derivation of words, it can help your understanding and speed of comprehending a difficult text. It means that you can work out things for yourself. It is worth purchasing a book on basic grammar and punctuation, e.g. *English Words: History and Structure* by Robert Stockwell and Donka Minkova.

If you have ticked 'no' to 4, 5 and 6:

You may find that your understanding of the whole text is inaccurate. In addition, you will be slowed down in finding your way around the texts and pulling out information that you need. Go to Chapter 3.2 on 'Finding your way around a text'.

If you have ticked 'no' to 7–11:

You need to increase your critical reading skills. Go to Chapter 3.3, 'Reading Critically'.

ACTIVITY 3 What reading strategies do you use?

	Reading strategy:	Solution
1	Do you read a chapter or journal article from start to finish and have a fuzzy/vague idea of what was said?	Set reading targets. Ask yourself what information you are looking for. Read a section which you think gives you the information you need. Read a short section, cover up the text, write brief notes about what you think you have understood and read. Then check your notes with the text.
2	Does it take you a long time to do the reading for your course?	You might be choosing texts which are too advanced for you at this time. Focus your reading more by posing questions to which you require answers. Set manageable targets. Give yourself some questions so that you can find out the answers.

	Reading strategy:	Solution
3	Do you find that the chapters or books or articles seem to go above your head?	You might be choosing texts which are too advanced for you at this time.
4	Do you read word by word?	You might be choosing texts which are too advanced for you at this time. Build up your self-confidence as an academic reader. Do this by letting your eye flow over a phrase at a time. Practise this with magazines and newspapers.
5	Do you 'say' the words silently to yourself in your head as you read?	Build up your self-confidence as an academic reader. Do this by letting your eye flow over a phrase at a time. Practise this with magazines and newspapers.
6	Do you find you have to read and reread sections?	This might be because you are tired or have lost concentration. If you are tired, take a short rest. If you have lost concentration, you need to reset your focus and set yourself new and possibly shorter targets. Ask yourself what you think the section is going to be about before you read it and then check to see if you are correct. You might be choosing texts which are too advanced for you at this time.
7	Do you try to avoid reading complicated/ advanced texts and articles?	It is the flexible and effective reader who makes appropriate decisions about the level of the text to read.
8	Do you vary the pace of your reading?	To start with, make a conscious effort to monitor your pace of reading. Evaluate its effectiveness. Then adjust according to the task.

References

Bloom, B.S. (ed.) (1956) *Taxonomy of Educational Objectives: The Classification of Educational Goals: Handbook I, Cognitive Domain*. New York, Toronto, Longmans, Green.

Buzan, T. (2006) *Speed Reading: Accelerate Your Speed and Understanding for Success*, 3rd edn. London: BBC Active.

Entwistle, N. and Tait, H. (1996) *Approaches and Study Skills Inventory for Students*. Edinburgh, Centre for Research on Learning and Instruction, University of Edinburgh.

Nicolson, R. and Fawcett, A. (1990) 'Automaticity: a new framework for dyslexia research', *Cognition*, 35, pp. 159–82.

Nicolson, R. and Fawcett, A. (2001) 'Dyslexia as a learning disability', in A. Fawcett, (ed.) (2001) *Dyslexia: Good Theory and Practice*. London, Whurr.

Palincsar, A. and Brown, A. (1984) ‘Reciprocal teaching of comprehension-fostering and comprehension-monitoring activities’, *Cognition and Instruction*, 1, pp. 117–75.

Seely, J. (2004) *The Oxford A–Z of Grammar and Punctuation*. Oxford, Oxford University Press.

Strang, R. (1967) *The Improvement of Reading*, 4th edn. Maidenhead, McGraw-Hill.

Stockwell, R. and Minkova, D. (2001) *English Words: History and Structure*. Cambridge, Cambridge university Press.

Truss, L. (2005) *Eats Shoots and Leaves: The Zero Tolerance Approach to Punctuation*. London, Profile Books.

3.2 Finding your way around text

There are many skills which expert readers use to get information from text. SMART readers will apply reasoning and thought:

- Which texts?
- Which sections are important?
- What is the writer getting at?

In order to decide if the chapter/book/journal article needs further study, you need to be able to get a quick overview. This overview will enable you to decide if the text is appropriate to your current task. However, these decisions are best made if you know your way around the type of texts you are directed to read by your academic tutors. If you are not sure what this means or how to do this, this section will give you guidance.

In this chapter you will:

1. find out about the purpose of different types of texts
2. learn about the ingredients of texts
3. become aware of the features of journal article layout.

USING THIS CHAPTER

Estimate your current levels of confidence. At the end of the chapter you will have the chance to re-assess these levels where you can incorporate this into your personal development planner (PDP). Mark between 1 (poor) and 5 (good) for the following:

I know the purpose of the text layouts.	I can find my way around (navigate) text to access the information I need.	I am aware of how text is constructed (text ingredients).

Date: ______________

1 Maximising efficiency

Taking into account the volume of reading you are expected to do while at university and the other aspects of studying for your units and course, time management and reading efficiency play crucial roles in ensuring that you cope with the course demands. Consequently, the effort you put into your reading should get the best results in terms of your time and the quality of information which you extract from texts.

It is possible to take short-cuts without watering down the quality of information access. This is achieved not only by developing reading speed and fluency but also by being able to navigate your way effectively and efficiently around your texts. You will be able to navigate more confidently if you are aware of how authors construct texts.

2 Finding your way around texts

As a reader you do not always consciously take note of the rules of text construction because you are concentrating more upon the message contained in the text. However, if you are to negotiate texts more efficiently, it is well worth while exploring how they are put together. Refer to Section 4, 'Text ingredients', to see the function of the various components of the text.

Finding your way around texts is often reliant upon:

- your knowledge of how texts are assembled and put together – in other words, the style of the text format
- your understanding and experience of the writing style of the type of texts with which you will have most contact.

You can increase your reading speed and improve your comprehension by being familiar with the way text is written for your subject. This is called 'genre' or the style of the text. You might also examine how the text is organised; and how the author has analysed (broken down) the material in order to set up an argument. Be aware that different disciplines (e.g. engineering, sociology, philosophy, psychology, neurology, etc.) will have different ways of arguing so the text may be set out in a different format and adhere to different 'rules'.

Different types of texts

Expert readers are able to navigate texts more quickly than novice readers and one of the reasons for this is that they know what to expect from different types of texts. In other words, they can recognise the hidden features of a text so that they are aware of the purpose of the text, and what they can get out of the text. The types of texts which are commonly found in university materials are summarised in the following table:

Type of text	Purpose	Typical contexts	General features
Discursive	To argue or persuade the reader	Social Studies/Sociology English History Geography Philosophy Law Health Sciences Environmental Sciences	Thesis or hypothesis Arguments Examples/back-up information Conclusions
Report	To classify information To present findings To record data and procedures	Education Engineering Health Sciences Chemistry Psychology Tourism and Leisure	Objective account Often contains graphical and statistical information interspersed with prose Many reports are procedural, such as journal articles
Narrative	To write a story or fictitious accounts in order to entertain the reader	English Media Studies	Text often contains inferential material Development of plot and characterisation

Authors tend to write using a type of text which is most suited to the subject material. Consequently, you will be exposed to one of the above types more than others. Whilst text layout for these different types varies, there are, nevertheless, general rules about communication so that the author's message is coherent.

3 Text features

One of the skills of the SMART reader (**S**kill **M**anagement in **A**cademic work through **R**easoning and **T**hinking) is to be able to move around text quickly in order to locate the information required. You need to get to know the type of text you are most likely to come into contact with, where specific information is found and how it is presented to the reader. Try Activity 1.

ACTIVITY 1 Text features and layout

Here are some things for you to think about when examining text to find your way around more efficiently:

1. Choose a text which your tutors expect you to read for your studies.
2. Analyse the text using the questions in the table below.

Chapter	Book title			
	Text features and layout	**Yes**	**No**	**Sometimes**
1	Are chapter summaries usually found at the beginning?			
2	Are chapter summaries usually found at the end?			
3	Are the chapters broken down into appropriate sub-sections?			
4	Do the sub-heading titles give me a summary/overview of the section?			
5	Is there a revision section at the end of each chapter?			
6	Is key terminology presented in: bold italics as a separate glossary?			
7	Does each section contain a summary sentence/statement at the: beginning end both?			
8	After the summary sentence/statement, does each section provide any or all of the following to explain information further: subsidiary and supporting material evidence examples?			

Chapter/ article title:	Text features and layout	Yes	No	Sometimes
9	Are diagrammatic features used to explain prose text?			
10	Are tables and graphs used to explain prose text?			
11	Is the sequencing of the information obvious in the text layout?			
12	Does the text rely upon: fairly simple sentences complex sentences?			
13	Does the bibliography contain books on my reading list?			

Finding the answers to the above points will mean that you have to examine the way text is put together for your subject. This will help with comprehension and speed of access to information. In the next section we will take a look at how a text is constructed.

4 Text ingredients

Maximising the Earth's resources

Summary or topic sentence ←	Biodiversity is the interactivity of diverse plant and animal life in a particular habitat in order to sustain equilibrium in the ecosystem.
Brief, factual information about the topic to be read	A look at invertebrates can demonstrate some of this complexity. Invertebrates are known as ectotherms and are dependent upon their environment for many metabolic functions. Scientists are beginning to investigate ways of preventing disease in invertebrates and in doing so can demonstrate that they may be part of a large food pyramid.
Supplementary example to back up topic sentence	Giant millipedes are an example of this. Most live in moist rainforests and eat decaying plant material. As they forage for food they become covered in parasitic mites. Human natural instinct would be to kill these small parasites because they
Further example, Note the language prompt: 'on the other hand'. This tells the reader that conflicting information follows	are thought to be harmful and irritating to the host. However, in millipedes they perform a vital role: they eat the fungi which grow in the joints. If the mites were killed, then fatal fungal infections would develop in the millipedes. On the other hand, in another species mites can be harmful. Varroa mites can infest bees and have been found to be irritants.
Conclusion sentence ←	Thus, scientists need to examine the role of parasites in the ecosystems to provide stable biodiversity for the future.

As you can see, sentences have a function in the text and this is the way that an author can guarantee that the text fits together, or, in other words, that it has **coherence**. Activity 2 asks you to analyse one of your unit/course texts.

ACTIVITY 2 Analyse one of your texts

Choose a section of a chapter from one of the books on your reading list and fill in the table below.

Text ingredient	Write example from text
Topic sentence	
Introductory information	
Supplementary example information	
Further example/opposing view	
Conclusion sentence	

Hot Tip

Not all texts are perfectly written! Some writers do not always think of their readers so you might find a text does not follow these 'good practice' guidelines. Therefore, if you can't find your way around sections of text it might not be your fault at all. Of course, in the main your tutors will try to guide you to texts which are well written but there may be an occasion when the only text available is not perfectly constructed.

How authors manipulate text

I don't know how to spot an argument or a theory when I'm reading. This is a serious drawback, and it means that I waste time worrying about what I'm reading.

Phil, first-year Chemistry student

Most of the texts that you will be expected to read at university reflect the author's ideas or thoughts. In some cases, the author takes an idea and presents it to his/her reader to provide factual information. However, in most cases, the ideas are related to current thinking and theories with the result that they are placed within a context of research and debate.

If a text is well written you will find that there is a well-established line of reasoning which should be obvious to the reader. The order and sequence of the evidence or factual information should be clear so that you can understand what the author is getting at and the points being made. To do this, expert writers will express their point of view (often referred to as their 'position') and then will proceed to select arguments or ideas to confirm and strengthen this. For example, 'Intelligence can be measured'. Such a statement would be followed by evidence to support this position.

To bolster a point of view or to try to persuade the reader, the author may draw upon theories (something which has been proved), arguments (reasons for or against) and truths (propositions which are well founded). In some scientific subjects theory is often referred to as a law. For example, the law of quantum physics.

Thus, you have to be alert to different types of information. SMART readers will be on the look-out for a statement which proposes a theory, position or argument, in the knowledge that subsequent sentences will provide examples and back-up to try to persuade the reader or simply to inform.

5 Reading journal articles

Many students find reading journal articles more difficult than textbooks and are daunted by the fact that journal articles are written by current experts in their field of study and sometimes their own lecturers. However, this source of information can be worth considering because many universities, for example, provide students with electronic access to journal articles. This can be useful when making notes about what you have read. (See Chapter 2.1, 'Making notes'.)

It is useful to adopt a twofold approach to reading an article:

1. **Read quickly to find out the main ideas and findings of the article**.
   - Read the **abstract**, which contains an overview of the article.
   - Read the **summary and conclusions**. If the article does not have a

summary, look at the titles, sub-headings and the **discussion section** of the article. As you read ask yourself whether the information is relevant to your own reading purpose or research. Will it be useful for your assignment?

2. **Read more thoroughly to familiarise yourself with the details.**
   - Ask yourself questions and search for the answers in order to focus your reading.
   - Read the article critically and analyse and evaluate the findings.

The abstract can be used not only to give you a snapshot of the article but also to guide you to the intended order or sequence of the article.

As soon as you told me that the abstract was a mini framework of the article, I was more prepared for what to expect and also for the order in which it would be presented. This made a big difference to the amount of time I spent reading the article.

Andy, second-year Psychology student

Locating the information you need quickly is part of your management technique as a SMART reader. For example, if you want to find out about the implications of the research, you would home in on the 'Discussion' section. Therefore, realising the hidden function of the different sections could save you valuable time and enable you to buy yourself some thinking time for critical reading. Look at the table below then tackle Activity 3.

Article sections	Author's purpose
Abstract	A summary of the article. It should contain the rationale for the study as well as the main results and a statement about interpretation of the results.
Introduction/background	This section will put the context of the article. It will often contain the researcher's position or the premise of the article. If the article is exploring a new or specific point of view, the theoretical context will be introduced so that the reader can relate the author's findings/ideas to earlier research. The hypothesis or the main argument is usually set out in this section so that the reader has some sort of anchor for the subsequent sections.
Methods	Much will depend upon the type of article you are reading as to the presentation of information in this section. If the research describes and explains clinical experiments, then the design of the experiments will be detailed. For example, the number and type of participants will be described. This section should also indicate the different methods used. For example, case studies, participant observation, etc. This is useful information when comparing two articles to interpret the reliability (or otherwise) of the research. This section may be omitted if the article is not an experiment-type of research. For example, the article may be a philosophical discussion of a theory or premise.

Article sections	Author's purpose
Results/findings	This section presents data (often in statistical format). However, social sciences' research may present qualitative findings. For example, pupils' perceptions of discipline in the classroom. This type of data may not be suitable for statistical analysis. This section is often descriptive.
Discussion	This section provides the reader with the researcher's interpretation of the results. In this section, the author may try to persuade the reader to a way of thinking. Sometimes, this section will be critical of the way in which the research was conducted so that the reader is aware of any flaws.
Conclusions/summary	This section will provide the reader with a snapshot of the research but also will give the implications of the research.

ACTIVITY 3 Navigating my way around a journal article

Armed with the information from the table above, now see how you can extract information efficiently from a journal article.

Name of article Article sections	Note down information
Abstract	
Introduction/background	
Methods	
Results/findings	
Discussion	
Conclusions/summary	

You can enhance your reading speed and understanding by getting to grips with the technical terminology. The sooner you start to tackle this the better. Key words are used as a sort of shorthand in communicating with others in the field. It is vital that you learn how they are specifically defined in your subject. Look out for glossaries of technical words and have these by your side when tackling new and difficult texts. You will be surprised how quickly you can get on top of this by frequent use and constant reminders of the meanings.

6 On reflection

Taking control of your reading means that you have to be aware of how the texts you frequently deal with work. This means that you have to have knowledge of how writers structure texts and what the hidden rules of structure are. This chapter helps you to analyse how texts are constructed and how to navigate these texts more efficiently.

Summary of this chapter

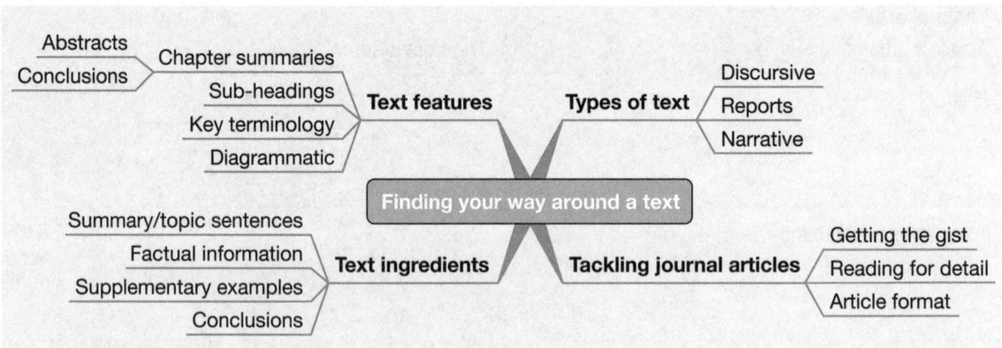

ACTIVITY 4 Update your personal development planner

Having read this chapter, gauge your confidence again – how does this compare with your confidence levels at the start of the chapter? What can you do to improve? You can incorporate this into your own personal development planner and of course add anything else you feel appropriate.

Grade your confidence on a scale of 1–5 where 1 = poor and 5 = good.

My developing skills	Confidence level 1–5	Plans to improve
I know the purpose of the text layouts.		
I can find my way around (navigate) text to access the information I need.		
I am aware of how text is constructed (text ingredients).		

Date: ______________

Getting extra help

- Go to the Students Union to find out where to go for skill development. Many universities and colleges have tutors who provide this service.

Consult a few interesting websites:

- A simple guide to reading journal articles, at: **www.coun.uvic.ca/learn/program/hndouts/Readtxt.html**.
- This page will help you to understand in more detail how to read critically a journal article: **www.oandp.org/jpo/library/1996_01_024.asp**. It takes you through the elements of an article and gets you to think about questions to ask as you read.
- If you need to read scientific articles you might like to browse this short information page: **www.fiu.edu/~collinsl/Article%20reading%20tips.htm**.

3.3 Reading critically

Critical reading is an essential aspect of academic study at university. It is more than reading all the entries on your reading list. Developing a critical approach to what you read will not only assist you in getting better grades, but will also be a skill that you will need for your professional career.

Critical reading involves flexibility and interactivity. You will take control of your reading in a way that enables you to develop your thinking in your subject.

In this chapter you will learn:

1. what skills are involved in critical reading
2. how to develop strategies to increase your interaction with texts
3. what is meant by 'inferential' reading
4. the best questions to use to interrogate texts
5. how to judge information you got from Internet reading.

USING THIS CHAPTER

Estimate your current levels of confidence. At the end of the chapter you will have the chance to re-assess these levels where you can incorporate this into your personal development planner (PDP). Mark between 1 (poor) and 5 (good) for the following.

I know what skills are involved in critical reading.	I know how to interact with texts.	I know how to read between the lines when reading.	I know the best questions to interrogate texts.	I know how to judge information I read on the Internet.

Date: ______________

What is the added value in reading?

When you get to university it will be constantly impressed upon you that tutors expect high-flying students to have that extra something. That something is the ability to demonstrate your critical thinking skills. This is done in two main ways: by being a critical reader (which is explored in this chapter) and by communicating your thoughts and ideas in written format in a critical manner (see Chapter 4.1, Section 3, 'The writing process'). If you look at the rubric for assessment criteria, you will notice phrases such as 'critical evaluation' and 'critical analysis' frequently appear in the descriptors for a First class or 2:1 degree. Students who can show that they have this capacity for dealing with information and resources are awarded more marks. Critical skills are the qualities which are often looked for by employers, no matter what profession you decide to take up. These qualities encompass:

- flexibility of working
- ability to question
- ability to analyse information
- capacity for independent thought
- an interactive approach to information and resources.

These are the underlying qualities that you will see in many of the chapters in this book.

1 What does critical reading mean?

They keep mentioning critical reading. But what are they getting at? I just read.

First-year Biological Sciences student

In a survey of academic skills at Southampton University (Price, 2001), the gulf between what the academic tutors expected of their students and the skills the students thought were needed for study was great. Academic tutors expect their students to be able to 'interact' with the texts. When your tutors talk about interacting with the texts, they are referring to readers who can question, reflect upon and evaluate what they are reading. You may even hear them talking about 'metacognition', which is simply a way of saying that you are in control of your learning and that you are making positive, reflective decisions at all times. A high level of reading autonomy is assumed (Barnett, 1997; Peverly *et al*., 2002).

Gaining high grades for your assignments involves your ability to engage with text in **a critical manner**. Most tutors will tell you that you will be expected to:

- understand the content of a variety of texts
- reflect upon what writers have said
- evaluate what you have read from different sources
- develop your own ideas
- use reading to develop your thinking.

Quite a tall order when you are bombarded by information, recommended reading and electronic resources.

Critical approaches to study are, therefore, vital. Much of this is to do with the way you interact with text whether it is text which you have generated or text in books, journals etc. Critical reading usually occurs when students have a working knowledge and understanding of the issues, theories or topics they are studying.

To read critically is to make judgements about *how* a text is argued. This is a highly reflective skill requiring you to 'stand back' and gain some distance from the text you are reading. You might have to read a text through once to get a basic grasp of content before you launch into intensive critical reading.

These are the keys:

- Don't read looking only or primarily for **information** (surface approach).
- Do read looking for **ways of thinking** about subject matter (deep approach).

You might like to refresh your memory about the eight stages of reading development which will support critical reading. If you intend to change your reading habits and wish to become a critical reader then you must consider how you can engage more with your texts.

2 Are you an active reader?

The key to success is being an **active** reader rather than someone who passively lets the information flow over them. To check your level of interaction with texts you should go back to Activity 1, 'What type of reader am I?' in Chapter 3.1.

Professor Noel Entwistle, a prominent researcher into how people learn, has been conducting studies for many years into what makes students tick and how they go about the business of studying (1991, 1992). His notion of 'surface' and 'deep' learners which is explained in Chapter 3.1 can be applied to the way you approach your academic reading.

Are you a surface or a deep reader?

Can you see the difference between the two approaches?

Surface approach = memorisation of facts/information

Deep approach = understanding of facts/information

All students should use both approaches at some time. If you understand your subject material fully you will be able to apply it successfully in your reading approach and your written work.

Characteristics of a surface approach to reading are:

- memorise information needed for assessment and assignments
- not able to distinguish principles/concepts from examples
- treat reading task as an activity which is imposed upon you by your tutors
- focus on the details without being able to integrate these into the 'big picture'
- no self-awareness of how you go about reading tasks.

Characteristics of a deep approach to reading are:

- intention to understand what the author is getting at
- vigorous interaction with content – constantly asking questions
- relate new ideas to previous knowledge
- relate concepts to everyday experience
- relate evidence to conclusions
- examine the logic of the argument.

Undergraduate as well as postgraduate students are expected to become **critical** readers and develop a 'deep' approach to reading. Relating this to 'Steps to proficiency', in Chapter 3.1, shows how you can build up your expertise. This means that you have to try to reach level 8 of the reading levels. How do you interact with texts? Try Activity 1.

ACTIVITY 1 How do I interact with texts?

How do you interact with the text you are reading?	Yes	No
1. Do you know exactly what you are looking for?		
2. Can you select important and/or relevant information for your purpose?		
3. Can you pick out key words and/or information?		
4. Do you use the same styles of reading, whatever the task?		
5. Do you soak up the information and then wonder what to do with it?		
6. Do you regularly monitor your own understanding of the texts you are reading?		
7. Do you know how to improve your reading comprehension?		
8. Do you try to anticipate what is coming next?		

Check the feedback section at the end of the chapter to find out your level of interaction and to see suggestions for improvement.

3 Getting started: becoming a critical reader

Now use Activity 2 to think about how you go about your interactive reading.

ACTIVITY 2 Are you using your critical skills?

Are you using critical reading skills?	Yes	No
1. Do you think about what you are reading and question what the author has written?		
2. Do you take what the author has said as gospel truth?		
3. What credibility does the writer have in the subject area?		
3. Do you challenge the ideas as you are reading?		
4. Able to distinguish different kinds of reasoning used?		
5. Are you able to synthesise the key information and make connections between what different authors are saying?		
6. Can you make judgements about how the text is argued?		
7. Can you evaluate how the information could be better or differently supported?		
8. Can you spot assumptions that have not been well argued?		

The above eight questions demonstrate what you are aiming for to become a critical reader. You should use these as keys to help you increase your criticality. Now you are in the right mind-frame for approaching your reading in a critical manner, you need to practise and generalise your skills. Activity 3 presents some questions to get you to interact and think about your texts. Gathering the evidence is the first stage: weighing up what you have found is the critical thinking you will have to apply.

You need to consider if the evidence or the way the author tries to persuade you is strong or weak. Ask yourself if it is substantiated (a) by the author's admission and (b) by other authors. This will give you a strength gauge. You will also have to consider whether the evidence you have looked at is flawed.

ACTIVITY 3 Weighing up the evidence

Choose a chapter or an article and find out answers to the following questions:

Your questions	Evidence from the text
Who is the author's audience?	
What are the central claims/arguments of the text?	
What is the main evidence?	
Give examples of how this is substantiated.	
What assumptions lie behind the evidence or arguments?	
Is adequate proof provided and backed up with examples of evidence?	
What are the general weaknesses of the threads of the argument/evidence?	
What are the general strengths of the threads of the argument/evidence?	
Give examples of what other leading authors have to say on the same subject.	

4 Taking a critical look at a text

I find it difficult to do the critical thing. After all, who am I, a lowly undergraduate, to make judgements about the ideas of someone who is the leading researcher in cognitive psychology? Yet my tutors are always going on about 'you must be critical and analytical of the information'. How do I decide?

Susan, second-year Psychology student

Many students want to be critical in their reading but are faced with the same dilemma as this psychology student. Your tutors want to see evidence of your ability to weigh up ideas and information. To do this effectively, you will need to interact with your text so that you get into the habit of questioning information and seeing links between what one author has written and what you find in another text. Do they corroborate each other or do the authors take a different stance?

Reading between the lines

All that glisters is not gold.
Often have you heard that told.

Shakespeare: *Merchant of Venice*, 11:vii

This quotation can be applied to texts you will come across. Texts may not be what they literally appear to be. Some authors hide their true meaning. Books cannot always be taken literally, i.e. word for word as a factual account. Being able to read between the lines is an important reading quality which you need to finely tune if you are to increase your critical approach to reading. Your tutors will mention **inference** skills which relate to reading between the lines. For example, an author, writing about the war in Vietnam, might state: 'The landscape was washed with blood.' This can be taken literally to mean that the fields had blood running in streams but it may be the author's way of depicting the horror of the situation.

Reading between the lines requires you to take an interactive approach to text. You are expected to put two and two together and come up with answers. However, you must take care not to come up with the wrong answers! At times, authors make assumptions about their audience and expect the reader to take for granted some information which is not explicitly stated. In these cases you will have to read between the lines to extract the full, intended meaning. For example: 'In Paris in the 1970s, the university students were revolting.' Here the author could be expressing a personal comment about what he thinks about students or he could assume that the reader knows about the tumultuous, political upheavals of the day when university students were actively involved in political change.

It is important to ask yourself questions about the information you are reading. It is also vital that you are aware of how the writer's use of language can give clues that help the reader to examine text critically. Try Activity 4.

ACTIVITY 4 Unpicking or deconstructing a text

Here is a short passage of information. Let's analyse what is going on behind the scenes.

Ancestral sensitivity

There are few species which take any interest in their dead. While there are studies which show that creatures which mate for life demonstrate loneliness at the death of a partner, most animals lose interest once the carcass has decomposed. This is contrary to the social practices among the human species whereby graves are tended and the memory of the loved one is often enshrined in some way.

However, a research team, led by Karen McComb at the University of Sussex, is examining the behaviour of elephants in a Kenyan reserve. The team have found that the elephants show interest in skulls and ivory of their ancestors. When given similar shapes made of different materials, for example wood instead of ivory, the animals appear disinterested, thus proving that they have an affiliation with the dead matriarchs. Dr Field, the head of animal care at London Zoo, suggests that this behaviour reflects the tactile nature and intelligence of elephants. Dr McComb corroborated this, referring to a study of 17 families of African elephants. When presented with skulls from their own matriarchs and those of buffaloes, the elephants only showed interest in their own species.

Let's take a look in more detail:

Sentence	Critical interrogation
There are few species which take any interest in their dead.	What evidence is there? Is this the writer's own generalisation?
While there are studies ...	What studies? I need to cross-check this to find out proof.
A research team, led by Karen McComb at the University of Sussex, is examining the behaviour of elephants in a Kenyan reserve.	How credible is this research? What type of research? What research methods have been used to validate the findings?
Dr Field, the head of animal care at London Zoo, suggests that this behaviour reflects the tactile nature and intelligence of elephants.	This statement seems to make many assumptions about these animals. The causal proof seems believable but is it merely the view of this one scientist?
Dr McComb corroborated this, referring to a study of 17 families of African elephants.	Is this convincing? Are the links between the previous idea of Dr Field and this sound? Do I believe in this evidence?

Remember that part of weighing up information, being critical, is your questioning ability. Can you ask yourself the right questions to ensure that you evaluate and analyse a text? Try Activity 5.

ACTIVITY 5 What to look for in a text

In the table below you will find some generic questions which you can apply to most texts you are studying at university. The table also provides you with ways of finding the answers to your questions and what to look out for in a text.

Question	Solution
Are these ideas the author's potted summary of someone else's research?	Look for words like: • according to ... • a research study by ... • evidence supplied by ... • (cited in Smith and Bloggs, 2007)
Is the argument sound/strong?	• Look for examples of other research/information which backs up the line of argument. You might have to dip into other sources to check this. • Look at other sources for disagreement. This will help you to decide which has the most convincing argument which is backed up by evidence.
Is the evidence reputable? Remember that evidence comes in many shapes: statistical/graphical/anecdotal/reports	• What is the track-record of the author? • Be guided by what is said in lectures, course handbooks etc. • Do a quick survey on the Internet to find out about the author. Has s/he been involved in research? What sort of publications are there – always question the type of publication? Remember that some have greater credibility than others.
Is the evidence refutable?	• Do a quick survey on the Internet to find out other people's views. • What methods were used to gather the evidence? If, for example, it was gathered from asking friends about the subject, you must question this.
Are there any threads in the text which have not been dealt with or any inconsistent statements?	• Take each idea and check what the author has said. This is where colour-coding information is useful. • Use the 'find' facility to survey an electronic text.
Does the conclusion reflect the evidence/information in the text?	• Take each conclusion statement and quickly scan the text to find out where this has been dealt with.

The old saying, 'Practice makes perfect', applies to the way you can develop your critical reading skills. Some students have never been introduced to this way of handling the texts they read. It is worthwhile exploring one of your course texts and using the above questions to guide your critical reading skills. Try Activity 6.

ACTIVITY 6 Interrogating a text

Choose a chapter or section from one of your texts on your reading list.

Question	Your findings
Are these ideas the author's potted summary of someone else's research?	
Is the argument sound/strong?	
Is the evidence reputable? Remember that evidence comes in many shapes: statistical/graphical/anecdotal/reports	
Is the evidence refutable?	
Are there any threads in the text which have not been dealt with or any inconsistent statements?	
Does the conclusion reflect the evidence/information in the text?	

5 Critical evaluation of Internet information

One of the advantages of the Internet is that it is so accessible and a wealth of information is available. For academic purposes, however, not everything on the Internet is considered valuable, and some students find that quotations they have found on an Internet search are scorned by their tutors. The reasons why certain search results may be scorned by tutors is that the information may have little credibility or the author is an inappropriate source. It is, therefore, important to apply your critical reading skills to this type of information.

For example, a search about perceptions of dyslexia yielded this information:

> *Dyslexia is often not identified at school. I had left high school before someone said that I might be dyslexic.*
>
> Barbara from Wisconsin, USA

If we unravel these statements, we can understand why using this as evidence in an essay would be thought inappropriate by your tutors. How much credibility would you set by it?

- Who is Barbara from Wisconsin?
- Has she conducted well-designed research into this subject to enable her to make the first statement that 'dyslexia is often not identified at school'?
- What evidence is there that dyslexia is often not identified at school'?
- What is the frequency of identification? For example, how often is 'often' in this information? It is too vague.
- What was the status of the person who suggested assessment for dyslexia? Was it a friend? Another dyslexic person? A trained assessor?
- You need to be alert to the fact that later in this information you find that Barbara is trying to sell you a product. Obviously, she will speak about it in glowing terms. You need to consider its worth and credibility.

Question credentials

The example in the previous section demonstrates that you must question the credentials of the person who has written the information; what evidence there is for the claims; and what the ulterior motive is for making this information available free to the whole world.

> *I only search for articles or e-journals on the* **www.scholargoogle.com**.
>
> Christiana, MSc student

Searching reputable sites is vital, and you may need to ask your tutors for guidance. Of course, you may need to analyse the information to see if it gives you information you can understand. If it is too technical, you may need to find out some basic information first before going to more technical and subject-specific sites, for example, **www.ask.com**. There are also online dictionaries and thesauruses to help you with getting to grips with technical terminology, for example, **www.askoxford.com**.

Types of information on the Internet

The array of sources can be baffling. Apart from the obvious e-journals which are available on your university site and library databases (which are often divided into subjects by your librarians), there are many other sources. However, some types of information are more useful to certain subjects. For example, newspapers will give up-to-date editorial information for Politics students; and Social Studies, Education, History and Environmental Studies students can benefit from government statistical data. There are downloadable, video-streamed interviews of professionals' case study findings for Education students on **www.teachers.tv/home.do**.

6 On reflection

If you want to obtain a good degree, then this chapter is vital reading. You must develop and increase your critical reading skills. This section has explored ways in which you can interact more effectively with texts. Reading at university is stimulating. However, it requires more effort and energy on your part. You need to use your interrogation skills and adopt an enquiring approach to reading. As a SMART reader, you will be utilising the 'R' and 'T' – the reasoning and thinking – aspects.

Summary of this chapter

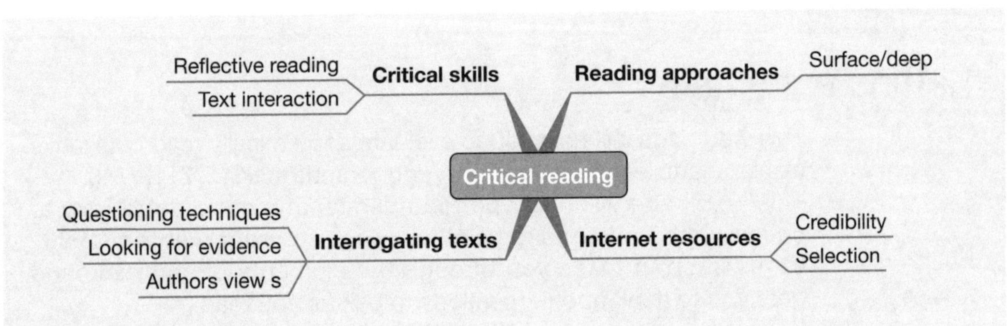

ACTIVITY 7 Update your personal development planner

Questioning what authors say and weighing up the information will ensure that you do not take what you read for granted and that you are more alert to reading between the lines. However, at the heart of critical reading is your ability to know what questions to ask and how you can find the answers to your questions.

Now reflect upon how critical a reader you are and how you intend to change and adapt your current approach to reading texts.

Grade your confidence on a scale of 1–5 where 1 = poor and 5 = good.

My developing skills	Confidence level 1–5	Plans to improve
I know what skills are involved in critical reading.		
I know how to interact with texts.		
I know how to read between the lines when reading.		
I know the best questions to interrogate texts.		
I know how to judge information I read on the Internet.		

Getting extra help

- This web page will help you to evaluate and critically read qualitative research articles: **www.bmj.com/cgi/content/full/315/7110/740.**
- This web page will help you to understand in more detail how to critically read a journal article: **www.oandp.org/jpo/library/1996_01_024.asp.** It takes you through the elements of an article and gets you to think about questions to ask as you read.
- If you need to read scientific articles you might like to browse this short information page: **www.fiu.edu/~collinsl/Article%20reading%20tips.htm.**

Feedback on activities

ACTIVITY 1 How do I interact with texts?

How do you interact with the text you are reading?	Yes	No
1. Do you know exactly what you are looking for?		
2. Can you select important and/or relevant information for your purpose?		
3. Can you pick out key words and/or information?		
4. Do you use the same styles of reading, whatever the task?		
5. Do you soak up the information and then wonder what to do with it?		
6. Do you regularly monitor your own understanding of the texts you are reading?		
7. Do you know how to improve your reading comprehension?		
8. Do you try to anticipate what is coming next?		

If you have answered 'yes' to 1, 2 and 3:

You are well on the way to becoming an active reader. These activities mean that you are thinking and questioning. If you want to increase these skills, look back to Section 7 'Are you an interactive reader?' in Chapter 3.1.

If you have answered 'yes' to 4:

You may be stuck in a rut and need to be more flexible in your approach to reading. You will find that it pays off because you will be more efficient and effective. Revise Chapter 3.2.

If you have answered 'yes' to 5:

You have not asked yourself why you are reading the text. Go to Chapter 3.4.

If you have answered 'yes' to 6, 7 and 8:

This means that you are giving yourself the best chance to add on your critical reading skills because you are monitoring your understanding and thinking about what you have read. Revise Section 2 in this chapter.

References

Barnett, R. (1997) *Higher Education: A critical Business*. Buckinghamshire, Open University Press.

Entwistle N. J. and Entwistle, A. C. (1991) 'Contrasting forms of understanding for degree examinations: the student experience and its implications', *Higher Education*, 22, pp. 205–27.

Entwistle, N. J., Entwistle, A. C. and Tait, H. (1992) 'Academic understanding and contexts to enhance it: a perspective from research on student learning', in T. Duffy and D. Jonassen (eds) *The Design of Constructivist Learning Environments*. Berlin, Springer Verlag.

Peverly, S. T., Brobst, K. E. and Morris, K. S. (2002) 'The contribution of reading comprehension ability and meta-cognitive control to the development of studying in adolescence', *Journal of Research in Reading*, 25(2), 203–16.

Price, G. A. (2001) *Report on the Survey of Academic Skills at Southampton University*. Southampton, University of Southampton.

3.4 Managing your reading

Managing your reading choices and reading environment can increase your efficiency and will certainly optimise the effort you put into your reading activities.

Reading lists are an essential feature of any study unit. They provide you with guidance but can cause stress. Therefore, the ability to manage and organise how you use the reading lists will increase your effectiveness.

In this chapter you will:

1. find out how much you know about the purpose of a reading list
2. learn how to make beneficial choices from your reading lists
3. learn how to choose books that are suited to your skill level and academic needs
4. explore solutions to make the best of your reading environment.

USING THIS CHAPTER

Estimate your current levels of confidence. At the end of the chapter you will have the chance to re-assess these levels where you can incorporate this into your personal development planner (PDP). Mark between 1 (poor) and 5 (good) for the following:

I know how to make skilful reading choices.	I know how to select reading materials at appropriate levels for my study.	I know how to make the most profitable environment in which to conduct my reading.

Date: ________________

1 The reading manager

An essential part of the SMART reader is 'M' for Management. Being an effective and efficient reader, like so many other things in life, relies upon how you manage your time and how you organise yourself – in this case how you organise your reading tasks which are an integral part of your academic studies.

Your course tutors will furnish you with much advice and guidance. They are experts in the field and are passionate about their subject. So it is little wonder that they want you to read in depth about their topic. Instructions for your reading are to be found in your course/unit handbooks. During lectures and seminars your tutors will refer to books and journal articles, putting pressure upon you to read more and more texts. In fact, there will be times when you feel overwhelmed by the sheer volume of reading that is expected of you. Some students go into panic mode and almost shut down. Although this is understandable, it will not help you to keep up with and keep on top of your academic reading (to remind yourself of how to cope with stress go back to Chapter 1.1, 'Managing your stress').

They (academic tutors) forget that their unit is one of six that I am doing this semester. They suggest reading this book and that book and are totally oblivious to the fact that all my other tutors are doing the same thing. If you did all the reading that each unit tutor suggested, you would not be able to do anything else for a whole year.

Martin, second-year Philosophy student

Managing your reading involves coping with your reading lists, making skilful choices and knowing what to do if the suggested books are too hard to understand. This section will delve into methods to manage your reading and to do so with minimum loss of quality.

2 How to cope with reading lists

I'm so confused by the reading lists. I've been told to choose the best texts but how do I know which are the best. I wish they would just give us a few books to read for an assignment.

First-year Geography student

The tutors think they are being so helpful giving us detailed reading lists. Frankly, I find them daunting. When am I going to find the time to read them all?

Part-time Sociology postgraduate student

Many students do not realise that academic tutors expect them to take control of their learning and that this also applies to the reading lists. They assume that students will make choices in their reading and that this premise is applied to how to deal with reading lists. Thus, they will provide course handbooks with lengthy reading lists, unit reading lists, lecture handouts with lists of references, and electronic course notes with further reading lists. This can be confusing and overwhelming. Do they expect students to read every single text to which they refer? The answer to this question is probably no: so why do they give so many lists?

Most academic tutors are aware that their students come from different academic and cultural backgrounds, with a variety of prior learning experiences. They provide what they hope are comprehensive lists to meet diverse learning needs. For example, in many first-year Law degrees tutors are aware that some of the students will have studied Law at 'A' level while others will be new to the subject. Reading lists have to cater for these different needs.

What are reading lists for?

If you understand what reading lists are for, you are more likely to make better use of them.

The tutor's perspective

Some tutors want to provide a rich source of background reading for their subject and will provide students with detailed reading lists. They do this because they want their students to 'read around' the subject and not be blinkered into reading only a few texts which would get them through the assignment. Often, these lists are for **guidance**. If a student has little or no knowledge of the content of the unit, then the list must include some texts which enable them to build up concepts and knowledge. The reading lists have to take this into account and provide basic texts as well more advanced texts to challenge and develop thinking.

As an academic tutor, I provide substantial lists because I am concerned about the availability of texts in the library, particularly for my part-time students. Therefore, I may include books about the same topic by different authors. These will contain very similar information. I do not expect my students to read every book but I am reassured that by including this variety the important texts will be accessible and available in the library.

Cultural perspectives

Of course, there are cultural aspects to this question. In some countries, notably in the Far East, students are expected to read every text on the list provided by the academic tutor from start to finish. Thus, when they come to do postgraduate studies in the UK, they think that the same rules apply, and they wear themselves out trying to keep up with the reading lists.

In addition, some students from EU countries embarking on postgraduate studies are perplexed because their academic tutor has not directed them to one or two important texts which will ensure that an assignment can be carried out successfully, and they are confused by such long lists.

Differentiating the lists

On some courses, the lists are essential readings. These are usually identified quite easily because the lists are relatively short! How do you make the appropriate decisions about the reading lists? Well, it is down to you. You need to differentiate the titles so that you can decide:

- which texts to read to help you understand the ideas (facts and knowledge)
- which texts will help you to build up different views about the topic (opinions and critical evaluation)
- which texts provide you with some detailed examples of research to back up your information (information to strengthen your argument).

Managing reading lists: personal control

Looking down a long list of guided and suggested reading can be daunting. Making skilful choices about what to read and what to leave aside for the present is an important feature of managing your reading, and is discussed in Activity 1.

ACTIVITY 1 How to make skilful reading choices

Gather together your reading lists for one of your units of study. If possible, get different coloured marker pens and try this out. You may need to do this in the library so that you have quick access to the titles, and you can skim the books/articles to make your decisions.

As a quick overview, look at the titles and authors on your reading lists and answer the following questions:

Question	Action
Does the title imply that the resource will help me to do my assignment?	1. Look for key words in the titles and cross-check with the assignment title. 2. Put ticks, crosses or some sort of system for categorising against each entry on your reading list.
Is the author important?	1. Check your lecture notes and electronic course notes to see if your academic tutor has mentioned the writer or made reference to his/her research in this field. 2. Has the writer's name come up frequently in any of your electronic searches?
Is this the right book/chapter/article for **my** purposes?	1. You need to make a judgement about the resource level. It might assume a lot of knowledge which you do not, as yet, have so this means it is too difficult for you at this time. 2. Have a simple system of 'easy', 'moderate' and 'difficult' against each of the titles on the list. You could colour-code this for ease of identification.
How can I make quick, practical decisions about the resources on the lists?	Categorising your resources is always helpful if you feel pressurised about time. You could divide the items on the list by colour-coding into: **Essential (E)** – this is vital for this assignment **Back-up (B)** – this would provide useful information for examples and back-up for some of my ideas and statements **Luxury (L)** – this would give me further, in-depth information if I have time to read it and it is possible to use it within my word-count.

How to choose the right resource will be dealt with later in this chapter in Section 3, 'Reading list solutions'. However, having made an initial start with taking control of the reading lists, you must not forget that **availability** is crucial.

By asking the questions in Activity 1, you are beginning to take control of your own learning and make educated decisions.

Managing reading lists: how to control your tutor

Full- and part-time students are often wary of asking academic tutors' help at the beginning of a course or a new unit. Often in these circumstances the tutor is new to you, and you do not know the ground rules they have set, nor how they like to operate. Obviously, you need to gauge what they are like and whether you can approach them.

One of the short-cuts to sorting out the best reads from your reading lists is to ask the person who has drawn up the list or the tutor who has set the question for your assignment. It is helpful to have the lists divided into **essential reading** and **background reading**. This way the choices you have to make about your own personal reading are more manageable from the outset. It is also comforting to know that your tutor directs you to a group of resources which you need to grapple with first (essential reading) before going on to other texts for additional information (background reading). Of course, if you are aiming at a First degree classification, then you must tackle some from both categories.

However, be prepared for some tutors to refuse your request to provide broad categories for reading. Some academic tutors think that these decisions are a vital part of learning at college or university and expect their students to show that they can make these reading choices.

3 Reading list solutions

My reading trophy

I found that it's no good choosing books to impress your friends. I once got a book out of the library and carried it to lectures in the hopes that the others on the course would think 'he's clever if he can read that book and understand it'. Of course, I found it far too difficult and never used it other than looking at a few pages, panicking because it was unintelligible and putting it to one side. I had to accept that I needed to get books which were at my level.

Pete, second-year Geology student

Reading lists are all very well but you must use them selectively to suit **your** needs. This means that there are some simple rules you can apply when searching the library or the web for reading material for your assignment, as shown in Activity 2.

ACTIVITY 2 Pragmatic decisions about reading lists

Ask yourself ...	Yes/No
Is this book available when I need it?	
Is the book only available in the reference section of the library? (This means that you have to make sure you plan your study reading so that you can do this in the library and not in your flat or room.)	
Is the book pitched at a level which I can understand? (Sample a chapter to see if you understand the ideas.)	
Does it contain chapters/sections which would be useful to help me complete my assignment? (Remember to go back to your assignment title to check what you are being asked to do.)	
Is it too difficult for me to understand? (Then you need to choose a book which you can understand before moving on to more complex books.)	
All of the books on the reading lists have already been taken out by others on my course. (You will need to be craftily creative in these circumstances. Some solutions follow.)	

The shelves are bare!

Of course, finding that none of your reading list titles are available on the library shelves is frustrating, to say the least. However, you must have a back-up strategy for managing this situation.

Firstly, you need to ask yourself why there are no books available. This could be important for future organisation. One of the criticisms which is often noted on the end-of-unit student evaluation form is that the resources were not available or they were insufficient. It could be that there were insufficient books for the number of students on your course. However, your department probably could not afford to purchase one book per student. Consequently, there may be only one copy or there may be a small number of multiple copies. This means that there are many students searching for precious resources.

Many essential reading resources are placed in a 'reserve' or 'reference only' section in the library. This means that there will be many of your fellow students chasing these precious texts. You need to ensure that you find out in advance the 'loan availability' of books. In most college and university libraries this is divided into:

- reserve/reference only/short-term loan
- one-week loan
- three-week loan.

Of course, if you have left it very late to look at your reading lists, the chances are that your fellow students have got there before you and taken out the books. Thus, it is vital that you organise and manage your work routines to ensure that you do not leave your reading to the last minute. Nevertheless, your tardiness may not be the issue. It may be that the materials and resources are scarce. In these circumstances, you have to be creative and to think laterally. You will need to revert to your key words for the topic to conduct some searches to see if there are any similar books which will do the job for you.

4 Is the text suitable for my purposes?

Test suitability is not just about choosing the right book for the assignment. It is also about choosing the right book **for you** at your stage in the learning process or your conceptualisation of ideas. Management of choice is an aspect of this.

The books are too hard

Whilst choosing books to suit **your** needs depends upon what you already know and bring to the task, you must remember that sometimes your tutors put books on the lists which are too difficult for many students. They have introduced these books to challenge the high fliers. Their expectations are high!

If the books are too hard for you, then you must draw upon strategies to cope with this. You need to start examining the suitability of the text for your purpose.

Is this text suitable for you?

Just because a tutor has placed a book in the reserve collection or on short-term loan does not always mean that you are ready to access that particular reading resource. (Reflect upon your level with the aid of Section 4, 'Steps to proficiency', in Chapter 3.1.) Some students forget that one of the elements of successful reading is the knack of matching your level of understanding with the relevant resources for the activity in which you are involved.

Some students become disheartened when they cannot understand a text on the 'book list'. This may be because they are still at an early stage of understanding, of both the new concepts and the new terminology. Some books are, therefore, at too high a level **at this stage** and are more like reading a second language where you have to look up all the new terminology to help you link the vocabulary with the meaning! If this applies to you, you should choose a text which gives you more help and briefer, more broad-stroke, explanations. If the subject is new to you, the various *Idiot's Guides* on the market are a 'must'! However, there may be some excellent 'A' level textbooks which serve this purpose as a bridge to exploring more complex journal articles, for example. It is important that you seek advice from your department, tutors and postgraduate students about what is available. It is well worth a visit to the campus bookshop where you may find second-hand textbooks. Amongst the titles, you may come across a simplified text which fits your purposes. Also, it is reassuring to know that some previous students on the course had recourse to just the sort of text which meets your requirements.

NOTE This advice may seem to contradict what your academic tutors tell you. There are few who would recommend *The Idiot's Guide to* ... This is because tutors expect their students to have a higher, starting point. You need to assess the knowledge **you** bring to this activity and choose accordingly.

Is this text suitable for my studies?

The question you need to ask yourself is 'Does this book or chapter or article contain the information or evidence I need for my assignment or task?' If it does then it is worth using. However, you will probably find there is no one book which conveniently and neatly contains all the information you need for your specific assignment. So you are expected to dip in and out of books, chapters and journal articles. Key words, and task analysis (see Chapter 4.1), will enable you to make effective decisions about what to use and what to discard.

At times, you will have to think about the usefulness of a section of text. Will it provide background information? Will be useful to help develop your understanding of the key ideas and concepts?

Remember that the books or chapters or articles have not been written especially so that you can answer the question posed by your tutor. They may go into a lot of complicated depth which is not relevant to your current needs.

Selecting appropriate texts

ACTIVITY 3 Selecting appropriate books

Try this out with a selection of **books** for one of your assignments. You will need to have a list of key words available. These words may be in your unit outlines or course handbooks.

Name of book: ____________	Possible	Discard
Has this book been mentioned/recommended by my tutors?		
Is it on the reading list?		
Are there some of my key words (or equivalent) in the title?		
Is the book fairly recent? Remember if the publication date is too old, the information may be out of date.		
Look at the back cover of a book. Do the summaries indicate that there may be some useful sections?		
Look at the contents list at the beginning. Are there any of my key words in the titles? If so, note the specific chapters in the 'possible column'. Look at the index at the back of the book. Search for specific key words (or equivalent). Note the page numbers in your 'Possible' column.		
Sample some of the chapter sub-headings. Do you think some sections may be of use? Make a note of page numbers in the 'Possible' column.		
Sample a small section of a chapter. Is the information accessible to me? Remember that if the style of writing is too academic or filled with many technical words which you don't know, you may not be ready for it yet.		

ACTIVITY 4 Is this the right journal article?

Try this out with a **journal article** which you have come across:

Name of article: ____________	Possible	Discard
Has the article been mentioned/recommended by my tutors?		
Is it on the reading list?		
Are there some of my key words (or equivalent) in the title?		
Read the 'Abstract'. This gives an overview of the article. Does it contain any useful information for my assignment?		
Examine the key words (usually located after the Abstract). Is there a high match factor?		
Is the article fairly recent? Remember if the publication date is too old, the information may be out of date.		

Name of article: ______________	Possible	Discard
Sample some of the sub-headings. Do you think some sections may be of use?		
Sample a small section of the article. Is the information accessible to me? Remember if the style of writing is too academic or filled with many technical words which you don't know, you may not be ready for it yet.		

Organising your reading lists, getting hold of the 'right' texts and analysing what is available are all aspects of managing your reading. However, there is another element of a reading activity which you ought to have in your control: finding out the type of environment which increases your reading effectiveness.

5 Managing the reading environment

Many students state that it is a matter of trial and error to find out the type of environment which helps you to absorb information and to concentrate for longer and longer periods of time. Getting the reading environment right will improve your stamina and ultimately will help you to gain better grades by raising your efficiency levels. Try Activity 5.

ACTIVITY 5 Environmental management

Do you manage your environment to produce the best solutions?

Do you ...	Yes	No
1. Make sure that the lighting is good?		
2. Make sure you are sitting in a comfortable position?		
3. Control the environment to maximise concentration while reading?		
4. Do you have all your back-up equipment ready to hand before you start reading?		

Check the feedback section at the end of the chapter to find out if you are managing your environment effectively.

6 On reflection

As this section has highlighted, becoming an effective reader involves managing your reading resources and environment. Making the right decisions about which reading materials to use is just one of the factors which will have an effect upon your understanding and knowledge of your subject. However, choosing your reading resources does not simply rely upon the availability of texts in your library. You must take into account the best texts for you at your stage in the learning process.

Summary of this chapter

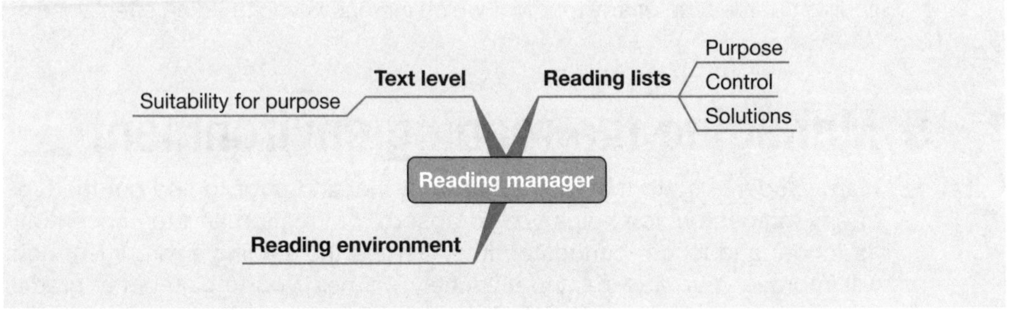

ACTIVITY 6 Update your personal development planner

Now reflect upon how you go about managing your reading and how you intend to change and adapt your reading habits so that you can spend your time more effectively. You may want to transfer this information to your own institution's personal development planner scheme.

Grade your confidence on a scale of 1–5 where 1 = poor and 5 = good.

My developing skills	Confidence level 1–5	Plans to improve
I know how to make skilful reading choices.		
I know how to select reading materials at appropriate levels for my study.		

My developing skills	Confidence level 1–5	Plans to improve
I know how to make the most profitable environment in which to conduct my reading.		

Date: ______________

Getting extra help

- Consult your academic tutor for advice about the different levels of the texts on the reading lists.
- Develop reading networks with friends on your courses so that you can sort out the logistics of borrowing textbooks.

Feedback on activities

ACTIVITY 5 Environmental management

Do you manage your environment to produce the best solutions?

Do you ...	Yes	No
1. Make sure that the lighting is good?		
2. Make sure you are sitting in a comfortable position?		
3. Control the environment to maximise concentration while reading?		
4. Do you have all your back-up equipment ready to hand before you start reading?		

Environmental management solutions:

1. **Lighting**: It is inadvisable to shine a strong lamp onto white pages of text. It can reflect glare and give you a headache.

2. **Seating:** If you are sitting in one position for some time, it is best to have a chair which provides support for your lower back. Some students prefer to be curled up on a settee or sprawl out on the floor while they are reading. Of course, what determines your seating is often whether you intend to make notes or not.
3. **Distractions**: Some students prefer to have background music whilst others can only concentrate upon difficult concepts if there is absolute silence. You need to find out which help you to absorb information most comfortably. Remember that one of the biggest distractions is a mobile telephone. You need to decide whether to switch it off or whether you still want to be in communication with the outside world.
4. **Back-up equipment**: Nothing stops reading effectiveness more than interrupting your flow of thoughts while you are reading. Think about the tools which help you to maximise your reading experience and ensure that you have these ready for use before you open your book. Equipment you might like to consider will be related to note-making, memory stimulation and marking up text to aid consolidation and understanding. Do you have the following ready for use:
   (a) coloured highlighter pens
   (b) small Post-it Notes to mark important pages
   (c) pens for underlining crucial information
   (d) notepad or laptop for making notes?

4 Develop your writing

Most students comment that adjusting to academic writing at university is stressful and time-consuming. This part will help you develop your critical writing skills by helping you manage the writing process, see Chapter 4.1, 'Taking control of the writing process'. You will also consider how to ensure that what you write is not plagiarised. This relies on organising your information for writing carefully and referencing your work meticulously, see Chapter 4.2, 'Understanding academic integrity: plagiarism'. If you want to improve your grades, then it is worthwhile looking at Chapter 4.3, 'Making the most of your tutors' feedback'.

4.1 Taking control of the writing process

Essays are a part of university life. In a recent student survey of academic skills writing essays was identified as the most stressful activity. However, your essays can make a big difference to your final grades so it is imperative that you are in control of the writing process right from the beginning of your studies.

In this chapter you will:

1. learn to manage the writing process effectively
2. learn how to probe essay questions
3. explore a system for gathering information, linked to essay title
4. learn the difference between drafting and editing
5. learn how to proofread your work effectively
6. examine critical writing.

USING THIS CHAPTER

Estimate your current levels of confidence. At the end of the chapter you will have the chance to re-assess these levels where you can incorporate this into your personal development planner (PDP). Mark between 1 (poor) and 5 (good) for the following:

I know the different elements of the writing process.	I can analyse what is required of an essay question.	I have a system for collecting relevant information linked to the essay question.	I can proofread my work accurately.

Date: _______________

1 Process and components

The academic essay ... is a kind of game in which the writer, according to the extent to which he or she is familiar with the rules and is able to use them, seeks to satisfy the demands of the reader/marker.

Houghton (1984), p. 21

Most university students have had some experience of writing essays prior to entry to the course. Undoubtedly, these experiences will have shaped the thinking about the writing process. However, what was expected of an essay when you were at school is different from your university tutors' expectations. At the outset of your studies, it is important to work out how you can meet those expectations. There are strict game rules for academic writing. The knack is knowing what these rules are, and where the goal posts have been positioned, so that you can play accordingly.

Writing is a social act (Hayes, 1996) and is one of many forms of communication. It is a means by which the writer can share information and thought with others. Usually, it is done within a specific context, e.g. writing e-mails to friends; making a shopping list for yourself; or showing your knowledge and understanding of what you have learned in an essay.

Taking control of writing essays is divided into two chapters. This chapter covers how you organise and manage the process of writing, in order to write a coherent essay. Chapter 4.3 is devoted to what you do with the feedback from an essay. In between these chapters, Chapter 4.2 looks at the issue of plagiarism, and how to avoid it in your essay writing.

2 What is an essay?

Although there are slight variations in the characteristics of essays in different subject disciplines, generally an essay is a piece of continuous prose writing which is divided into paragraphs. There are different types of essays and these will be explained in Section 3, 'The essay structure', in Chapter 4.3.

An essay has diverse purposes. The most obvious is that it is a method of assessing your performance on the course. However, your tutors will tell you that the essay has many other functions: It can be used to:

- develop your thinking processes
- increase your understanding and knowledge of a subject
- organise your thoughts to communicate with others.

Written communication at university is complex because there are many layers to control. Being aware of and developing expertise in the construction of well-written English for academic purposes is but one of the aspects you have to manage. This will be dealt with in Section 3 in Chapter 4.3. However, writing is a process or a journey and, as such, requires careful management. You need to be in control of this process – the essay should not control you.

3 The writing process

Expert writers do not adopt a linear approach to the writing process. It is not simply a matter of 'do this' and then 'do that'. You may have used this approach when you first started writing essays at school but you will need to develop a more sophisticated way of working to respond to the more complex needs of writing at university.

One of the baffling things about writing essays is that, although it is not a linear experience, you are expected to produce information in a linear format so that your paragraphs hang together effectively and your information is presented sequentially.

Many students become obsessed with the fine detail of sentence and paragraph construction to the extend that they do not reflect upon how they managed the whole process. If you want to improve your grades while you are at university, you need to look back upon how you went about the whole business of writing your essay from the time you were told your essay title to the hand-in and submission. Could you have achieved a more efficient way of managing how you worked?

The writing process can be divided into discrete elements which you have to manage:

1. **Cracking the code** – deciding what the essay question is asking of you – not just a matter of the content or **what** information has to go into it but also **how** you need to select and draw together (or reshape) information.
2. **Gathering together the information/content** – pulling together information from different books, notes and articles and grouping this information effectively.
3. **Putting your ideas together** – drafting and editing how you express this in written format.
4. **Tidying up and checking** – proofreading your work to eliminate irritating errors.

What's the difference between an expert and a novice writer?

Researchers Bereiter and Scardamalia have spent the last thirty years exploring what makes an expert writer. They have examined how schoolchildren and academic writers go about the process. One of the interesting findings is that expert writers go about managing the writing process differently from novice writers (Bereiter and Scardamalia, 1987).

Novice writers adopt a linear approach to their writing and tend to take each of the writing process elements in turn. The reason they do this is because they are not at the stage of managing and controlling more than one element at a time. Consequently, they gather information for an essay without giving thought to how they are going to use the information at a later stage in the writing process.

On the other hand, expert writers keep a mental map of the finished product or essay in mind while they are gathering information and during the drafting process. Consequently, they keep moving backwards and forwards through the various elements of the process. In addition, they do this with ease and skill.

Thus, if you wish to become an expert writer, it is vital that you take firm control of the different elements. If you wish to improve your marks, you need to start considering how good a manager you are. Most students have to write assignments within tight deadlines – either self-imposed or externally imposed by tutors. Therefore, you need to be effective and efficient in your control of the whole process.

4 Cracking the code

Most essays start with the giving out of an essay title. In some subjects, you are given a choice of essay titles. In this case it is even more important to ensure that your choice will gain the most marks and will enable you to show off your knowledge and understanding most effectively.

Essay titles: the key to a good essay

- Contrary to popular belief, the essay question has been very carefully worded by your tutor.
- The wording of the question is there to help you to understand what is required. If you can crack the code of the title, you will unlock the often hidden agenda of the title.
- The title will also help you to decide how to approach the topic/subject. By careful use of language, it leads you into a specific type (genre) of writing.

Probing the question

If you are not sure what you are supposed to do when you read an essay title you need to develop some strategies to help you to decipher just what the title is getting at and what is expected of you. The best way to start is to ask yourself some questions:

- How does the essay question fit in with the course, the lectures and the lecturer's expectations?
- What is being asked for? Is it a description, an explanation or a well-documented argument?

Interacting with the words in the title

- If you can crack the code, the **title** will help you to narrow your research and focus more carefully.
- If you crack the code, you will make better choices for the selection of reading materials and the selection of information to be considered.
- If you crack the code, you will start looking for the right evidence and information to include in your essay.

Hot Tip

It is worth spending time solving the language of the title – the key to good marks starts with cracking the code of the essay title.

Getting started: the BUG technique

The **BUG** technique stands for:

1. Box

2. Underline

3. Glance back to check

1. Put a box around the action/instruction word(s). An action word tells you what you have to do or what type of essay is expected – explain, evaluate, analyse, etc. These are important words because they are telling you something about the type of structure expected for the essay.
2. Underline the key words in the question. This will help you sort out not only the content expected but will also tell you any limitations, e.g. only a specific time scale or one facet to be analysed.
3. Glance back – have you missed out any words which are important and change what you have to do?

How 'the BUG' works

The BUG is a system which has been developed by the author in response to concerns expressed by university students (Price, 2001). It has been used successfully by hundreds of students in different subject areas. Here is what the students have to say:

> *I used to frequently get comments like 'you have not answered the question' from my tutors. I couldn't understand what they meant because the way I read the essay title, I thought I* ***had*** *done what was asked. When my tutor told me I wasn't tuning myself into the language academics use and showed me the BUG I found that at last I had something which I could use for any essay title or exam question. It's brilliant and saves so much time.*
>
> Dave, second-year Mechanical Engineering student

> *I can't tell you how much time I used to spend worrying about whether I was doing the right things for the essay. It caused me sleepless nights. Then to be told you haven't done what was asked was just devastating. As soon as I started to use the BUG, I felt more confident and, even better – my grades have improved.*
>
> Sharon, third-year Nursing student

The reason it is important to box and underline specific words is that it helps differentiate the function of the language used. It is easy to pick out the type of essay required because the clue word(s) is boxed. This also serves as a quick reminder when you come back to the title at different times. Thus, the type of essay required is singled out, and you immediately know what type of structure your tutors are expecting.

If you go through the process of underlining the key words, you will have had to weigh up which words you think are important. Conversely, this means that you will have had to eliminate words which are not so vital. By doing this activity, you will have started the thinking process and will be analysing language to help you to get to the heart of what is required. Similarly, the physical act of underlining chosen words helps them to stand out so that they act as memory joggers later on when you are embroiled in your sentence construction and writing – a time when you could forget your way and wander from the point.

The 'glance back' is the part which is often overlooked by students anxious to get started with the essay. However, this is the part which helps you to develop critical skills. More importantly it is a self-check to ensure that you have not got stuck into a thinking rut and taken things for granted. This makes you check that you have done the job properly.

The BUG in practice

Let us explore how this works with a question which was set for first-year Law students:

Essay Title: 'Mentally disordered offenders should be the responsibility of health rather than the criminal justice system. Discuss.'

Mentally disordered offenders *should* ***be the responsibility of health rather than the criminal justice system. Discuss.***

It is well worth noting that the action or instruction word does not always come at the beginning of the title so you must be on your toes to identify this first. This essay requires students to consider the arguments for and against by using 'discuss'. Your next question must be 'What have I got do discuss?' If you probe the title your answer becomes immediately apparent. You are being asked who has responsibility for 'mentally disordered offenders'. Is it the health system or the criminal justice system?

The '**glance back**' part of the BUG technique requires you to weigh up whether any important words have been left out which could make a difference to how you manipulate the facts.

Of course, a crucial word is **should**. Did you spot this? This makes a difference to **how** you answer the question. This word is asking you to make decisions, based on the evidence you find. Noticing this will make a difference to how you organise and manage the gathering of information which is linked to the next part of the writing process.

So having carried out the BUG on this essay title, you now have a clearer idea of what your tutor wants, what type of essay he or she is expecting and the type of information you are looking for. This means that your research reading has been primed so that you are not led astray. You can ask yourself questions about the information to help you find the answers you need for this essay. With experience, this technique will inform you about how to collect your facts and information more efficiently.

Essay title instruction words

Each subject uses instruction words in a slightly different way so it is important that you check with your tutors what type of essay structure they expect when they use words such as 'discuss' or 'evaluate', etc.

As a general guideline the following definitions give an indication of what you are expected to do and what sort of essay you are supposed to be constructing and structuring. The list below gives some of the most frequently used terminology. It gives general guidelines for working out what kind of essay is required. You are advised to check with your department. Some terminology is used in a very specific way by some departments.

Account for	Give the reason for. Not to be confused with 'Give an account of' which is only asking for description.
Analyse	Describe the main ideas in depth, showing why they are important and how they are connected.
Assess	Discuss the strong and weak points of the subject. Put your own judgement clearly in the conclusion.
Comment	State your views on the subject clearly. Back up your points with sufficient evidence and examples.
Compare	Look for similarities and differences.
Contrast	Show how the subjects are different.
Criticise	Give your opinion/judgement about the merit of theories/facts; back this up by discussing the evidence or reasoning involved.
Define	Give clear, concise meanings. State limitations of the definition.
Describe	Give a detailed or graphic account of.
Discuss	Give reasons for and against; examine implications.
Evaluate	Weigh things up; look at the strengths and weaknesses and assess.
Examine	Look closely at all aspects.
Explain	Give reasons for something.
Illustrate	Make clear by the use of examples/diagrams; clarify points.
Interpret	Express in simple terms. You are usually expected to include your own judgements.
Justify	Show adequate ground for decisions/conclusions/ideas/theories.
Outline	Give the main features or general principles of a subject – should not include all the details.
Prove	Establish that something is true by presenting factual evidence or giving clear, logical reasons.
Relate	Show how things are connected to each other; how they affect each other.
Review	Make a survey of something.
State	Present brief, clear information.

Summarise	Give a concise account for the main points – should not include details.
Trace	Follow the development of a topic.
To what extent ...	Another way of saying evaluate but suggests that you bring out how much (or how little).

Having worked out what your tutor wants in the essay, it is important to develop efficient ways of gathering information so that you group and categorise information/ideas/arguments from an early stage. Doing this systematically will help with the 'joined up thinking' or 'synthesis of ideas' in your communication in your essay. Adopting an appropriate system will also ensure that your essays are structured more effectively so that there is cohesion.

5 Gathering information for essays

Some students spend too much time and effort on this part of the writing process, working inefficiently. You need to make sure that you streamline your working habits. This will have an effect upon your time management and will also have a knock-on effect upon the grade you can achieve. Activity 1 asks you to identify how you gather information.

ACTIVITY 1 How do you gather information for an essay?

Ask yourself	Solution
Do you spend a lot of time gathering information for an essay?	This sounds as if you are not really sure what you are looking for. Carry out the BUG to clarify what your tutors want.
Do you find that you have gathered information for an essay which is irrelevant?	Go back to the essay title and do the BUG to find out exactly what you need to find.
Do you find it difficult to decide what is needed for your essay from the information you have?	Check back at the underlined words in your essay title. Ask yourself how relevant your notes are and whether you have information to answer the question.
Do you end up with lots of notes and spend too much time picking out information that you need when you come to write your essay?	You have no system for gathering notes. You need to be more efficient. Look at the next section and go back over the different ways of making notes in Chapter 2.1.
Do you feel overwhelmed by the amount of notes you have made?	You have no system for gathering notes. You need to be more efficient. Look at the next section.
Do tutors comment that you have not answered the question and that there are irrelevant sections in your essay?	This is probably because you have not carefully analysed the wording in the essay and conducted the BUG.

Organising the paper-chase

This section will give you tips about how to organise yourself when gathering information for an essay. Time is a precious commodity for all students, and it is important that you work effectively and efficiently. Perhaps, you are not well **organised** when researching your information. If you have analysed your question well, you will have a better idea of what to look for. A little time invested in the early stages of essay writing can have huge pay-offs in terms of time management and improving your marks. Different note-making and note-taking systems are explored in Chapter 2.1, 'Making notes'. This section looks specifically at how to link gathering information with your essay title.

The matrix: a tool for categorising information for an essay

Many of the essays set by your tutor would benefit from the adoption of the information grid/matrix system of gathering **relevant** information.

A matrix or grid:

- can help you categorise and compare information
- can help prevent copying out word for word what is in books and journals because there is a limited space available for making notes
- can prevent plagiarism if you do not copy out word for word information into your matrix
- can develop your summary skills
- is useful for those who like to see an overview of information
- is very good for those of you who have difficulty with sequencing and structuring essays because they act as a first stage in this process by allowing you to gather the information randomly. Once this has been completed, you can then order the information as you wish.

Using a matrix or information grid linked to essay titles

Let's use the essay title which was used earlier to unpick the language.

Mentally disordered offenders should be the responsibility of health rather than the criminal justice system. *Discuss.* → *Not describe!*

Your 'evidence' can be collected from different sources and as you make decisions about who says what, you can place your summarised bullet points in the most appropriate part of the grid.

Mentally disordered offenders

Keep this title so that you remember what it is you have to focus on. Not any old offenders but mentally disordered ones.

	Who argues for this?	Who argues against this?	Alternative (?)
Responsibility of criminal justice system?			
Responsibility of health system?			

It is important to use the language of your question in your matrix. This will act as a constant reminder of what you are supposed to be finding out and will help to prevent you wandering from the point.

Having set up such a grid before you start to do your reading and information gathering, you are on the look-out for information from different sources which will provide arguments and evidence. This means that as you conduct your background reading, you can decide which box the information goes into – even though the chapter or article was not written for the purposes of answering your essay for you.

If you are using printouts of e-articles from your university website, you can colour-code the information so that it fits into your matrix or grid. For example, all arguments for the health system taking responsibility could be highlighted in a specified colour, while you choose another colour for arguments against the health system taking responsibility. In this way, you can quickly identify and categorise information from an article to suit your essay.

Hot Tip

1. Buy some A3 paper for this system.
   - With this size paper you will have room in the boxes to place the source of your information/idea as well as a brief summary of the point being made.
   - A3 gives you a complete overview of your ideas on one sheet. Consequently, links will be more obvious.
   - Having all the information on a single page will help you to sequence the ideas more carefully because you can see your 'train of thought' more easily.
2. With a large A3 piece of paper you would have room in the boxes to place the source of your information/idea.
   - However, the size of the boxes will only be sufficient for you to develop bullet points and will help with your summary skills.
   - The size of the boxes forces you to put the information into your own words and thus avoid plagiarism.
3. You need to develop your own cross-referencing system – not only the name of the reference but possible page number references if you quote from this source.
   - Such a system will help you to **cite references** with greater accuracy. And will actually save you time when you are the stage of checking the final draft. (For further reading see Chapter 4.2, 'Understanding academic integrity: plagiarism'.)

If you are concerned about how to get your ideas to hang together in paragraphs, you might like to go to Section 3 'Essay Structure' in Chapter 4.3, where you will look at the role of essay sections and how you can ensure that your essay structure has cohesion.

6 Putting your ideas together

Having made up a comprehensive matrix of evidence for your essay you are now ready to manage the drafting and editing stages. Are you aware that these are different activities? Some students start to compose or draft their ideas into prose and at the same time edit what they are writing. For novice writers, it helps to keep these activities separate. Some students have said that they don't have the luxury of time to go through the drafting process and then go through the whole essay again editing what has been written. It is **not** a luxury. Students who try to combine these activities are often unaware of the purpose of the two processes. Trying to cut corners by combining these activities may lead to a drop in the quality not only of your sentence and paragraph construction but also in terms of the overall structure of your essay.

Drafting

Drafting is often referred to as the composing part of the writing process. It is at this stage that you are ordering and structuring your ideas. It should be considered as the first stage of your finished product. During the drafting phase you have the chance to get your initial thoughts into sentences and paragraphs. It is the time when you can try out ways of communicating to your audience. When you are drafting an essay, it can be enough of a struggle just to get the ideas down in the right order. Do not add to it by worrying too much about finding the right word or a particular reference. In fact, when you're stuck for a word, it is often better to leave a gap and fill it in later. Be sure to remind yourself to go back and find the word later, Some writers do this on screen by using the coloured highlighter function to pick out spaces or phrases which you know will have to be edited later on. Others remind themselves by putting a note in square brackets, i.e. [find the word].

Editing

When you have finished your first draft and left it alone for a day or two, you need to put on your editor's hat. Many people find it helps to print out the first draft and mark it up in a different coloured pen – you can choose the alterations you would like to make without losing sight of the original text. Also, many find it easier to flick from page to page as you check the draft.

Read the essay as if someone else had written it. Now is the time to check that you have included all the references you need (and not left any unattributed), and filled in any blanks that you left in your draft.

When you are happy that you have marked up all the changes which you can cope with, go back to the computer and edit the document.

Checklist for editing

The checklist in Activity 2 helps you to operate on different levels of your essay. It ensures that you check structure, paragraphs, sentence construction and, above all, cohesion.

ACTIVITY 2 Editing checklist

Ask yourself ...	Solutions: where and how to check
Have I answered the question?	Locate the places where this is obvious to the reader.
Are there any issues (obvious or assumed) in the title that are not answered in the essay?	Remind yourself of the BUG technique for teasing out hidden issues.
Do I have an overall argument/theme upon which the whole essay hangs?	Think of your main argument/theme and go through each section to find evidence.
Is the structure clear?	Think about logical sequences of ideas.
Is the information presented in the right order?	Think about cause/effect; problem/solution.
How strongly have I presented my points/arguments?	Look for evidence to back up your points.
Is all the information accurate and relevant?	Double-check your notes and references.
Have you chosen appropriate points to include?	'Glance back' to the title and instructions. Look at your essay plans.
Are your ideas/arguments well supported with examples and evidence?	Go through each point separately and make sure you have got examples to back up.
Do your paragraphs develop only one main idea? Have you summarised your main idea for the reader?	This main idea is often best at the beginning of your paragraph.
Is there sufficient backing/detail to support this main idea in your paragraph?	Examine your sentences after your 'topic' sentence. Do they follow on and develop this sentence?
Have you repeated yourself?	Read through sections.
Have you explained/defined important/technical terminology in the essay introduction?	Treat your reader like an idiot and explain everything accordingly.
Do the paragraphs hang together as a whole?	Look for signal words which glue paragraphs and ideas together.

Ask yourself ...	Solutions: where and how to check
Does your reader know what to expect next in your essay?	Have you given explicit clues to signal what comes next?
Do your paragraphs have more than one sentence?	Don't just go by the number of full stops you have put but rather by the number of separate ideas/examples.
Do your sentences make sense using correct grammar and punctuation?	Don't rely on what you think makes sense. Read each sentence aloud and don't pause until you come to a full stop. Or get a friend to read your paragraphs to see if they make sense.
Is your language academic?	Check that you have not used slang phrases and words.
Is your style of writing formal?	Check that you have not put in abbreviations such as 'aren't', etc.

7 Tidying up and checking your work

Tidying up your essay and checking that there are no irritating errors is the final part of the process.

Editing versus proofreading

Once again these are different processes and have a different purpose. Editing is a way of polishing your work by checking that your ideas flow and that the language you have used really does express your ideas. Proofreading is more to do with the mechanics of writing. This is the part of the whole process where you need to iron out any errors and omissions which will irritate your reader. Activity 3 gives you a checklist to follow.

ACTIVITY 3 Proofreading checklist

Go through your essay and think about the following:

Proofreading checklist
Spelling errors
Punctuation
Do my cited references appear in my bibliography/reference list at the end of my essay?

Proofreading checklist
If quotations have been used, have I put in the page reference?
Have all the details required of items in the bibliography/reference list been included? You need to check the system your department prefers.
Have I included all my page numbering? Check your headers and footers.
Is the font style acceptable to my academic tutor?

How to spot your own errors

Many students are so pleased to have finished an essay (or they have left it to the last minute and have run out of time!) that they do not want to undertake or do not have time for this essential aspect of writing. Proofreading is different from editing in that it is all about spotting your own errors. These fall into various categories: typographical errors (the type of errors you can make when you are trying to type too fast); irritating spelling errors; and poor sentence constructions. Once again you cannot afford to skip this part of the writing process. It could make a difference of five to ten marks. However, it is an activity that you have to plan for. This means that you must take it into account when working out your time management and the lead-time you need to complete all parts of this writing process and still hand in your essay on time.

- The time it takes to proofread will vary according to:
  - the length of your essay
  - the complexity of the essay structure – third-year projects/dissertations/theses are going to take different lengths of time to proofread because of the number of chapters and sub-sections involved
  - your own ability to spot your own errors.
- You need to **estimate** the time you need to spend on this activity. You will become more accurate in your estimations as you learn about your own proofreading abilities and judging the 'tidying up' process.
- Whatever system your prefer you **must** leave at least one day between finishing your essay and reading through it for errors. The longer you can leave it the better because you will prevent yourself reading what you want to be there (because you can remember what you wrote) and reading what makes sense. You will need to experiment with timings to ensure that your memory is flushed out before you do your own proofreading. Remember that everyone is different, so what works for your friend will not necessarily work for you.

Spotting spelling errors

Many students have difficulty spotting their own errors yet seem to be able to identify problems in friends' writing. Remember that proofreading requires a special expertise:

- You need to have a very good memory for the look of words when spotting spelling errors as well as knowing something about spelling rules.
- If you are checking your work for spelling errors only, the way that some professional proofreaders go about this aspect of the job is to start reading backwards. In other words, start with the last word and read the previous word and so on. This makes you look at the spelling because you have taken away the element of 'making sense' of the sentence and you only look at one word in isolation. This only works if you have a good memory for the spelling of words.

Use technology to help you to identify spelling errors. Spelling checkers have their limitations. They will not pick out a 'wrong' word, for example a homonym. This is where you have spelled the word correctly but used the wrong one as in 'your' for 'you're'. You need a sound knowledge of language to spot these types of errors.

Over-reliance on computer spelling and grammar checker: a word of caution

Many students, understandably, rely on word processing software packages to do their spelling and grammar checks for them. In the main, many of the computer spelling/grammar checkers do a good job. However, they are often set up for the American system which is subtly different from UK English. It is worth noting that most of your tutors will be irritated by American spellings, and some may even find them unacceptable. For example, colour (UK English) and color (US English). Ensure that you have set your language and put UK English as the default before turning on your spelling checker. (To do this go to the button marked **Tools**, then **Language** then **Set Language** – make sure you change the default to UK English.)

Of course, it has to be said that not everyone is good at spotting spelling errors so if you are never going to be efficient you must develop alternative ways of doing this – don't simply avoid it.

'Other' error-spotting support systems

You need to be able to make decisions about whether the whole essay hangs together **for the reader**. This means that you need to be on the lookout for the structure of paragraphs and the construction of sentences – does what you have written make sense?

Proofreading 'buddies'

These may be difficult to find – especially from your own year group – because of the work pressures of your fellow students. However, it may be a useful service that you and a group of friends can provide for each other. You have to decide on a mutual deadline and place to get together to form a 'proofreading' group to critically examine each other's work and make helpful suggestions.

Get a proofreading 'buddy' to read your work aloud while you listen for errors in construction and structure. You have to really trust your buddy and not feel embarrassed or threatened as they read your work while you are sitting next to them. This often appeals to auditory learners who can spot their own errors when they hear what they have written.

It is worth noting that your reading buddies will probably look at your work with the same critical eye that you use in your own research reading.

Listening for errors

Reading your work aloud or onto a tape recorder is an alternative strategy to getting others to read your work to you. If you are an auditory learner, this strategy can work well. **But** you must read exactly what is written not what should be. When you hear what you have written, you may be able to spot poor sentence structure.

Of course, you could let the technology help you. Using voice recognition software can be useful for those who prefer to work alone. You can listen to your sentences and paragraphs being read aloud to you by the computer so that you can hear if your essay makes sense.

Learning from errors: frequency patterns

If you want to improve your writing, you need to reflect frequently upon your writing. It is frustrating and time-consuming to keep making the same errors while you are writing. Therefore, you ought to reflect upon the types of errors you make so that you can make a difference in the future.

Look for spelling error patterns – do you frequently get certain words incorrect? Do you often miss off the endings of words or the middle bits?

By findings patterns of errors you will get a focus on what you need to tackle to improve.

For example, trying to memorise lots of words which you misspell is tedious and difficult.

- Think about a manageable number to work on at any one time (ten is the absolute maximum).
- You will have to find the best memory strategies to match learning the word.

- You will need to work on these and test yourself every day – it will only take a few minutes if you limit what you are trying to achieve.
- Remember that spellings have to have 100% accuracy rates so you cannot move to another word until you can spell the word without thinking about it – in other words it just comes automatically.
- Remember to concentrate upon the 'irritation factor' in your choice of memorising spellings. People get irritated if you can't spell some of the small, everyday words, e.g. advice/advise – practice/practise. It gives a bad impression to your tutors who are marking your work. An immediate reaction is 'if this person can't spell these ordinary, frequently-occurring words what are we dealing with?'
- Make sure that you concentrate upon the specialist terminology for your subject. It doesn't look good if you are trying to argue a complex point and you can't even spell the topic words correctly!

Developing skills and strategies for taking control of the writing process will make a difference to your grades. However, another aspect of gaining high grades is closely linked with many aspects of the process. Your essay should demonstrate that you have analytical and critical writing skills.

8 Critical writing

Critical writing utilises the same general principles as those explained in Chapter 3.3 on critical reading. Critical writing indicates the ability to communicate critical thinking, analysis and evaluation of information and the development of your own ideas.

You need to show in your writing that you can take part in the academic debates. You will be judged on:

- how you state your argument/evidence/information
- how you back up your argument/evidence/information
- how you analyse what the opposition says
- how you evaluate and weigh up all your evidence, both supporting and opposing your claims.

In his helpful book *How to Argue*, Alastair Bonnett (2001) identifies six types of academic argument. It will depend upon the subject discipline as to which is best. To find out which is most appropriate for you, you may need to go back to the way the leading writers in your subject present information. These are the most frequently used types of academic argument:

- identifying tensions (discussing the existence of points of conflict in a discipline)
- cause and effect
- starting with observation or starting with hypothesis
- arguing about words
- contributions and impacts
- comparison and context.

Each type of argument gives you opportunities to engage with your material.

If you're new to this level of academic writing, you'll find it helps to arrange your facts so they represent the balance of ideas. Remember that part of critical writing is about how to present other people's ideas which may diverge. Unless expressly asked to do so, you are not writing a diatribe about your personal views.

When constructing an argument, each argument (topic) and supporting evidence (topic development) should be **critically argued** in relation to your claim or hypothesis. In other words, you are expected to debate an idea, stating what other writers think. However, to do this **critically** means that, by your careful choice of language, you can infer your own view, whilst explaining what other writers have stated.

Here is a simple framework for constructing an argument:

Main argument/hypothesis or idea should be stated clearly at the beginning. You need to let the reader know what it is that you are doing.	
Reasons in favour of the essay title or essay statement/hypothesis	Evidence and examples from things different people have written about
1.	1A
	1B
2.	2A
	2B
3.	3A
	3B
Opposing ideas	Evidence and examples from things different people have written
4.	4A
	4B
5.	5A
	5B
6.	6A
	6B
Conclusions: This is where you can interpret or summarise the views discussed. You can discuss what the evidence suggests.	

Hot Tip It is important that your main argument/hypothesis or idea is clearly set out at the beginning. It is the point from which you develop your supporting arguments. You will gain marks for substantiating your argument, using different sources.

9 On reflection

If you explore how you take control of the writing process, you will be well on your way to increasing your writing skills. Taking the pragmatic approach set out in this chapter will make a difference not only to the quality of your essays but also to your time management effectiveness.

Excellent essays rely upon your organisation and management of the whole process and not just on digging out the information. If you take control of the process from the moment you are given the essay titles, you give yourself a better chance of producing coherent essays.

Summary of this chapter

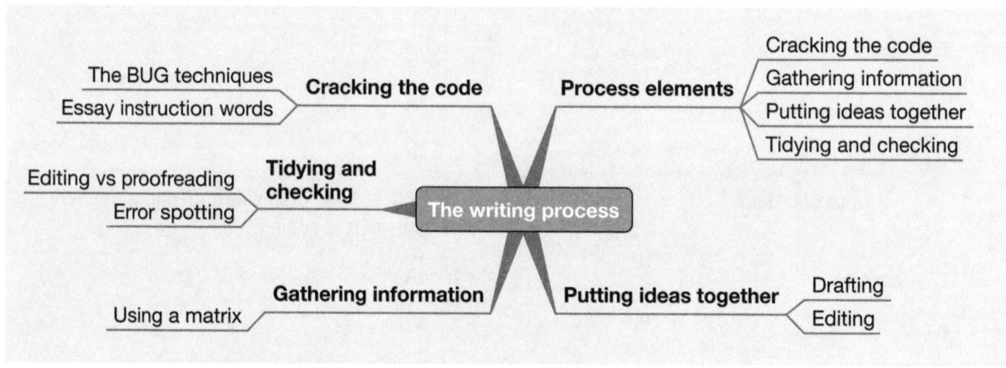

ACTIVITY 4 Update your personal development planner

Having read this chapter, you can see that organisation and management play key roles in writing your essays. From the moment you receive an essay title to the time you hand it in, you need to be in control of the process.

Now reflect upon how you go about the writing process and how you intend to change and adapt your habits so that you can spend your time more effectively. You may want to transfer this information to your own institution's personal development planner scheme.

Grade your confidence on a scale of 1–5 where 1 = poor and 5 = good.

My developing skills	Confidence level 1–5	Plans to improve
I know the different elements of the writing process.		
I can analyse what is required of an essay question.		
I have a system for collecting relevant information linked to the essay question.		
I can proofread my work accurately.		

Date: ______________

Getting extra help

- Go to the Students Union to find out where to go for skill development. Many universities and colleges have tutors who provide this service.
- If you are unsure about what you have got to do, make an appointment to see the academic tutor who set your essay title. Make sure you have given some thought to the possible ways of interpreting the question so that you have specific questions to ask, and it does not look as if you want them to help you write your essay.
- Find out if there is a proofreading service at your college or university if you have trouble spotting your own errors. However, make sure that the service does not correct your errors – your text may be changed into something you did not want to write.

Consult the following:

- Bonnett, A. (2001) *How to Argue: A Student's Guide*. Harlow, Pearson Education.
- Sussex University's study skills website has helpful information to guide you through the writing process: **www.sussex.ac.uk/languages/1-6-8-7.html.**

References

Bereiter, C. and Scardamalia, M. (1987) *The Psychology of Written Composition*. New York, Lawrence Erlbaum.

Bonnett, A. (2001) *How to Argue: A Student's Guide*. Harlow, Pearson Education.

Hayes, J. R. (1996) 'A new framework for understanding cognition and affect in writing' in Levy, C. M. and Ransdell, S. (eds.) *The Science of Writing: Theories, Methods, Individual Differences and Applications*. Mahwah, NJ, Lawrence Erlbaum Associates.

Houghton, D. (1984) 'Overseas students writing essays in English: learning the rules of the game', in James, G. (ed.) *The ESP Classroom*. Exeter, University of Exeter.

Price, G. A. (2001) *Report of the Survey of Academic Study Skills at Southampton University*. Southampton, University of Southampton.

4.2 Understanding academic integrity: plagiarism

Academic integrity is a code of practice which is strongly adhered to in any type of academic writing. You must ensure that you are able to give recognition to the work of others in your own writing. To do this effectively, you need to understand the rules of referencing your work and how to cite others' work within your text. If students do not reference their work properly they are in danger of being accused of plagiarism. Learning how to reference the work of others also demonstrates your background reading.

In this chapter you will:

1. learn that there are different forms of plagiarism
2. learn steps to prevent plagiarism
3. learn how to cite references in your written work
4. learn how to build up a bibliography or reference list
5. find out how to organise and manage your bibliographic data.

USING THIS CHAPTER

Estimate your current levels of confidence. At the end of the chapter you will have the chance to re-assess these levels where you can incorporate this into your personal development planner (PDP). Mark between 1 (poor) and 5 (good) for the following:

I know the variety of ways in which plagiarism can take place.	I know the difference between presentation of in-text citations and references at the the end of my written work.	I know the difference between a bibliography and a reference list.	I know the rules for presenting different types of references.	I am able to manage the collection of references in a systematic manner.

Date: ______________

1 What is academic integrity?

Your tutors set great store by academic integrity. Two essential ingredients of this are plagiarism and how you reference your written work. They are closely linked as you will see by exploring this chapter. Referencing your work properly will substantially ensure that you are not accused of plagiarism. However, some students are genuinely unaware that they have plagiarised work because they do not understand what plagiarism is. It is much easier nowadays to inadvertently fall into the trap because of the ease of access of information. Andrew Hammett, the principal of Strathclyde University, stated that many students are part of the 'Google Generation' (Hammett, 2006), which results in the authorship boundaries being blurred and could lead to more frequent instances of plagiarism.

Academic integrity is a code of practice which is strongly adhered to in any type of academic writing or exposition. It relates not only to essays but to PowerPoint presentations, examinations, dissertations and theses.

2 What is plagiarism?

I didn't know that I'd plagiarised things. I took words and phrases on the Internet and re-arranged them into my own sentence. I was shocked and humiliated when I was told to go to my tutor about cheating.

Chris, first-year Geography student

Plagiarism can take many forms. *The Oxford English Dictionary* gives a straightforward definition:

PLAGIARISM: *to take and use as one's own, the thoughts, writings or inventions of another.*

It cannot be stressed strongly enough that plagiarism is grounds for failure on your course. All universities and colleges have regulations which can be found on the main institutional website or repeated in your course handbooks and departmental guidelines. The wording is strong to emphasise the severity of the offence.

> *It shall be an offence for a student knowingly ... To represent as one's own any idea or expression of an idea or work of another in any academic examination or term test or in connection with any other form of academic writing, i.e. to commit plagiarism.*
>
> University of Southampton (2006)

Of course, the significant word is 'knowingly'. Like Chris, the first-year Geography student above, some students are not aware that they have plagiarised. However, trying to establish your innocence when you are being questioned by your tutor may be difficult to prove. Therefore, it is vital that you are aware of what plagiarism is and its many forms (see Activity 1).

ACTIVITY 1 What constitutes plagiarism?

Look at these statements and answer 'yes', 'no' or 'possibly'.

Which of the following are considered plagiarism?	Yes/no/possibly
I quoted the words from my textbook in my essay.	
I used inverted commas around the words I took from a text I was reading.	
I used different phrases from different sources and put them into a sentence in my essay.	
I used information from an Internet page which did not have a title or author so it is not plagiarising.	

Check the feedback section at the end of the chapter to find out the answers.

Patchwriting

The term 'patchwriting', penned by Howard (1995), aptly conjures up what you may be doing when writing. When you are drafting your ideas, you look at information from a variety of sources: books, articles and information which your tutors have given you. You may alter the odd word from lots of sources. This is termed paraphrasing. Some students think that since they have written the sentence then it is not plagiarism. Much depends upon how close your text is to the originals and how you have referenced your work.

Patching together other people's ideas is not a good way of demonstrating your understanding and knowledge. Remember to think about your reader. This type of writing can appear to be disjointed and fragmented.

Plagiarism defined

You will be accused of plagiarism if you:

- borrow or copy words from texts
- copy words/phrases word for word from texts
- do not identify and acknowledge all your sources of information
- download text from the Internet and do not acknowledge the source
- play around with (paraphrase) the text of others to create your own text
- copy another student's words without acknowledgement
- use someone else's ideas or theories without acknowledgement
- download pictures and diagrams from the Internet without acknowledgement.

Fiona Duggan, manager of the Plagiarism Advisory Service (PAS), is convinced that many students in the early part of their studies are not aware that they are committing an offence against academic integrity (Curtis, 2004).

3 Steps to prevent plagiarism

Sticking too closely to the words of others without acknowledging or referencing the source can be avoided. These problems stem from weak reading techniques as well as inexperienced writing strategies. Some of these problems are identified in Activity 2.

ACTIVITY 2 Problems and solutions to plagiarism

Students often lack confidence in their own ability to write authoritatively, which is understandable. Look at the following statements and reflect upon which ones apply to you. They could be the precursors to plagiarism.

Check the feedback section at the end of the chapter to find out the solutions to your problems.

Do any of these statements apply to you?	Yes or no
I can't possibly write this better than the author.	
When I look at the notes I've made on the texts I've read, I can't remember which are my words and which are ones from the author's text.	
I can't remember where I got the information to make my notes so I can't check whether the notes are in my own words or not.	
My sentences and paragraphs are like a patchwork quilt. That's how I write up my information.	
I think I can avoid plagiarism just by listing every single source in the bibliography at the end.	

Although plagiarism is detected at the final stage of your writing, viz. when you are drafting your ideas, prevention measures have to be taken much earlier on in the writing process. It often begins unwittingly at the note-making stage. Thus, it is vital that you distinguish in your notes direct quotations and your own paraphrasing. See if you can idenitfy the text that contains plagiarism in Activity 3.

ACTIVITY 3 Can you spot which texts contain plagiarism?

Read the original text and the following samples and identify which are cases of plagiarism.

Original text

The cognitive resources used in the writing process are considerable, and memory capacity and storage are often overloaded by competing, simultaneous operations. The ability to synthesise information is one of the essential skills required by HE students. Price (2006)

Version A

The cognitive resources used in the writing process are great and memory capacity and storage are often overloaded by many mental, simultaneous operations.

Version B

In Higher Education, the cognitive resources used in the writing process are often overloaded by competing, simultaneous operations. One of the essential skills needed is to synthesise information.

Version C

As Price (2006) indicates in her research, writing is complex and draws upon many of the mind's resources. One of the difficulties is that at times the writer runs out of memory space because of the need to do many tasks at the same time.

Check the feedback section at the end of the chapter to find out which texts would be considered to contain plagiarism.

Hot Tip

You can prevent plagiarism occurring by:

- **organising** the way in which you collect information for your essay or written work
- developing good **summary skills** so that you put information in your own words and are not tempted to use the words of others
- getting into a routine of **accurately recording your sources** – either using your own lists or an electronic reference manager software program.

The key to success is management and organisation right from the start. Efficient strategies will support your way of working. To ensure that you develop the appropriate skills, techniques and strategies, explore the chapters on reading and writing, where you will find information to help you to develop methods for recording information systematically which will reduce your chances of plagiarising work.

Although students find referencing confusing, once you understand the logic and principles behind it you will be able to ensure that you do not lose valuable marks in your essays and project work.

4 Referencing your work

Referencing your work accurately is a means of demonstrating the ownership of information. It is also a way of showing off the background reading which you have conducted in order to formulate your ideas on a subject. Citing references provides your tutor with confirmation that you are aware of what is going on in your subject and the research field. Thus, it has a positive effect if it is carried out properly.

Referencing is complicated because there are three different systems which are closely related to one another:

- citations within the text (in-text citations)
- references: a reference list at the end of your essay
- bibliography: a list at the end of your essay.

In-text citations are short but are linked to the reference list or bibliography at the end of your essay. The latter should provide the full information about the item which has been cited within your text.

Is a reference list different from a bibliography?

A reference list and a bibliography serve similar purposes. Some departments use the two terms interchangeably and make no distinction between the two. Some departments have a preference for one or the other, while some departments like to see both included at the end of your work. You must check your department's guidelines about this.

A **reference list** is a full and accurate description of all of the citations which are found in your text. Some departments prefer these to be listed chronologically. Thus, each item in the list is in the order in which it occurs in your text. This means that it is **not** alphabetically presented but rather the items appear in a numbered list which is cross-referenced with each in-text citation. However, many departments ask students to prepare 'references' at the end of the essay, and these are formatted in alphabetical order.

A **bibliography** has a different purpose. It contains an alphabetical list of **all** the books, articles, Internet information, etc. you have used in the process of formulating your ideas and thoughts about the subject. Not all of the items in this list will be given an in-text citation. For example, you might have read a chapter in a book to help you understand a difficult concept but you have not used this as a specified citation in your essay. In a sense it is a hidden resource which has helped in the accumulation of your knowledge.

5 In-text citations, references and bibliographies

Why bother?

These can be used to good effect and can give your writing the academic integrity it needs.

1. They give the reader of your text the opportunity to read the original source for themselves.
2. They provide a record of what you have used in your piece of work, so that you can easily find it in the future – there is nothing worse than knowing you once found something **really** useful, but you cannot remember where to find it!
3. They give authority to what you are writing and are an excellent way of strengthening your point or argument – if you are making reference to other people's research, it shows you are not just 'making it up'.
4. You avoid the risk of plagiarism. By giving your information sources, you are making it clear that you are not pretending that someone else's work is yours.
5. It is only courteous and polite to acknowledge the work of another person.

When should you use them?

We have just examined **why** you should use in-text citations and references. The question now is '**when** should you use them?'

Here are some possible answers:

1. When you have quoted directly from someone else's work.
2. When you have paraphrased the work of another author, rather than quoted directly from them.
3. When you have referred to previously published work of your own.
4. If someone's work or ideas are the source of a particular theory, argument or viewpoint.
5. When you have used specific information, e.g. statistics or case studies.
6. When you have used something as background reading, but where it still has influenced your thinking towards your piece of work.

6 How to present citations and references

The key purpose of any citation and its corresponding reference is to enable you, or someone else who is reading your work, to identify and locate the original text. So, be accurate and give full details. There are a variety of different conventions for the compilation of in-text citations and references for bibliographies. Two of the most common are the Harvard system and the British Standard Numeric system.

In-text citation rules

The Harvard system

The Harvard system is the most commonly used. In this system in-text citation must contain the author's name and the year of publication together with page numbers if a direct quotation is used. For example:

Price (2006) states that ...

In a recent study, Price (2006, p. 21) demonstrated that 'memory capacity and storage are often overloaded by competing, simultaneous operations' ...

The British Standard or Numeric bibliography

The British Standard or Numeric bibliography allocates a number to each citation and uses footnotes with numbers for references in the text. This is used often by the Humanities.

For example, round or square brackets are chosen (be sure to be consistent in use) and the citation is given a number which is cross-referenced to the reference list at the end of your essay or writing:

Price (1) states that ... (round brackets)

Price [1] states that ... (square brackets)

A recent study[1] ... (as a superscript number)

It is likely that your department or subject area will have a preference for one particular system, and it would be wise of you to use that system.

Whichever system you choose, you must use it consistently, accurately and following the rules. It is also worth checking individual academic tutors' preferences. This is especially important for those following joint honours courses in two departments. Do not be worried if there is inconsistency of approach within a department.

What information is needed for referencing?

For each reference that appears in your reference list or bibliography you must record specific pieces of information. It is vital, therefore, that you get into a routine of noting down this information in a safe place. This will be dealt with later in this chapter. The presentation of the information has to be carefully punctuated, and the source of your information will have a different method of presentation. However, the main details that you need to collect are:

- author's or editor's surname and initials
- title, with any sub-titles
- year of publication
- edition if other than the first
- location of the publisher
- name of the publisher
- the name, volume number, part number and pages of the journal
- for electronic resources, the web or e-mail address.

The remainder of this section contains information and examples of how to record a wide range of resources and draws upon the Harvard system because it is the most widely used. You may choose to practise creating references for the types of resource that you feel you will need to use in your studying. The most common sources for students are books, chapters from edited books, journal articles and websites.

Books

References to books should include the follwing details:

author's name and initials

year of publication, in brackets

title of the book, <u>underlined</u> or in *italics*

edition, if other than the first

place of publication

publisher.

For example, Smith, P. and Jones, W. (2006) *The Art of Academic Referencing,* 2nd edn. London, Made-up Publishing.

Chapters from edited books

Some books contain chapters written by a number of different authors. These books will have an overall editor who has compiled the book. You should include the following details:

name and initials of the author of the chapter

year of publication, in brackets

title of the chapter,

title of the book, <u>underlined</u> or in *italics*

edition, if other than the first

place of publication

publisher

page numbers of chapter.

For example, Smith, P. (2005) 'The role of punctuation in referencing', in Smith, P. and Jones, W. (2006) *The Art of Academic Referencing*, 2nd edn. London, Made-up Publishing, pp. 56–72.

Note that the main source, i.e. the book into which you have dipped, is still the part which is in italics **not** the name of the chapter.

Journal articles

References to journal articles should include the following details:

author's name and initials

year of publication, in brackets

title of the article (not underlined or in italics)

title of the journal, underlined or in *italics*

volume no. and (part no.)

page number(s).

For example, Price, G. A. (2006) 'Creative solutions to making technology work: three case studies of dyslexic writers in Higher Education', *ALT-J Research in Learning Technology*, 14(1), 21–28.

Electronic information

There is a wide variety of types of information which you might use from electronic sources. The main ones are:

- Internet pages (Uniform Resource Locators or URLs)
- articles in electronic journals
- electronic books
- articles in Internet journals
- photographs and images
- information from your department's virtual learning environment, e.g. Blackboard
- online newspaper articles
- personal e-mail correspondence (with a leading researcher, for example)
- course discussion board information.

As a rule of thumb it is important that you provide the URL address and the date upon which you accessed the information. The rules for books and journal articles remain the same, with the additional URL and accession date:

Author's name and initials

year of publication, in brackets (if there is no date, put: [n.d.] – NB use square brackets)

title of the website, underlined or in *italics*, followed by '[online]'

place of publication

publisher (if ascertainable)

available from: URL [date accessed] – NB use square brackets: the http:// may be left off if the URL also contains 'www'.

For example, Williams, S. (2002) 'Avoiding plagiarism' [online]: New York, Hamilton College. Available from: **www.hamilton.edu/academic/Resource/WC/AvoidingPlagiarism.html** [accessed 18 December 2006].

Overview of components of references

	Author	Year of publication	Title of publication	Title of article/chapter	Issue	Place	Publisher	Edition	Page no.	URL	Date accessed
Book	✓	✓	✓			✓	✓	✓			
Chapter in book	✓	✓	✓	✓		✓	✓	✓	✓		
Journal article	✓	✓	✓	✓	✓				✓		
Internet	✓	✓	✓							✓	✓

Punctuation of citations and references

There is nothing more irritating to your tutor than to have to correct incorrectly punctuated citations and references. It is imperative that you are meticulous in this to maintain your academic integrity. It is also important to ensure that you do not lose vital marks because of silly errors, omissions and lack of proofreading. The examples above provide you with the correct punctuation so it is worth spending a bit of time looking carefully at these and using them as templates for your own work.

In-text citations

Short quotations – single words or short phrases – are included in the body of your text and brought to the reader's attention by single inverted commas. For example,

> *Price (2006, p. 21) intimated that a person's capacity, the 'cognitive resources' are significant ... .*

Longer quotations are best delineated from your text by placing them in a separate, indented paragraph. The reader is alerted to the fact that you are going to use someone else's words by a colon. For example:

The centrality of using language in particular ways in subject disciplines is at the heart of the sociolinguistic theory relating to discourse:

> *The student who is asked to write like a sociologist must find a way to insert himself into a discourse defined by this complex and diffuse conjunction of objects, methods, rules definitions, techniques and tools ... In addition he must be in control of specific field conventions, a set of rules and methods which marks the discourse as belonging to a certain discipline.*
>
> Ball *et al*. (1990), p. 357

Note that the quotation was taken from a book by Ball *et al*. '*Et al.*' is Latin for and all of the rest. This is a shorthand method of referring to a number of different authors. Note also the punctuation of this.

If you have paraphrased information and ideas which are related to your reading of a specific author, you can strengthen your statement by letting your tutor see that you have read a relevant text. It is important to note where this is located in your text in order to avoid confusion. For example,

> *Expert writers need to be able to multi-task when they are drafting their ideas (Price, 2006). They have to draw upon ...*

Notice that the full stop does not come until after the brackets, thus indicating to which sentence the reference is related.

Make sure that the minute you put a citation in your own writing, you also take time to put it into your reference list or bibliography.

7 Frequently asked questions

Do I have to name every author or just the first one in my essay?

It depends upon the location. In-text citations require the first author only followed by '*et al*.' if there are more than two authors (see example above). If there are only two authors, it is usual to name both in your text. For example, Smith and Jones (2006) state ...

How do I cite and make reference to something which is referred to in a book or chapter which I have read?

These are called **secondary sources**, and the rules for dealing with these are slightly different. The important thing to remember is that you are showing, by your citations and references, which sources you have actually used. If a secondary source is not properly identified it will be taken that you have read the original text or research – which clearly you have not. This would be less than honest.

In-text citation:

According to a study by Smith (2001, cited in Jones, 2005).

When you transfer this into your reference list or bibliography, you can only include the Jones (2005) reference because this is the only one which you have actually read. You have not read Smith's original research but rather Jones's interpretation of it. Thus, Smith is a secondary source.

Do I have to keep repeating a citation from the same book?

If you have used the same reference on a number of consecutive occasions in your text then a way round this would be to use the Latin term **Ibid.**, which means 'from the same place'. However, it is often not used with the Harvard system.

What if I want to refer to a number of books by one author?

One method of getting around this with your in-text citation is to use the Latin term **Op. cit.**, which literally means 'in the work cited'. It is often used to refer to the work of the same author which you have last cited. However, it is often not used with the Harvard system.

8 Bibliographic reference management

Remember that your bibliography should include all the resources you have used to complete your assignment. This means both resources you have referred to in the text of your document and also relevant background materials that you have used, but not necessarily discussed. It is essential that you keep meticulous records. A little time spent recording the details of a book, a chapter, an article or an electronic reference will be time well spent.

> *What advice would I give to future students? It's simple. Keep a record of everything you read in the proper format so that you can use it for your written work. I know my tutors kept impressing on us the need to do this but you know how it is. I was in a rush, didn't think I had time to get out my list and update it. I was convinced that I would remember the reference anyway. So what happened? Yes, when it came to using the reference for my essay I didn't have the correct information. I could not believe how much time it took me to find that one single reference.*
>
> Natasha, third-year Fine Arts student

Natasha's advice is so important if you want to become an efficient student and prevent the disproportional amount of time it takes searching for vital references.

There are different ways of recording your information and much depends upon what you prefer. However, if you are doing a lengthy project which will depend upon a lot of references, it is often well worth spending time learning how to manage software which is dedicated to this purpose, such as

EndNote or Reference Manager. Whilst, such programs can be used in a simple way, they, nevertheless, take time to master. If your third-year project starts in the summer term of your penultimate year, it is worth setting aside the Easter vacation to get to grips with the software. It will save you much time and stress later on.

Whatever system you use, it is imperative that you record all the details, accurately following the system used by your department. Check with your tutor or the course handbook if there is a preferred style and look carefully at the rules which govern this system.

Low-tech management

You can either use a handwritten list or separate card index system. The handwritten list has the advantage of being accessible at all times if you carry this paper around with you. However, the disadvantages are that the lists are not automatically put into alphabetical order and, second, you will have to enter the separate items into a text document eventually.

Writing out separate index cards is another option. The key to success of this system is that each reference is written on a separate index card. There is usually sufficient space to jot down page references and useful quotations. The advantage this system has over the handwritten list is that you can shuffle them around into alphabetical order manually before you enter the separate items into a text document.

Dedicated bibliographic software systems

If you are using or would like to use a bibliographic database like EndNote (see below or refer to the user guide) or Reference Manager, then this is an ideal way for you to keep track of your notes and references. Although it does not always appeal to those who are not comfortable with computers, it is nevertheless a time-saving method, once you have mastered some of the basics. The advantage of this type of system is that the computer will sort out your lists into alphabetical order, you can cite-while-you-write by clicking onto a reference in your list and the citation is automatically in text and in a list at the end of your work. However, the disadvantage is that you need to have a laptop or access to computer facilities whenever you are working on your essay. This may not be feasible for some students.

Disabled Students' Allowance

Remember if you are eligible for this allowance, ask for EndNote or Reference Manager software to be purchased for your sole use. This means that it will be installed on your machine and you will be entitled to individual software training.

Hot Tip

Tips for management

- Put everything you read for a topic into your database.
- Key word the items in your database so you can find a group of references on a related topic you are working on.
- Store the hard copies (if photocopies or paper articles) in alphabetical order, but always make a note in your database if you have a hard copy and where it is.
- Finally, if you make notes on something you've read, also record where your notes are on your database entry too.

What will electronic bibliographic managers do for me?

The specific program that you choose will depend upon:

- the preferred system used by your department – for example, many medical departments use Reference Manager
- personal preferences
- the system to which your university or college has subscribed – many institutions now provide a cut-down version of EndNote for undergraduates which is found on the network system at workstations around your university. It is worth looking into this before you rush out and purchase the costly full program out of your own money.

This sort of software is very powerful and can save much time, providing that you have set it up for your personal use. Many students (and tutors) do not use the full potential of these programs but rather are content to select the features of most use to them.

Common features of electronic bibliographic managers

Electronic bibliographic managers allow you to do the following tasks:

- Create a separate reference 'library' for each of your essays.
- Add information for each entry – this can be personalised to include key words (for later grouping of references).
- Choose the referencing style you need to use (most software provides extensive lists from which to choose).
- See an example of what each item in the list will look like at the end of your writing.

- Sort the items in your 'library'. There are many options available for sorting your data so that you can extract the specific items for any written assignment.
- Search for authors or key words (if you have meticulously put these in).
- Automatically create term lists from the author, journal title, and keyword fields.
- Create term lists – these are particularly useful if you regularly consult specific journals, and to ensure that key words are being used consistently as an additional research tool.
- Use the system with Word so that you can select a reference from your database and cite-while-you-write. This means that the referencing and cross-referencing are carried out by the software, and it can save you time.
- Sort your selected bibliography into alphabetical order at the touch of a key.
- Import references from electronic sources, provided you have set up your system correctly. This can save time typing in each individual reference.

These are just some of the basic tools available in these systems. However, like all technology, you must set aside time to become familiar with its workings and use it frequently so that you do not forget the procedures for carrying out specific operations.

Hot Tip

A comprehensive and accessible booklet on the subject of citing and referencing is *Cite Them Right* by Pears and Shields (2005). It is inexpensive and provides a wealth of examples of different types of references which might be applicable to your subject.

9 On Reflection

Being aware of the pitfalls and the regulations for referencing your written work will ensure that you are less likely to be guilty of plagiarism. An awareness and understanding of the principles which are behind the regulations is essential. With this knowledge you can begin to appreciate why your tutors are so particular about your referencing.

The essence of this is to organise and manage your time and efforts effectively. Getting into good routines early on in your studies will reap rich rewards and higher grades.

Summary of this chapter

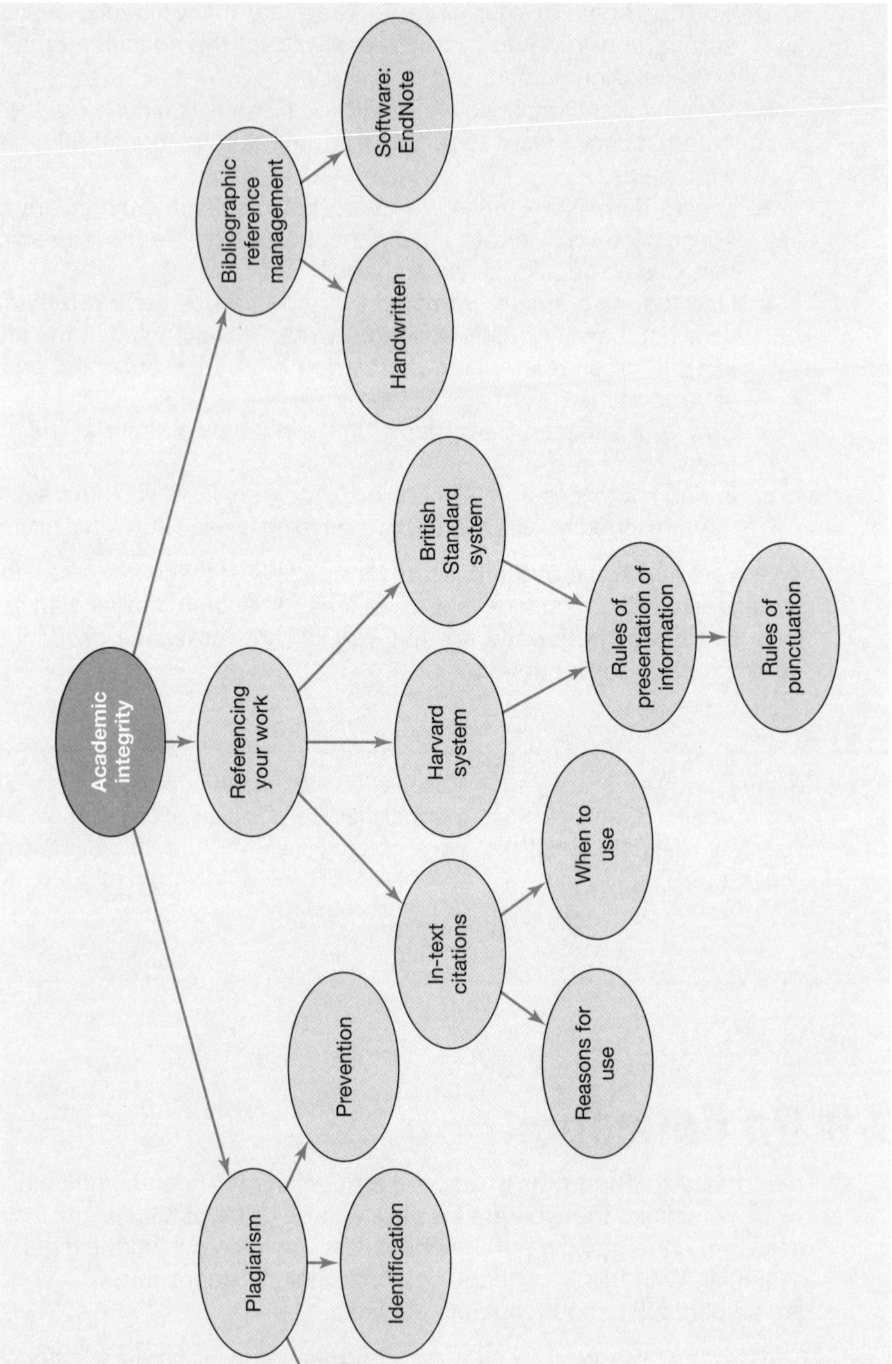

ACTIVITY 4 Update your personal development planner

Having read this chapter, you can see that organisation and management play key roles in the way you reference your written work. Knowing the rules for in-text citations and compiling accurate bibliographic data will ensure that you do not plagiarise work.

Grade your confidence on a scale of 1–5 where 1 = poor and 5 = good.

My developing skills	Confidence level 1–5	Plans to improve
I know the variety of ways in which plagiarism can take place.		
I know the difference between presentation of in-text citations and references at the end of my written work.		
I know the difference between a bibliography and a reference list.		
I know the rules for presenting different types of references.		
I am able to manage the collection of references in a systematic manner.		

Getting extra help

- Go to the Students Union to find out where to go for skill development. Many universities and colleges have tutors who provide this service.
- Closely examine your department's guidelines to make sure that you are aware of their rules and regulations.

Consult the following:

Pears, R. and Shields, G. (2005) *Cite Them Right: Referencing Made Easy*, 2nd edn. Newcastle, Pear Tree Books.

Feedback on activities

ACTIVITY 1 What constitutes plagiarism?

Look at these statements and answer 'yes', 'no' or 'possibly'.

Which of the following are considered plagiarism?	Yes/no/possibly
I quoted the words from my textbook in my essay.	Yes
I used inverted commas around the words I took from a text I was reading.	Possibly
I used different phrases from different sources and put them into a sentence in my essay.	Yes
I used information from an Internet page which did not have a title or author so it is not plagiarising.	Yes

'*I quoted the words from my textbook in my essay.*'

If you quote the words of others and do not acknowledge that you have used the words of others, this is considered plagiarism.

'*I used inverted commas around the words I took from a text I was reading.*'

Just because you have put inverted commas around the quoted words, does not mean that you have not plagiarised work. If you have not stated your source as well, this is considered plagiarism.

'*I used different phrases from different sources and put them into a sentence in my essay.*'

Patching together lots of phrases from different authors and sources without showing the reader that it is not your own words still constitutes plagiarism. Just because you have put the words into your own sentence does not exempt you.

'*I used information from an Internet page which did not have a title or author so it is not plagiarising.*'

Many students think that because there is no obvious author or title to the work that they can use such Internet information freely. This is not the case. You are still expected to indicate where you got the information.

ACTIVITY 2 Problems and solutions to plagiarism

Do these statements apply to you?	Yes or no	Solutions
I can't possibly write this better than the author.		A. Read what the author has said. B. Cover up the text. C. List the key words/ideas in your own words. D. Try to explain it simply in your own words.
When I look at the notes I've made on the texts I've read, I can't remember which are my words and which are ones from the author's text.		There are two solutions to this: 1. Colour code your notes so that you can immediately 'see' which are the notes written in your own words. 2. Improve your summary skills by following A–D above. Look at the 'Hot Tips' on p. 288 in the section entitled 'Organising the paper-chase' in Chapter 4.1.
I can't remember where I got the information to make my notes so I can't check whether the notes are in my own words or not.		The solution to this problem is to adopt a more organised routine to recording your notes. You need to record not just the 'what' but the 'where' – using cards/software/electronic lists will help. (See Section 4, 'Referencing your work' in this chapter.)
My sentences and paragraphs are like a patchwork quilt. That's how I write up my information.		Firstly, develop your reading skills in getting the global picture. (See Section 6, 'How to get a quick overview' in Chapter 3.1, 'Reading efficiently'.) Secondly, become a more critical and active reader of information. (See Section 4, 'Taking a critical look' in Chapter 3.3, 'Reading critically'.) Also look back at the 'Hot Tips' on p. 288 in the section 'Organising the Paper-chase' in Chapter 4.1.
I think I can avoid plagiarism just by listing every single source in the bibliography at the end.		You need to incorporate your acknowledgements into what you are saying to avoid plagiarism. (Go to Section 4, 'Referencing your work', for examples of how this is done effectively.

ACTIVITY 3 Can you spot which texts contain plagiarism?

Read the original text and the following samples and identify which are cases of plagiarism.

Original text

The cognitive resources used in the writing process are considerable, and memory capacity and storage are often overloaded by competing, simultaneous operations. The ability to synthesise information is one of the essential skills required by HE students. Price (2006).

Version A

The cognitive resources used in the writing process are great and memory capacity and storage are often overloaded by many mental, simultaneous operations.

Comment: This is clearly plagiarism. Even though there has been some attempt to substitute some words, the original author's sentence structure is intact and no acknowledgement has been given.

Version B

In Higher Education, the cognitive resources used in the writing process are often overloaded by competing, simultaneous operations. One of the essential skills needed is to synthesise information.

Comment: This is still plagiarism. Although the writer has moved the sentences around a little, it is too close to the original and this version does not acknowledge the source. In addition, this version does not use inverted commas to identify the original text: e.g. 'cognitive resources used in the writing process'; 'overloaded by competing, simultaneous operations'; and 'to synthesise information'.

Version C

As Price (2006) indicates in her research, writing is complex and draws upon many of the mind's resources. One of the difficulties is that at times the writer runs out of memory space because of the need to do many tasks at the same time.

Comment: There is no plagiarism with this version. This version clearly indicates the source and appropriate paraphrasing of the original has taken place.

References

Ball, C., Dice, L. and Bartholomae, D. (1990) 'Developing discourse practices in adolescence and adulthood', in Beach, R. and Hyndes, S. (eds.) *Advances in Discourse Processes*. Norwood, NJ, Ablex.

Curtis, P. (2004) *Guardian*, 30 June.

Hammett, A. (2006) *Guardian*, 17 October.

Howard, R. M. (1995) 'Plagiarism, authors and the academic death penalty', *College English*, 57, 788–806.

Pears, R. and Shields, G. (2005) *Cite Them Right: Referencing Made Easy*, 2nd edn. Newcastle, Pear Tree Books.

Price, G. A. (2006) 'Creative solutions to making technology work: three case studies of dyslexic writers in High Education', *ALT-J Research in Learning Technology*, 14(1), 21–8.

University of Southampton (2006) *QA Handbook: Guidance for Schools. Section 1V: Encouraging Academic Integrity – Procedures for Handling Possible Breaches of Academic Integrity*. Southampton, University of Southampton.

4.3 Making the most of your tutors' feedback

Managing the writing process is one aspect of developing your writing skills. Making the most of the feedback you receive is an essential part of increasing your grades. You have written your essay and handed it in. At times students are surprised by the mark they receive and gloss over the feedback commentary. Reflecting upon your tutors' comments is one of the keys to improving your essay writing techniques.

In this chapter you will learn how to:

1. analyse typical essay comments
2. structure your essays
3. ensure that your essays are coherent and cohesive
4. state your message clearly.

USING THIS CHAPTER

Estimate your current levels of confidence. At the end of the chapter you will have the chance to re-assess these levels where you can incorporate this into your personal development planner (PDP). Mark between 1 (poor) and 5 (good) for the following:

I am able to judge the correct length of an essay.	I know how to achieve coherence in my writing.	I know how to use signal words to achieve cohesion in my writing.	I can develop a strong paragraph, using good paragraph structure.

Date: ______________

1 Never mind the quality, feel the width!

Spending a long time writing essays and writing a lot of pages does **not** equal high grades. Improving your techniques, strategies and style will help you to gain better marks. You need to think about what your tutors consider worthy of good grades but equally what do they regard as adequate work for a bare pass.

Essay feedback is a significant aspect of developing your writing skills and improving your essay grades. If you reflect upon the comments which your tutors make at the end of your essays, you can identify how well you managed the writing process and which elements need to be worked upon in the future. In this way you can extend your essay writing techniques and improve your writing skills.

> *Academic writing is regarded by some academics as a process of socialising the student into the research community, be it Engineering, Medicine, Sports Science etc.*
>
> Ivanovic (1998, p. 76)

Your tutor's commentary will provide you with vital clues about academic communication and writing in your subject. If you want to improve your marks, you may to have to consider doing something slightly different. As the old adage says: 'If you always do what you've always done. You'll always get what you've always got!'

Taking stock of your position

- Are you satisfied with the grades you are getting for your assignments?
- Do you think you could do better?
- Are you puzzled by the grades you have received?

Writing is such a complex process that there are many aspects which you might need to change in order to improve your grades.

Do you need to change the way you **construct and structure your writing** – in other words how you organise language? This is making changes to the way you manage the **writing product** itself.

Do you understand what your tutors mean when they comment upon coherence and cohesion, weak essay structure and plagiarism? Try Activity 1.

ACTIVITY 1 Understanding your essay grade

Take a recently marked assignment and consider the following statements. If any of the statements apply to your essay place a tick in the right-hand column. This might help you to understand where you gained and where you lost marks.

Evidence in your essay: look for comments from your tutor	Does this apply to you?
1. Did not answer the question.	
2. Did not provide evidence in the essay of having met the tutor's objectives for the essay.	
3. Essay was considered to be descriptive.	
4. Simply restated, even in your own words, what you have read in a book or heard in a lecture.	
5. Lacked analysis.	
6. Took one point at a time and did not integrate ideas which were in books and articles.	
7. Weak structure and organisation.	
8. Poor paragraph structure.	
9. Weak sentence construction, paying little heed to formal grammar and punctuation rules.	
10. Developed a clear and sound argument.	
11. Provided supporting evidence for arguments made.	
12. Selected appropriate information, theories and issues.	

Evidence in your essay: look for comments from your tutor	Does this apply to you?
13. Showed relationships between different and sometimes conflicting information, theories and issues.	
14. Showed evidence of understanding of the subject by synthesising (pulling together) other people's ideas and views.	
15. Showed reflection and thought.	
16. Selected appropriate quotations to back up ideas.	
17. Used referencing systems with accuracy.	

Check the feedback section at the end of the chapter to gauge where you could improve and to find out some solutions.

2 What tutors say about students' writing

Your essay lacks any structure and ideas have been thrown onto the page.

You need to develop synthesis and analysis of your subject if you are to gain higher marks in the future.

This is not proper English usage. Your sentences are undefined, and your paragraphs lack cohesion.

Many students comment that they do not look closely at the comments made by their tutors. Some students admit that they are unsure about the comments and do not know how to move forward and improve upon the points mentioned. The following sections will provide you with the most common essay problems and solutions to enable you to gain higher grades next time.

3 The essay structure

This section will help you to improve the quality of your writing. It will get you to think about your skills relating to the basic components which are essential for good communication.

Traffic lights: starting blocks to better writing

Different subject disciplines may emphasise different features but, broadly speaking, essays should meet the following requirements:

1. Basic writing components	2. Hidden rules	3. 'Critical' writing components
Be a piece of **continuous** writing. This means that your tutors will not accept note writing and expect that your writing is in good prose style.	Some departments encourage the use of **sub-headings**. Check what your department guidelines state.	The writer has analysed the question and answered it with clarity.
Be clearly written so that your ideas and knowledge are communicated to the reader. This entails using language effectively and **constructing good sentences**.	Use the preferred bibliographic style of your department. Check departmental guidelines.	Demonstrates an understanding of the key theories and ideas. The key here is 'understanding'. Your tutor will not get a sense of this if you simply regurgitate and describe what you have read in chapters and articles.
Have **clear paragraphs**. Your tutors will expect your paragraphs to flow logically so that they can follow your line of thought and the threads of your discussions.	Some departments allow students to intersperse sentence constructions with information in bullet and list format. Check to see what your tutor prefers.	Have a clear line of thought. This may involve the **development of an 'argument'** in response to a central question or proposition.
Contain **relevant** information to ensure that you answer the question which has been set.	Some departments encourage students to present appropriate information in tables. Check the regulations in your course handbooks.	Contains supplementary 'evidence' or examples which you are required to analyse and which support or contradict perspectives.
		Contains a conclusion which pulls together the threads of your essay.

These 'traffic lights' can help you to decide what you need to work on. Column 1 contains the components of essay writing which are considered the nuts and bolts and provide a foundation for structures. The skills in column 2 build upon the foundation skills. While the skills in column 3 are what you are aiming for to get high grades and marks. Tutors value all of these skills but look, particularly, for those in column 3 to award First-class degrees or distinctions.

You now need to consider where your writing 'stress points' are and turn to the appropriate section in this chapter to strengthen your writing skills.

The essay components

The basic framework of any essay is its paragraphs. These are the foundations that should provide a vehicle for communicating your thoughts and ideas in a logical and structured manner. Written work comprises, by definition, a grouping of paragraphs. These paragraphs should be linked coherently so that the document you write hangs together and develops a thread of ideas or line of argument. A group of paragraphs forms a section of an essay.

Novice writers often ask how many paragraphs/sections an essay should contain. This is rather like asking how long is a piece of string. Much will depend upon your essay title, the prescribed word length, and what the author has to say. However, as a general guideline the five-section model is often used (Figure 1).

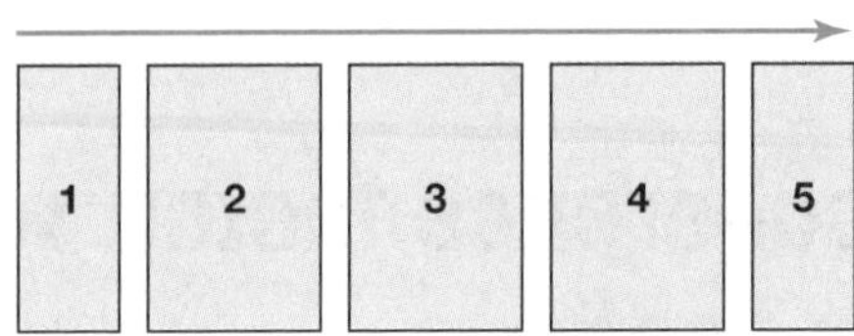

Figure 1 The five-section model

As you can see from Figure 1, sections 1 and 5 tend to be smaller than the main body sections 2, 3 and 4.

Section 1 will constitute the **introduction** and will contain the following:

- A **motivating statement** – this is optional. You may find you add this statement after you have found an interesting fact or position that sums up what you want to talk about. It could be a provocative question. Whatever it is its role is used to catch the readers' attention.
- A **topic statement** – this is essential. The topic statement is a clearly focused statement as a result of your research and analysis for the essay. It makes a clear statement about what the essay will cover and the structure it will take.
- The **role of the introduction** is to lead the way for the reader to the ideas which will be discussed and elaborated in subsequent paragraphs in the body of your essay. It is the place where you can set out your stall, organising items which will be written about and explained in detail later. In a sense it gives the mindset for your readers and prepares them for what to expect.

Sections 2, 3, 4 will constitute the **body of your essay**:

- Section 2 will be your first topic for discussion. You may have indicated in your introductory paragraphs what topics you will be discussing, so the reader will be prepared for this. It is important that you make sure that the order of your themes/topics, as set out in the introduction, is followed. You have told the reader to expect them in a specific order so keep to that sequence in these paragraphs.
- Section 3 could be a sub-topic of the above. You could use this section if you want to discuss further some aspect of the topic mentioned in section 2. However, you may wish to introduce another sub-theme and strengthen what you say by giving some examples.

- Section 4 can be used to link back to your introductory section, or some more generalised statement about the topic from section 2. Alternatively you may use this as a space for exploring another sub-theme and strengthen what you say by giving some examples.

Section 5 is your **conclusion** and will sum up key factors of the topics discussed and relate back to issues in your introduction. Never introduce new topics in this section.

This five-section structure is simply a model for the role of paragraphs/sections in an essay.

4 The coherence factor: working within essay sections

Your ideas are all over the place.

Tutor's comment

Expert writers produce paragraphs where the messages are clear, and the reader is able to understand the points that are being made. Good paragraph structure ensures that the train of thought flows – the essential 'coherence' factor looked for by your tutors.

If you have been told by your tutors that your essays are disjointed and that there is weak structure, they may be referring to the way that you write paragraphs and to the sequencing of your paragraphs. Often the problem is that you launch into minute details and examples before telling the reader what point you are trying to make. In other words, you have forgotten to flag up the main idea to the reader. This is done by a **topic or summary sentence**. These types of sentences are usually found at the beginning of a paragraph, because it is more helpful to the reader to be prepared for your supporting or complementary ideas which expand this main thought. Of course, some expert writers make a point of leaving this sentence until the end of the paragraph because they want to build up tension or get the reader to start thinking and questioning. However, this depends upon the type of writing community to which you belong, for example, Sociology, History, Engineering, Health Sciences, etc., so you should always check first.

ACTIVITY 2 Does my essay hang together?

Take a recently marked assignment and consider the following statements. Decide whether any apply to your work. This will give you indicators for future development.

Ask yourself ...	Commentary to look out for
Is there a logical sequence to my paragraphs?	Your ideas are muddled. Your paragraphs do not follow on. Your essay structure is weak.
Is my train of thought obvious to my reader?	A question mark in the margin. What are you getting at?
Is the thread of my argument obvious?	Can't follow your argument. This section is jumbled/muddled.
Are my paragraphs well structured?	Your paragraphs do not seem to follow on from each other. Your ideas are all over the place. Your sentences are muddled within this section.

There are two ways in which you can improve upon your writing if you have received these sorts of comments. One is by improving the **coherence** of your writing structure and the other is ensuring that your essays are well glued together – that is, that they have **cohesion**.

Just as was noted in Chapter 3.2, 'Finding your way around a text', in Section 4, 'Text ingredients', there are ground rules to follow to produce coherent paragraphs which can be easily followed by your reader.

Paragraph structure

To ensure that your paragraphs have clarity examine your paragraph structure. The following table explains the function of the sentences in a paragraph. These functions are then applied in Activity 3.

Link sentence from previous paragraph	**Optional** If you can make links between paragraphs your essay will hang together more effectively.
Topic sentence	**Essential** Let your reader know what to expect in your paragraph.
Develop topic	**Essential** Expand upon your topic sentence. Give more detail. Flesh out your idea.
Move towards next topic/ next paragraph	**Optional** Letting the reader know what is coming next helps the reader to understand your logical sequencing.

ACTIVITY 3 Exploring paragraph structure

Let us look at a paragraph written by Michael, an Education student, and examine the way he ensures that there is coherence to his paragraph. He is writing about working memory.

Sentence	Function/purpose
1. Newell and Simon (1972) were the first to propose that there was a computational workspace between the Short-Term Memory and the Long-Term Memory, which they termed the Working Memory (WM).	This is the **topic sentence**. It introduces the reader to the main idea which is to be explained in the paragraph. Notice how he succinctly tells the reader the main ideas so that the reader is primed for the rest of the paragraph and what follows will make sense.
2. It is here that the reader stores the theme of a text, where the reader's own representation of the situation is referred to and major syntactical elements, from surrounding sentences, are accumulated.	**Develop the topic**: This sentence gives an explanation of what the Working Memory does. By using the word 'here', the writer links back to the previous sentence to provide strength and cohesion.
3. In this way, the individual can make sense of the text.	**Develop the topic:** This sentence is further explanation of the topic sentence.
4. The Working Memory is also the space where the reader can temporarily store earlier parts of a sequenced story in order to relate them to later sequences.	**Summary sentence** to draw the paragraph to a close.

Writing a good main statement

ACTIVITY 4 Capturing the reader's attention: topic sentences

Look at these topic sentences. Can you identify why one of each pair is a good statement and the other is a poor statement? They have been taken from: University of Toronto, *Advice on Academic Writing*, available at: **www.utoronto.ca/writing/advise.html**.

A.		
Poor	Shakespeare was the world's greatest playwright.	**Why poor? Why is it difficult to develop from this point?**
Better	The success of the last scene in Midsummer Night's Dream comes from subtle linguistic and theatrical references to Elizabeth's position as queen.	**Why good? How could you develop this?**

B.		
Poor	Having an official policy on euthanasia just causes problems, as the Dutch example shows.	**Why poor? Why is it difficult to develop from this point?**
Better	Dutch laws on euthanasia have been rightly praised for their attention to the principles of self-determination. Recent cases, however, show that they have not been able to deal adequately with issues involving technological intervention of unconscious patients. Hamarckian strategies can solve at least the question of assignation of rights.	**Why good? How could you develop this?**

Developing your topic sentence

Supporting evidence shows that you are looking at the evidence and findings of other researchers and writers in support of your main/topic statement. You need to show that you are looking at this information fairly and with a critical eye. **Any conclusions you come to are due to the evidence you discuss.** This is what your academic tutors call 'your voice' in the essay. This is how you demonstrate what you want to say. The choices **you** make from the array of ideas in books, articles and web sources are what makes your writing analytical.

5 Cohesion: cement, glue and linkages

Many students know the meaning of the words cohesion and coherence in isolation but do not know how they can be achieved when they are writing. Signalling to your reader what your thoughts are will achieve coherence. Similarly, ensuring that your sentences and paragraphs link together into one large jigsaw will help communicate your ideas to others more effectively.

> *I kept getting comments on my work about 'lack of coherence and cohesion'. Although I understood the words themselves, I have to admit that I didn't really understand what my tutors were getting at. When my academic skills tutor was talking about signalling things to my reader and showing me examples, the penny dropped. It all suddenly made sense, and I realised what my tutors were getting at.*
>
> Second-year History undergraduate

Coherence and cohesion are closely linked. An essay which has logical sequencing and guides the reader through the ideas and thoughts will have coherence and will make sense. Cohesion is achieved by making sure that all the parts fit and stick together. This is done by careful choice of language to point the reader in the direction you want them to go.

If you are stating a new idea or giving an example in a paragraph, it is a good idea to use '**signal words**'. These are words or phrases that prepare the reader for what is to come, be that an example, a comparison with what went before, a contrast, a continuing description, etc.

Signal words help the reader through the text. They act as small, mental arrows that keep the reader on track. Without signal words, a text is quite difficult to read and can seem very stilted. Different types of essays will call upon different types of signal words and phrases. Some common signals are listed below:

Purpose of the signal	**Examples**
Comparison or similarities	Similarly Likewise In the same way In comparison
Contrast or differences	In contrast On the other hand, Not only ... but also In comparison But Even though However,
Cause and effect	As a consequence (effect) Because (cause) Consequently (effect) As a result of (effect) Due to (effect) The reason for..... (cause) Therefore (effect) If ... then With the result that ...
Listing	A major development ... To begin with Next ... Later ... Furthermore In addition Afterwards Finally In conclusion
Problem solution	The dilemma facing ... The problem facing ... A major difficulty ... A resolution to this ...

6 Is your writing too descriptive?

Your writing needs to be more analytical – it is too descriptive.

Tutor's comment

Let us now examine how Alison, a second-year student, tightened up her essay introduction from a descriptive piece of work to one which shows that she has critical abilities.

Her essay title was 'Is a mass transport system the answer to Hong Kong's problems?'

First draft

Traffic congestion is a problem which all cities world-wide are having to face. There have been many solutions to this problem adopted by different countries. The basic network of the Hong Kong mass transit system was designed in the early 1970s and construction started in 1974. It included three lines, one along the northern shore of Hong Kong island and two crossing Hong Kong harbour to serve Kowloon which is situated on the Chinese mainland. The Mass Transit Railway (MTR) system now has five lines: Island Line (blue), which runs along the north side of Hong Kong island; Tsuen Wan Line (red), which crosses under the harbour from Admiralty on the island and passes through Kowloon on the way to the western New Territories ;Tung Chun Line (orange), which follows the same line as the Airport Express but makes local stops to Lantau Island; Kwun Tong Line (green), which links Kowloon's Yau Ma Tei station to Tiu Keng Leng and Tseung Kwun O Extension (purple), which begins on Hong Kong Island, then crosses the harbour and heads northeast to Po Lam in Kowloon. These underground trains have a close resemblance to those found in the London Underground which is not surprising because a company called Metro-Cammell in England was responsible for designing and building the trains and carriages. Thousands of people use the MTR every day.

Whilst this essay gives many interesting facts about the MTR it is too descriptive. It makes no attempt to comment upon why the system was introduced and the sociological and financial pressures which brought about this radical change in transport provision in a country where there were considerable limitations on space.

Second draft

Traffic congestion is a problem with which all cities world-wide are having to contend. The roots of the problem often reside in the lack of space in cities for every citizen to use his car. However, the situation is exacerbated by sociological issues and government policies. Hong Kong is an excellent example of how a strategic approach was taken to solve the space problems linked to an ever-increasing population. The government made a brave *decision to finance a new underground system which would meet the needs of its citizens and introduce partial bans on certain types of transport systems in the city. Thus, the mass transit railway system was developed in the 1970s into what is now a comprehensive transport solution which links all the main areas by a five-line system which is closely reminiscent of the London Underground system. This close resemblance is not surprising because a company called Metro-Cammell in England was responsible for designing and building the trains and carriages. Thousands of people use the MTR every day. This essay will examine the efficacy of the Hong Kong system as a solution to the financial, sociological and geographical factors.*

As you can see she has retained the topic sentence because it is a useful tool to signal to the reader what she is about to write about. However, the next two sentences summarise her views about the reasons there are problems globally. She then explains to the reader that she is going to use Hong Kong as her platform to discuss the issues.

Notice how she brings her own critical voice subtly into the writing by the use of 'brave'. She is making her own point which will be explained later. She goes on to succinctly summarise the system, bringing out the key points from the lengthy description of her first draft.

Eventually, Alison produced an essay which she felt answered the question and put forward her view of why the current MTR is the answer to Hong Kong's dilemmas. She was awarded a distinction for her critical writing.

7 Persuading your reader

Students who get the top grades are those who can persuade their audience with their writing. Students on the same course have access to the same reading lists, the same lecture handouts and the same electronic guides to help them to write an essay. How come some students get a mere pass grade while others achieve a sound grade 'A'? It hinges upon what you choose to include in your essay, and how you put the ideas together. It also relates to the way in which you merge the ideas to make a convincing argument or message.

How can I make a unique contribution to the topic when my tutors are the leading researchers in this field?

Peter, first-year Geology student

This 'uniqueness' relates to the choices you make. Other students may use different examples from sources to strengthen their ideas. The choices you make need to convince or persuade your reader. One piece of research could be used in different ways, according to the point the writer wishes to make. To do this effectively demonstrates that you are analysing what is being said by others, making critical choices to blend in with the way you wish to argue your point. An effective essay is discussed in Activity 5.

ACTIVITY 5 What makes effective essays?

Whilst this is only part of Andrew's essay, it may appear a long sample. However, it is worth going through the various sections to see how he gained top grades.

Essay title: 'The role of metacognition in learning for dyslexic students'.

Numbers have been inserted in order to categorise the function of each sentence/section.

Essay paragraphs	Function
Introduction: 1. Effective learning involves a number of interactive cognitive activities and processes. 2. Metacognition, which essentially means thinking about thinking, is one of the most important cognitive activities (Reid, 2003). Metacognition has an important role in how people learn and this can be vital to help dyslexic children clarify concept, ideas and situations and therefore make reading and writing more meaningful.	**Notice how this sets the scene for the rest of the essay and gives clear summaries.** 1. Topic sentence which gives a clear summary. It informs the reader that Andrew is going to write about many processes. 2. Clear definition of technical terminology as the writer intends it to be used. Notice, he has put it into his own words but the definition is strengthened by reference to Reid (2003).
3. Moreover, metacognitive awareness refers to higher order thinking and is thought important for learning about yourself as a learner (Price, 2004). 4. In addition, the learner who is taught metacogniton can involve themself in learning situations efficiently and effectively. 5. Furthermore, Reid (2003) stated that the skill of metacognition, that associated with learning, needs to be developed from an early age in order to help the learner to have a successful life. 6. In this essay we will try to explore what metacognition is, examine the role of metacognitive approaches in learning carefully and discuss how we can teach it to children. Finally, after giving a descriptive picture of metacognition and its aspects, we will explain why it is so vital for dyslexic learners. It is considered important at that point to clarify that we are going to give a definition of dyslexia later on, making clear to readers what dyslexia is and why it is necessary for dyslexic learners to be taught the skill of metacognition.	3. The use of 'moreover' lets the reader know that there are other ideas, and Andrew has put into his own words what Price (2004) has said. 4 and 5 expand and give further examples of the purpose and role of metacognition. He signals to the reader that there will be more by using 'in addition' and 'furthermore'. 6. This part of the introduction clearly lets the reader know what to expect and how the ideas are to be structured.

Essay paragraphs	Function
First section:	
7. THE CONCEPT OF METACOGNITION 7. Metacognition is one of the latest buzz words in educational psychology (Livingston, 1997). 8. As Metcalfe and Shimamura (1996) noticed, in recent years metacognition has emerged as a major focus of interest in cognitive psychology. 9. Interest about metacognition grew in early 1970s. 10. Two major seminar papers were presented in 1978 by Brown and Flavell and since then many papers were written on this subject. The two theoretical approaches of Brown and Flavell were both cognitive in essence and centered upon self (Brown, 1978) and upon individual's relationship with external (Flavell, 1979). Brown's approach was about cognitive self-management and how individuals control the process of planning, monitoring, checking and revising (Price, 2004). The main questions that concerned Brown were about how to control thinking, how memory works and how our brain controls the incoming information (Brown, 1978).	7. He uses a subheading to state what this section is to be about. This is the section topic sentence but it also links back to what has been said in the introduction. 8. This sentence sets the scene for giving some historical detail. 9. Takes the reader back to 1970s as the starting point of discussion. 10. 'Seminal' papers shows that Andrew has chosen these to build up his discussions.
11. Furthermore, the concept of metacognition is most associated with John Flavell (1979). According to him (1979, 1987), metacognition consists of both metacognitive knowledge and metacognitive experiences or regulation. Metacognitive knowledge refers to acquired knowledge about cognitive processes, knowledge that can be used to control cognitive processes ...	11. Notice the use of 'Furthermore' to let the reader know that he is going to give more examples to back up his discussion.

Andrew's essay is too long to include in its entirety but you can see how he develops his arguments and ideas very clearly, making sure that he:

- signals to the reader what he is thinking
- sequences his ideas so that they not only look back to previous statements but take the reader forward to new statements.

Andrew was given a grade 'A' for his essay.

'Hidden rules' checklist

Having considered some of the nuts and bolts of writing essays, it is worth checking the format your department/tutor prefers. It would be regrettable to lose marks because of some cosmetic or superficial elements.

Tutor/departmental preferences	**Rules/regulations**
Accepted paper size	
Typed scripts	
Preferred font style	
Use of colour	
Size of margins	
Sub-headings	
Indented first line of paragraph	
Tables	
Bullet lists	
Type of referencing /bibliographic style	
Line spacing: single, double?	
Name and/or student number on each page	
Page headers and footers:	
Position	
Detail	
Use of appendices at the end of the essay (what is permissible in an appendix)	
Use of numbered reference notes at the foot of the page	
Use of personal pronoun 'I' – writing in the first person	
Use of passive voice – 'This essay explores ...'	
Use of active voice – 'I shall explore in this essay ...'	
Title page details: Department Institution Tutor's name Unit title/number Student name and/or number Essay title Date	

8 On reflection

The sure way to improve your writing skills is to pay attention to the comments made by your tutors on your essays. Well-structured essays rely upon a number of features. Clarity of thought can be expressed by:

- good structure
- well-planned paragraphs
- adherence to the rules of paragraph structure
- coherent and cohesive writing
- persuasive writing.

This section has provided guidance upon these features. Only by constant reflection will you improve your writing for academic purposes.

Summary of this chapter

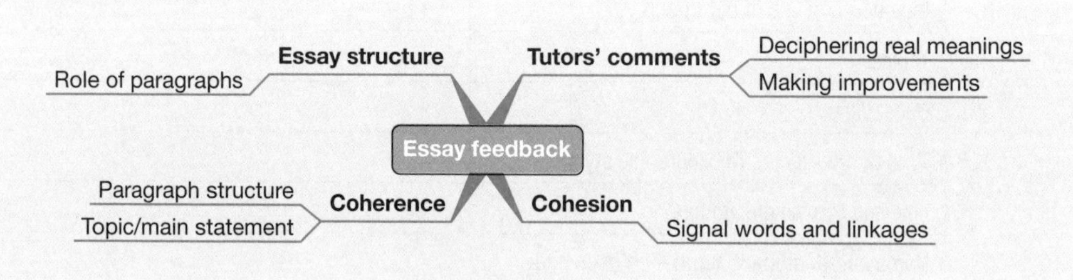

ACTIVITY 6 Update your personal development planner

Now reflect upon how you go about ensuring that your essays are well written and how you intend to change and adapt your habits so that you can spend your time more effectively. You may want to transfer this information to your own institution's personal development planner scheme.

Grade your confidence on a scale of 1–5 where 1 = poor and 5 = good.

My developing skills	Confidence level 1–5	Plans to improve
I am able to judge the correct length of an essay		
I know how to achieve coherence in my writing.		

My developing skills	Confidence level 1–5	Plans to improve
I know how to use signal words to achieve cohesion in my writing.		
I can develop a strong paragraph, using good paragraph structure.		

Date: ______________________

Getting extra help

- Go to the Students Union to find out where to go for skill development. Many universities and colleges have tutors who provide this service.

Feedback on activities

ACTIVITY 1 Understanding your essay grade

Evidence in your essay: look for comments from your tutor	Does this apply to you?
1. Did not answer the question.	
2. Did not provide evidence in the essay of having met the tutor's objectives for the essay.	
3. Essay was considered to be descriptive.	
4. Simply restated, even in your own words, what you have read in a book or heard in a lecture.	
5. Lacked analysis.	
6. Took one point at a time and did not integrate ideas which were in books and articles.	

Evidence in your essay: look for comments from your tutor	Does this apply to you?
7. Weak structure and organisation.	
8. Poor paragraph structure.	
9. Weak sentence construction, paying little head to formal grammar and punctuation rules.	
10. Developed a clear and sound argument.	
11. Provided supporting evidence for arguments made.	
12. Selected appropriate information, theories and issues.	
13. Showed relationships between different and sometimes conflicting information, theories and issues.	
14. Showed evidence of understanding of the subject by synthesising (pulling together) other people's ideas and views.	
15. Showed reflection and thought.	
16. Selected appropriate quotations to back up ideas.	
17. Used referencing systems with accuracy.	

If you answered 'yes to 1 and 2:

This means that you have not analysed the question sufficiently. You need to look back on Section 4, 'Cracking the code', in Chapter 4.1.

If you answered 'yes' to 3, 4, 5 and 6:

This means that you need to develop critical writing skills and you may need to examine your skills of writing coherently. You need to look back on 'Critical writing'. You will also find guidance in Section 4, 'The coherence factor'.

If you answered 'yes' to 7 and 8:

This means that your essays do not hang together well. You will find guidance in Section 4, 'The coherence factor'.

If you answered 'yes' to 9–17:

You are well on your way to becoming a critical writer. Re-read this chapter to find out if there are any more tips you can pick up to increase your grades.

References

Ivanovic, R. (1998) *Writing and Identity: The Discoursal Construction of Identity in Academic Writing*. Amsterdam, John Betjamins.

Index